DR. SEAT BELT:

the Life of
Robert S. Sanders, MD
Pioneer in Child Passenger Safety

written by
Robert S. Sanders, Jr.
© 2006-2008

March, 2009

To the Tennessee and Regional History section

Robert S. Sanders, Jr.

This book is a biography of Dr. Robert S. Sanders, who was born in middle Tennessee in 1927. He was educated and trained at Vanderbilt University Medical School. He became a well known pediatrician and was the director for 25 years of the Rutherford County Health Department in Murfreesboro, Tennessee. Sanders was the catalyst for the "grassroots" lobbying that resulted in Tennessee's being the first state in the nation with a child restraint law (Child Passenger Protection Act) in 1977.

By his focus on children, Dr. Sanders leveraged the combination of his passion for the well-being of children, his warm and unassuming personality, his rich network of colleagues and friends, with the guidance and contributions made by the pioneers to become the father of Tennessee's Child Passenger Protection Act.

With respect to serving humanity, Dr. Sanders' prime directive was saving lives. Bob Sanders made this world a better place. Many thousands of children will live who otherwise would have died. Hundreds of thousands will be spared disability because of Sanders' work.

DR SEAT BELT:
the Life of Robert S. Sanders MD
Pioneer in Child Passenger Safety
Copyright © 2006-2008 by Robert S. Sanders, Jr. All rights reserved.
First published printing: April 2008

photos on book cover by: Alan Loveless, & Chattanooga News Free Press

interior photo credits to: Bob and Pat Sanders, also:
Harry Cravens, Tom S. England, Walden Fabry, Kathy Ferris,
Henry Huddleston, Alan Loveless, Benjamin Porter, Jim Ramsey,
Bealer Smotherman, the Insurance Institute of Highway Safety,
Volvo Cars of North America, Inc., Chattanooga News Free Press,
the Daily News Journal, & Tennessee gov't photos

Acknowledgment to Clifton K. Meador, MD,
one of Bob Sanders' medical school classmates,
for reading the manuscript for this book.

Library of Congress Control Number: 2008924488

ISBN: 1-928798-09-8
13 digit ISBN: 978-1-928798-09-5

type: Non-fiction, Biography

Armstrong Valley Publishing Company
P.O. Box 1275
Murfreesboro, TN 37133-1275

printed in the United States of America

Table of Contents

"Bobby"
a poem written by his aunt Louise Sanders Brendle, 1995

In 1927 was born a fair-haired baby named Bobby.
His hair was curly and thick, but alas and alack, time took a whack.
At an early age, he was concerned with those who were ill,
So he decided to help people, was his niche to fill.
To increase his perspicacity for learning, for Vanderbilt he was yearning.
So to that school he did go, and was proclaimed no slo Jo.
He spent a year in Sweden to sharpen his skills,
So in Carolina he could handle all the ills.
For Murfreesboro, in pediatrics, his practice was draggy,
So his purse became saggy
From a friend came this suggestion:
"To Public Health, Bobby, that's your career."
So he made that change without even a tear.
He learned from statistics, how on the road so many babies are killed.
So his heart said, "Bobby, do something about this ill."
To pediatricians and politicians he made his way, with laws they did sway.
So mandatory restraint seats are the law of the land,
And he is held in great array.
For Public Health he made quite a name.
In fact, his accomplishments brought him enviable fame.
To the politicians, for the seat belt, again did he lobby.
Now, for lives saved, the whole nation can say, "Thank you, Bobby."
So broad in scope were his efforts and influence felt,
That Governor McWherter named him **"Dr. Seat Belt**."

Louise Sanders Brendle, Murfreesboro, Tennessee

Introduction and Executive Summary

courtesy: Chattanooga News Free Press

Dr. Robert S. Sanders was a remarkable man who was nationally known and recognized chiefly for his pioneering efforts in child passenger safety in vehicles in the 1970s and for causing Tennessee to be the first state in the United States and first place in the world to have a child restraint law in passenger vehicles.

Born and raised in Tullahoma, Robert Smith (Bob) Sanders was a native of Middle Tennessee. Both his father and mother were from Murfreesboro and Rutherford County. He would spend time in the summers at his mother's homeplace with his aunts, uncles, and cousins.

Bob Sanders attended Tullahoma High School for two years, and then transferred to Castle Heights Military Academy in Lebanon, Tennessee, after which he entered the U.S. Army for a year and a half. He spent several months in Okinawa and the Philippines, returned home in 1948 at which time he was discharged from the military.

Via the G.I. Bill, he attended Vanderbilt University. At one time, he considered being a Methodist minister, but he soon realized that his calling was medicine and that more lives could possibly be saved in that field. He studied three years at Vanderbilt in undergraduate arts and science, majoring in chemistry. Then he studied four more years at Vanderbilt

1

Medical School and did his residency training there and also in San Francisco, California; Stockholm, Sweden; and in Chapel Hill, North Carolina.

Bob married Patricia Ozburn Pelot from Crossville in 1962, and in 1963 he moved to his mother's old homeplace and farm, where he lived the rest of his life.

He raised sheep and cattle and was engaged in private medical practice as a pediatrician for three years. His son Robert was born in 1965, and his daughter Priscilla was born in 1967.

In 1966, with private practice not bearing much fruit, he moved on over to the Tennessee Department of Public Health and began a job at the Rutherford County Health Department in Murfreesboro. He became director in 1969 and kept that job until he retired in 1991. In 1983, Bob also took on a side job and became the medical examiner for Rutherford County, a job he kept until 1999.

In the midst of working at the Health Department and while raising his two children with his wife Pat, he became involved in child passenger safety. He spent countless hours showing safety belt films at medical conferences and meetings throughout the state.

Both Bob and his wife Pat lobbied at the state legislature for two separate years to bring about the Child Passenger Protection Act in 1977. Dr. Sanders was flown to several states, expenses paid, to have interviews and speak about his milestone accomplishment of how Tennessee was the first state in the nation with its Child Restraint Law.

He also became interested in other related medical issues, one of them being the field of autism and Asperger's Syndrome. His son Robert wrote two books on that subject: Overcoming Asperger's: Personal Experience & Insight: 2002; and On My Own Terms: My Journey with Asperger's: 2004. Bob and his wife attended several important meetings and conferences on the above subject.

In 2000, Bob was diagnosed with a type of lymphoma, a blood disease. He was in and out of sickness and treatments, but what really brought him down was shingles, resulting in several strokes, incapacitating him and making him an invalid for the last year and a half of his life. He spent the last year of his life (2005) at home being cared for by his wife, but he still got out and attended meaningful events. He attended some of Robert's book signings and photo exhibits. He also attended Priscilla's CD release concerts of her new album, "Ride a Wave With Me."

He passed away at the age of 78 in January 2006.

A Tribute by Robert S.Vinetz, MD, FAAP
April 15, 2007

Bob Sanders made this world a better place. Thousands of children will live who otherwise would have died...and tens or hundreds of thousands will be spared disability because of Bob's work. The parents of millions of children will, every day, do something that their own parents never knew to do to protect their own children: buckle them up in a child car safety seat in accordance with child passenger protection laws. That's only part of what pediatrician Robert Sanders, MD has given us all.

Bob, affectionately known as Dr. Seat Belt in his beloved home state of Tennessee, with his gentle manner and nearly transparent but enormous strength, spearheaded the passage in 1977 of Tennessee's child buckle-up law, the first of its kind in the world. Shortly thereafter, he was instrumental in fusing a few hundred passionate but disconnected child passenger safety advocates (I among them) into an inspired, coordinated grassroots army of advocates and activists. We were mothers and fathers, policemen and lawyers, nurses and physicians, engineers and business people and others of every stripe, who came from around the country to meet in Nashville to celebrate the law and convene at the 1st National Child Passenger Safety Conference in May of 1978. It was then that I and most others first met Bob. There Bob was, and grew to become even more, the guiding spirit of a national (even worldwide) movement. Within a few years this led to child buckle-up laws in every state and many nations, a change in the morés and behavior of how we protect our children and ourselves on our roads and highways.

In the broader sense, this was the culmination of a monumental change in public consciousness about motor vehicle trauma. The old consciousness that injury and death in motor vehicles was an "accident" (something pretty much beyond anybody's control) was transformed. Motor vehicle safety pioneers Dr. William Haddon, Ralph Nader, Joan Claybrook, Dr. Seymour Charles, Annemarie Shelness, Dr. Robert Scherz, many safety engineers and others created the invaluable scientific and socio-political foundations upon which Bob built. They enabled the reformulation of motor vehicle trauma from one of numerous and isolated "accidents" to that of a public health issue...the leading cause of death and disability of Americans between 1 and 34 years of age, annually causing hundreds of

3

thousands of preventable injuries, tens of thousands of preventable deaths and many billions of dollars in unnecessary costs. It came to be seen as an "epidemic", and one over which we have substantial control through scientific understanding, socially responsible commercial activity, individual expressions of social and self-interest, and publicly supported law and governmental regulation. What was missing was the ingredient to transform this relatively sequestered knowledge into wider awareness and into effective, preventive action.

By his focus on children, Bob intuitively hit upon that missing ingredient. He leveraged the combination of his passion for the well-being of children, his warm and unassuming personality, his rich network of colleagues and friends, with the guidance and contributions made by the "pioneers" to become the father of the Tennessee Child Passenger Protection Act. Pat, his wife and constant co-worker, was surely the law's mother. This law was Bob's unique contribution. It was instrumental in transforming motor vehicle trauma prevention from a relatively obscure public health problem to a sort of national "cause celebre". The American Academy of Pediatrics (and many other organizations) joined to help lead the cause. Child safety seats in cars and "Buckle-Up Your Baby" stickers decorating innumerable bumpers became a universal presence…as did Tennessee-inspired laws that changed the world of passenger protection. Indeed, the impact of Bob's work spread beyond child passenger safety, helping to make socially acceptable and politically possible the ensuing adult seat belt laws and automobile airbag safety standards which now protect virtually every person in the United States. Suddenly, against the earlier and prevailing dictum of Henry Ford II, safety "sold".

More than country music poured out of Tennessee in 1978. The state that had produced the Grand Ol' Opry also gave birth to an extraordinary son of the South. Bob Sanders composed and inspired a focused, national revolution in individual and social behavior, and helped make this world a safer, more secure place for us, our children, and their children for generations to come.

The story of Bob Sanders' life does not, of course, begin nor end with his activity as Dr. Seat Belt. That activity, while a personal and public highlight, is neither a light from nowhere nor a solitary light. He comes from a small town in the rural South; spends childhood summers in the sunlit and naturally-watered soil and limestone hills of his mother's family farm outside of Murfreesboro, Tennessee; grows, matures and builds a rich, enduring, international network of friends and colleagues in the medical schools and scientific centers of the great universities of Vanderbilt in Nashville and the Karolinska Institute in Stockholm, Sweden. Bob marries Pat who becomes his lifelong companion and collaborator. They move to that same family farm where they raise their children, Robert (who wrote this book) and Priscilla (who has written the next tribute). Bob practices pediatrics, later combined with public health as the health officer of Rutherford County. To help financial ends meet, (there was not much money in serving the poor), he cultivates crops and husbands livestock in the fields around his home, and he accepts appointment as the county medical examiner. Many of the details of his life story are told in this volume. His life and this book are a testament of a life well-lived, a beacon and guiding light that have shone and will continue to shine for so many, for years to come.

On a personal note, a few years before Bob's death in January 2006, my wife Nancy and I had the great pleasure of hosting Bob, Pat, and Priscilla during part of their visit to Los Angeles. Bob had been ill for quite a while, struggling against small B cell lymphoma, with Pat ever at his side. His spirit and enthusiasm still shown brightly through his questions and reminiscences, and with his appreciation for our hospitality and his thorough enjoyment of a Mexican dinner, Mariachi music and a flamenco dance performance at a downtown restaurant. At my home, Bob and I privately talked about his declining health and possibly impending death. His main concerns were not about himself, but about the security and well-being of Pat, Robert, and Priscilla . . . and for the integrity of their 140-year-old family home and farm. This was characteristic of Bob: self-effacing, generous and ever-caring for others and for the environment (physical and social) from which we all spring and to which we all return.

Thank you my friend.

Robert S. Vinetz, MD, FAAP

Reflections from his Daughter, Priscilla Sanders

From as early as I can remember, I treasured every moment with my Dad. We had a special connection we would often speak about and marvel over. I'd look forward to his coming home each night after he got done with work, and often would serenade him with my piano practicing as he came up the sidewalk.

I loved to visit him at his office at the Rutherford County Health Department. I felt so proud of him because I knew he was helping people. Classmates of mine in the public schools of Murfreesboro would say, "Is Dr. Sanders your dad?" "Yes," I'd say proudly. "I just LUV him." They'd drawl. My heart would warm. I figured he was as tender and sensitive a doctor as he was a father, and I was glad to share him, and glad they appreciated him.

He was very dedicated to my Mom, Robert, and me. He decided to go into public health because he wanted to have weekends off so he could spend more time with us, and have a salary he could count on to support us. He didn't like charging people for services, and the years he was in private practice as a pediatrician he barely broke even. He was not a cut-throat capitalist by any means. His medical training and fellowship in Sweden introduced him to socialist medicine and government, and it very much influenced him on his choices and world view. He often spoke about the responsibility of the government to educate and care for its people. This drove him and his vision to see kids in car seats in Tennessee.

The Health Department was our extended family, and I knew almost everyone there. They were so friendly to me, and respectful, and I felt special—and it was because of Dad. I had a lot of lovely life lessons from that staff. I also look back and appreciate them for their support of him as he worked tirelessly to get Tennessee to pass the law to put children in car safety seats. They knew he was working around the clock to make that happen, and I'm sure it had ramifications in the workplace. I think we were all skeptical it would pass, and then rooting for him at the same time. He was so passionate about it.

I remember wanting to spend time with him on the weekends and often having to patiently wait for him to finish with grassroots phone calls to physician allies or representatives he was working to convert. There were many Saturday afternoons spent sitting with him by the fire in the living room reading a book or doing homework while he wrote a letter or speech longhand on his yellow legal pad. I was so happy when he'd put the pen down, and we could go play tennis, or work in the yard together, or get ready to all go to a movie in town.

There were a lot of times I was jealous of his efforts at child passenger safety. We coined it "The Subject." Both Robert and I got tired of it being the topic of conversation at every meal at the dinner table and in every car ride. Dad and Mom were completely consumed. I realize now that *that* consumption and commitment is why the law passed, and the reason so many children's lives have been saved. I feel a little selfish for my 4th grade jealousies, but I was just a kid.

I also got made fun of by classmates for the multiple bumper stickers on our family car that reflected the obsession with educating the masses about seat belts and car seats. "Buckle Up your Baby!" was one, but "My baby's first ride was a safe ride," was the one that I really got taunted for. There were frequent eye rolls and sighs when "the Subject" came up, but of course now I see that it was all necessary, and I burst with pride that my parents were so significant in creating that movement that is now taken for granted, and that every state has a law. It's pretty incredible, actually. So many lives have been saved.

I remember having such mixed feelings in 6th grade when our whole class gathered around the classroom television to watch Dad get interviewed by David Hartman on "Good Morning America." I was proud, embarrassed, and worried for him all at the same time. He did really well on that interview. I know it was challenging for him. He was by nature a shy man who didn't really like to draw attention to himself, or brag in any way whatsoever. He was the very definition of humbleness, almost to a fault. Later in life, I wanted him to feel better about himself as a person, but he was never satisfied—ever a perfectionist. He never felt he could do enough for his community, friends, or family.

I appreciate all the people who contributed to the writing of this book: friends, colleagues, and family. I appreciate my mother for her many conversations with Robert about Dad, and recollections about that time some 30 years ago. I know she misses him, and it makes her sad to remember sometimes—they were true soul mates. I also admire my brother, Robert, for taking the initiative to write and compile all this information. It is an important story of a sincere, sensitive, humble man with a vision to help people, and especially children, to be safe on our nation's highways. I hope it will inspire you, warm your heart, and provide an example of how each of us really can make a difference in this world, and how we affect everyone else. Dad's life and efforts were like loving drops of water going into a pond and the ripples going out. They are still going out. May they now touch you.

Bob Sanders with his daughter Priscilla, 1970
courtesy: Jim Ramsey

Ancestry

Robert S. Sanders had his ancestral roots in Rutherford County right back to the early 1800s, the days of the pioneer settlers, or better said, European settlers. His father's family originally settled in the northeastern part of Rutherford County near Halls Hill, but later settled in the Leanna (or Bethel) community between Murfreesboro and Smyrna in later generations (mid 1800s).

His mother's family lived near the Salem (or Overall) community, her great-great grandfather Major Robert Smith having received a Revolutionary land grant in that area in the early 1800s.

Bobby Sanders' grandfather was William Josiah Sanders (Joe), born during the Civil War, December 1, 1862, son of Drury Josiah Sanders and Frances Jane Stockard. Drury was a Confederate soldier at the time.

WJ and Fannie A Sanders and their 8 children (William, Jr. in middle), 1920

William Josiah Sanders grew up in the Leanna Community, married Fannie Adams, and had eight children, (William, Jr., being the oldest). William (Joe) was first a physician and then a well-respected dentist and photographer in Murfreesboro for many years. He was a descendant of

Rev. Ebenezer McGowan of the Bethel Church in the Leanna Community. William J. and Fannie Adams Sanders' children were: William (1893), Frances (1895), Brockman (1898), Marthame (1900), Richard (1904), Henry (1907), Louise (1910), and Harvey (1911).

William J. Sanders' wife Fannie Adams was born December 13, 1871. She was the daughter of William Harvey Adams and Nancy Atkinson. She was a fine homemaker and had a talent for music and poetry. Her grandfather William Atkinson, who lived near the Leanna Community, was a big, tall man, weighing 350 pounds. He was a farmer and was known to walk the 7 miles to Murfreesboro instead of riding in a buggy for fear of breaking a buggy spring.

Bobby Sanders' other grandfather was Robert Andrew Smith, born February 16, 1846, son of John Parke Smith and Elizabeth Kennon Sims. Robert grew up on the old stagecoach road leading to Shelbyville, now known as Armstrong Valley Road and Midland Road.

Robert A. Smith   Florence E. McLean

He married Florence Elizabeth McLean, had ten children, seven living to adulthood. Inez was the youngest. Robert was a full-time, prize-winning shorthorn cattle farmer off of what is now Armstrong Valley Road. Robert A. and Florence M. Smith's children were: Katie (1870), Clifford (1872), Leonard (1877), Neva (1879), Alma and Howard (1881), Dana (1882), Missie (1884), Celene (1887), and Inez (1890).

Robert A. Smith's wife, Florence Elizabeth McLean, was born February 3, 1846. She was the daughter of Charles Grandison McLean and Temperance Catherine Joslin (earlier Jocelyn) who lived in the Middleton (now Midland) Community.

Bobby Sanders had mostly English, Scottish, and French ancestry, the majority of them settling in Virginia and North Carolina. Some of his ancestors were prominent, among them Nicolas Martiau, who lived in

Yorktown in the early 1600s and served in the House of Burgesses; Augustine Warner and Mildred Reade, the great-grandparents of the first President, George Washington; John Lewis, Jr. and Elizabeth Warner, whose descendant was Meriwether Lewis, the explorer. Another prominent ancestor was Nicholas Meriwether, who owned over 11,000 acres in Virginia and lived to be over 100 years old.

Swepson Sims   Jane Meriwether Lewis

Closer to home, Bobby Sanders' great-great grandfather Swepson Sims, MD was one of the first doctors in Rutherford County in the early 1800s. He lived on a farm on what is now Kimbro Road, southwest of Murfreesboro. Sims was also a Methodist minister. His wife was Jane Meriwether Lewis, first cousin to the explorer.

Charles G. McLean, 1850

Florence McLean's father, Charles Grandison McLean, was of Scottish descent, and he lived in Middleton (now Midland) in southern Rutherford County. He was a merchant who travelled back and forth to Philadelphia, and he was affluent and wealthy enough to send his children to prominent schools, such as Wards Seminary in Nashville.

Temperance Catherine Joslin's grandfather was Lazarus Crawford, one of the earliest settlers in Rutherford County. He lived near Wilkerson Crossroads, now known as the Blackman community. Her other grandfather was Benjamin Christopher Joslin, who was a large landowner and founded Joslin's Station near what is now Bellevue southwest of Nashville. Both the Joslins and the Crawfords have a long line of ancestry, dating way on back into the early days of England and France.

To put it mildly, many of Bobby Sanders' ancestors were well respected, hard-working individuals of good upbringing. They cared about educating their children and seeing to it that they were successful, all of which helped make Dr. Robert S. Sanders the well respected man that he became.

Childhood and Family Relatives

Bobby Sanders as a newborn in the arms of his father William

Dr. Robert S. Sanders was born in Tullahoma, Tennessee, October 24, 1927, the second and youngest son of William Josiah Sanders, Jr. and Inez Smith, both of whom were natives of Rutherford County, of which Murfreesboro, Tennessee is the county seat. As he grew up, he was called "Bobby," and he would later be known as "Bob."

Even though William and Inez had grown up in Rutherford County, they made their home in Tullahoma after they were married in 1920.

The Sanders family lived at 405 S. Jackson Street in central Tullahoma, the house having been built in the mid 1920s by his father William, who ran and owned Builder's Supply Company, a business that would remain in the family right into the new millennium.

Bobby Sanders had an older brother, Bill (William Josiah Sanders, III). Born July 3, 1922, he was five years older than Bobby, and he was a fine person who always set a good example for his younger brother.

Bill and his baby brother Bobby, 1928   Bobby, 1935

William and Inez' home on 405 S. Jackson Street, Tullahoma

Bob's father William was born October 29, 1893, in the home of his grandparents Drury J. Sanders and Frances J. Stockard. He was the oldest of eight, and he had the respect of his 7 younger siblings, all of whom called him "Brother." Even though his father WJ was a well respected dentist and the founder of the Rutherford County Creamery, he was too strict with his children. One day when William was a grown teenager, he decided to relax in the spring after a hard day's work on his parents' farm. WJ came after his son with a switch, telling him to get back to work, that there was more to do. William, being considerably bigger than his father, stood up, grabbed his father, picked him up, and dropped him in the water! Then he told him, "I'm a grown man now, Father. I've got my own life ahead of me." William didn't believe in nonsense, and he knew that a father's taking a switch to an 18-year-old son was just that . . . nonsense. After all, both he and his oldest brother Brockman had sacrificed going to college so they could help with the farm chores and help raise the younger siblings. It wasn't so much disrespect as much as it was that William had to assert himself to his father.

William's brother Brockman was a mechanic, and he had the first Ford dealership in Murfreesboro. He spent his whole life in Murfreesboro and raised his family there.

William had earlier been dating a Lillian Jarratt out in the Salem (Overall) community, but then WWI broke out, and William went off to South Carolina to train in the U.S. Marine Corps. Fortunately, the war ended before William was shipped out, and he never went to war. When he returned to Tennessee, he discovered that Lillian had not waited for him. She had married William Riggs.

So, William began courting Inez Smith, who lived further down the road. He already knew her and her family from Sunday gatherings and picnics. Inez was nearly four years older than William, but that made no difference to him. He used to ride out from Murfreesboro in a horse and buggy to visit Inez regularly. Upon returning home, since his horse Mac knew the way, he would sleep in the buggy, putting the buggy on "automatic." One night, he was awakened and startled by the sound of the train in Murfreesboro, and he was relieved to see that his horse had known to stop at the railroad crossing to let the train go by.

Bob's mother Inez Smith, was born January 2, 1890 at her parents' home off of what is now Armstrong Valley Road. Being the youngest of ten, she lost her mother to pneumonia when she was barely 11. Her father Robert never remarried, and she was raised by him and her older siblings. She had a good childhood, growing up on the 370 acre farm, and she became a good tennis player, as well. She attended Soule College in Murfreesboro. Inez's father, Robert, lost his life to a heart attack in 1916, while he was separating a dog fight. He was 70.

Inez was late getting married, and when she finally did in 1920, her oldest brother Clifford had to give her away. William and Inez were married October 20, 1920 at the Salem Methodist Church, soon after which they moved to Tullahoma where William was running and operating Builder's Supply Company.

William and Inez, around 1920

Bobby grew up living a good life in Tullahoma. It was a small town in those days, and everybody knew each other. He had plenty of friends while growing up, and he played childhood games with neighbors up and down the street. Grammar school was directly across the road from his house, and he enjoyed the luxury of going home for lunch each day.

William and Inez regularly took their sons to Murfreesboro to visit both William's parents on Sulphur Springs Road and Inez's family out on the Smith farm southwest of Murfreesboro.

William & Inez, around 1930

15

On William's side, all seven of his siblings had gotten married and had children. Nearly half of them moved to Atlanta, Georgia and lived there, and one of the families lived in North Carolina. They had family reunions on a regular basis and William, Sr. (WJ), being a photographer, always took plenty of photos. William, Jr. also took lots of snapshots at these family gatherings.

the Smith grandchildren, except Pon, mid 1940s

On Inez's side, the Smith farm was a great place to visit, and Bill and Bobby used to stay for several weeks every summer while growing up. Inez's older sister Celene, who married John H. North, used to bring her family from Dallas, Texas. There were 3 children: Florence (Pon), Mary Ruth, and Johnny. Mary Ruth was Bill's age, and Johnny was Bobby's age.

Celene with Mary Ruth, Pon, Inez with Bill, 1923
Missie and Neva Smith in back, Missie McLean Hill in center

All of them used to run around barefoot on dusty paths and play together. They enjoyed the barn and hayloft, playing on the haystacks. Their favorite area to play was the rocks. These were a group of large standing rocks, most of them several feet apart with the creek running between them. This group of rocks was midway between the Smith farm and Dana Smith's farm to the north. They used to enjoy jumping from one rock to another, sometimes over the water, and they played hide and seek.

Dana lived in the original John Parke Smith house on his farm to the north, but he used to visit and eat meals regularly at his homeplace with his sisters, Missie and Neva. Leonard had married and moved off to West Tennessee (Memphis), and Clifford had died already of a heart attack in 1931. Dana loved milk, and he used to drink it at meals and then say, "Ah, Lee Anthony!" He also loved baseball and used to take his nieces and nephews to Nashville to the games.

Missie and Neva were Sunday school teachers at the Salem Methodist Church. They were very interested in genealogy, and they found out as much about their ancestry and family connections as possible. They made charts and wrote dates on wrapping paper and other scraps and notebooks. They also compiled a wealth of old photographs, including hiding an extra photo of Dana with the Salem baseball team. Dana was very camera shy and had cut himself out of what he thought was the only photograph of him.

There were several tenant families who lived in houses along the edge of the woods. Some of those children, both black and white, were the ages of Bill and Bobby, and they used to join in the fun and play at times.

Dana, being a full-time farmer, had plenty of cattle, some sheep and goats. Among both farms, there were two big barns and silos, two smaller sheep and horse barns, and a corn crib. Snake rail fences made of split cedar rails, ran the edges of several fields to keep goats and sheep in their places.

Dana was well known throughout the district, and he used to trade with and buy cattle from a place out in Texas, having the cattle brought in on trains, and he would bring in sheep from Idaho.

Dana's older brother, Clifford, had travelled to the Klondike in Alaska in the 1890s, when he was in his twenties. He and his second cousin John Joslin travelled up there together to search for gold. It was 40 degrees below zero and they used to take turns in deep vertical holes, as they would dig for gold. Clifford never struck it rich, but he did bring back a few small gold nuggets as momentos or souvenirs.

Bobby Sanders enjoyed his childhood, growing up in Tullahoma. He had numerous friends. There was Goochie who lived next door. He also knew Laddie Harton, Sam Carney, Bob Couch, Lester Freeman, Mary Ann King, Charles Pikle, Dick Smartt, Tommy Wiseman, and others.

some of Bobby Sanders' friends in Tullahoma, 1942
Charles (Buck) Pehle, Corky Smartt, Mary Ann King, & Laddie Harton

Some of them used to play kick the can, and as a means of small mischief, several of them would stand on either side of the street, and when a car would come along, they would act like they were pulling a rope across the street. Sometimes cars would slam on their brakes and come to a screeching halt. Bobby and his friends would run and hide!

The neighborhood enjoyed knowing Bobby. He also liked to draw cartoon images, and he would include them with notes he would write to people.

One day, his brother Bill, on the spur of the moment, offered to take him out to Tullahoma's airport. Pilots were taking people up for $5 a piece. He carried Bob over there on his bicycle handlebars, and somebody took them up in an airplane. They flew all around Tullahoma and had the best time looking down at the town and surrounding countryside! Once back on the ground, Bill bicycled Bob back home. They kept their excursion a secret.

Of course, Tullahoma being a small town, gossip spread, and word reached Bill and Bob's parents. They were upset to say the least! Plus Bill and Bob had gone without permission! They sent Bob to his room upstairs.

Bill was told to stay downstairs where he was punished. Bob never found out what they did to Bill; seems like Bill didn't want to talk about it.

In adolescent years, Bobby dated Laddie Harton, Mary Anne King, and others. He and his friends would go to the movies or go get a soda at the drug store. They went to dances which were held on the floor of the old Coca Cola plant. They enjoyed swimming at Lake Tullahoma in the summers. Bobby Sanders and Bob Couch used to do diving antics to show off to the others.

Bobby also played the cornet in the school's band. He was a good student and a good athlete, as well. He did Boy Scouts and became an Eagle Scout at age 16.

In his childhood and teenage years growing up, Bobby used to love going to see Laurel and Hardy movies. He and Bob Couch used to make funny faces, especially liking to imitate Stan Laurel. Oliver Hardy used to say to Stan Laurel, "Well, this is a fine mess you've gotten us into!" That was said in every movie.

Bobby had a lot of antics like his father. He had that flare like his father did for making funny comments.

Bobby's father William had several hunting dogs, mostly beagles, and he used to take them hunting on the weekends. Sometimes Bobby accompanied his father on hunting rounds in the countryside.

William was a member of the Masonic Order, doing Eastern Star Work, and he was the Grand Master for a while. He travelled all over Tennessee to different Masonic meetings. William had a phenomenal photographic memory. Bill and Bob used to hold the book on their father, and they marveled at how he recited page after page of text and got every word right.

When Bobby was an early teenager, his father traded in the family car for a new 1941 Buick Super Deluxe, straight 8 motor with a 3 speed. It was nice to have a new car, and when they drove to visit relatives in Murfreesboro, they averaged 43 miles per hour on the narrow 2-lane highways. They didn't know they'd be keeping the car for so long, but WWII broke out later that year, and rationing came with it. It was well into the 1950s before they sold that car.

The war brought on the mentality in everybody's mind of a need for military training, so Bobby went off to Castle Heights Military Academy for his last two years of high school, not just for the military but for the sports and athletics offered, as well.

Anti-Segregation Viewpoint

Bob Sanders was anti-segregation from early on in his life. He realized that people were people, and that they were equal, regardless of race or color. Bob had considered the possibility of being a minister, back when he was a teenager. He believed in doing good, and he enjoyed the togetherness at church and being with friends.

One summer when he was still a child, his church took a weeklong trip to Lake Junaluska in North Carolina for their retreat. There were several black children also along on this trip, and as they were about to go swimming in the beautiful lake, the camp authorities suddenly informed them that the black children would not be allowed to swim in the lake! That really irked the church leaders, and as a means to try and be fair, they decided that *none* of the children would swim in the lake. They boycotted the lake!

That was very displeasing to Bobby. He had so much looked forward to swimming in that beautiful lake! And now he couldn't, due to a bunch of racist segregationists! That experience was a rude awakening to Bobby about the segregation of black people. It weighed heavily on his social conscience and had quite an impact on his way of thinking, and it came to influence him to be anti-segregation.

A lot of people were really narrow minded in those days. Thank goodness segregation was abolished with the Civil Rights Act in the late 1960s. Good thing too, because little did anyone know the number of races would increase from two to four by the turn of the millennium. A significant number of Asians and Mexicans have arrived in this country since the days of segregation. Segregation would have become very complicated and expensive by this day and time, with four separate schools and four separate facilities, four separate bathrooms, four separate seating areas on planes, trains, buses, theatres, restaurants, etc. Can you imagine the headaches it would have caused by this day and time?

Castle Heights Military Academy, 1944-1946

As the United States was fully entrenched in WWII, both in Europe and in the Pacific, Bobby Sanders decided to transfer to Castle Heights Military Academy in Lebanon, Tennessee, after going to Tullahoma High School for two years. His brother Bill was on a destroyer in the Pacific, and Bobby felt sure he was going to be drafted into the war, right out of high school. He entered Castle Heights as a junior in the fall of 1944. His junior and senior year, from a military standpoint, would help him understand things better, in case he got drafted, especially in terms of junior ROTC training and structured discipline.

Not just for the military, other attracting factors for Castle Heights were its academics and its athletic program. Granted, Tullahoma High School was a great school, and in retrospect maybe Bobby should have stayed there, but during the war, they tore down the gymnasium and a lot of the sports had been eliminated.

A school with a military atmosphere like Castle Heights applied a certain amount of discipline in academics and homework. There was a set time for that each night in the dorms. Bobby had to get used to the very structured guidelines and rules.

No women attended the academy in those days. Bobby and his classmates would only see women three to four times a year at socials or dances, proms, things like that.

In addition to the military and academics, Bobby participated in a number of sports. He ran track, doing the high jump, broad jump, sprinting, and he played grid iron football. In the end, he was voted best all around athlete.

Bobby carrying the football at Castle Heights
courtesy: Henry Huddleston

In the Huddle, by Henry Huddleston

SPRING FOOTBALL

Although not many people notice them over behind Bullard Hall every afternoon, the spring football candidates are still "sweating it out." Of the fifty who reported to coach Gwynn when he first issued the call in the second week in March only about 28 remain. The others have dropped out after finding there was a little more to football than meets the eye. The remaining boys are beginning to bear down to hard work on the few plays they have been given.

Already it is evident there has been plenty of conditioning, and football fundamentals have been drilled into the squad from the start. During the first few weeks the entire practice period was divided into three parts—calisthenics, blocking and tackling.

Now that the "goldbricks" have been weeded out, the boys are beginning to get a taste of scrimmage. The coaches are still feeling out some of the local high schools for a scrimmage game before spring training ceases in about three to five weeks.

PINGPONG CHAMP

Heights has crowned a ping pong champion! Bill Stonestreet turned the trick as he outclassed all opposition in the recent tournament sponsored by the Heights "Y." He emerged the winner from 62 guys who formed the two brackets in the tournament. In the finals, he flashed through on four straight games to beat out Irvin Griffin, who was runnerup in the tourney. In these games Stonestreet played almost flawlessly and his smashing forehand was the deciding factor. The entire tourney seemed to be enjoyed by all and no doubt should be made an annual affair.

SWIMMERS FINALLY SCHEDULE MEET

At last after four months practice the Bengal aquastars have found an opponent. Saturday, April 14, the McCallie swimmers are slated for a meet in the Heights pool. This means the Mid-South meet will be held in Chattanooga at McCallie again. After four months of work without reward the swimmers deserve the best support from the corps and we should all pack the pool next Saturday. With all the swimmers—Heyl, Jackson, Blank, Brink and Miller—ready and raring, they ought to put on a fine show.

THINLIES SHOW PROMISE

Don't let that first defeat of the track season fool you! They have plenty of power and potentiality. The most outstanding feat in the Heights-McCallie meet was Irvin Griffin's hurling of the javelin. He was the only participant in this event to throw the javelin over the 140-foot mark and he did it consistently. His heave of 158 feet, only a few feet short of the Mid-South

23

record, left the larger McCallie athletes gasping. Versatile Bobby Sanders, however, seems destined for the largest amount of work this year.

In this meet, the first of his career, he entered in five events, winning the high jump, placing second in the broad jump and one hundred yard dash, and brought home the baton in the first place team in the 880 yard relay, as the anchor man. That's 19 points in his first meet. Not bad at all!

However, the meet with McCallie cannot be mentioned without saying something about Owen, who won the meet for McCallie almost singlehanded. Incidentally, he is from the same town, Bluefield, West Virginia, as "Dancer" Draper, who was Heights' nemesis in the McCallie football game plus second in the 220 yard dash.

A few of Bobby's friends from Tullahoma were with him at Castle Heights, including Sam Carney. Bobby also made friends from other places, including Bascom Cooksey, Henry Huddleston, Enfield (Flicky) Ford, Hubert McCullough, Jack and Dick Reeves, and Jim Rich Roberts.

Class Officers Named at Heights

LEBANON, Tenn., Feb. 9—(Spl)—Bobby Sanders (seated), son of Mr. and Mrs. W. J. Sanders, Tullahoma, has been elected president of the senior class at Castle Heights Military Academy. Other officers are (standing, left to right), Kenneth Clevenger, Narrows, Va., Richard Blank, Tampa, Fla., and Richard Pennell, Nezperce, Idaho.

Castle Heights names officers

Even though Bobby was away from Tullahoma High School his junior and senior year, he still kept up with his Tullahoma friends and classmates, and when he was home during the holidays and the summers, he did activities with them.

In the spring of 1946, Bobby graduated from Castle Heights. He spent the following summer being a camp counselor at Lake Tullahoma and doing lifeguard duty.

Bobby Sanders with his father William

Bob and Bill Sanders, 1945

The 18 Months in the Army, 1946-early 1948

Bobby Sanders with his parents, 1946

In August of 1946, even though WWII was over, most people were still influenced to think about serving in the military. It was the thing to do, and no one knew if or when the next war might break out! One of Bobby's Tullahoma friends, Lester Freeman, told him that there was an offer from the Army to join for 18 months, and then you would never be drafted.

On August 12, both of them signed up for the U.S. Army at the Tullahoma Post Office recruiting office. As it turned out, they were together for the whole 18 months. The very same day, they left on a bus for Chattanooga, and Fort Oglethorpe, Georgia. The physical took place the next day, and he was sworn in. He was moved to Bragg, North Carolina, where he was given his shots, then on to Fort Belvoir, Virginia, where he underwent eight weeks of basic training. He was also at Fort A.P. Hill, Virginia.

Bobby managed to take leave long enough to be best man in his brother Bill's wedding to Jean Etheridge November 2, 1946 down in Norfolk, Virginia, Jean's home town.

After basic training, Bobby trained in survey classes for three months, shooting stars, the Azimuth, etc. He went home for Christmas, then returned to Fort Belvoir, for more training.

26

In March Bobby set sail for the Philippines. He met and became friends with Willie Jones from South Carolina, and Bob Reichenbach from Nebraska. They remained lifelong friends.

Once in Manila, they were assigned surveying duties, such as astronomical observations, topographical engineering, etc. It was fun work for Bobby and was not combat oriented. Much of his time in the military was spent waiting in lines.

While waiting in lines, Bob Reichenbach read books, so Bobby read books, too. His favorites were the Lloyd C. Douglas (Aerosmith) books written by Sinclair Lewis.

He spent several months being stationed at Okinawa, and in the Philippines.

Before returning to the U.S., he visited Omami Oshima in Japan. In December 1947, they set sail back to San Francisco, arriving on Christmas Eve. On January 8, 1948, Bob Sanders was discharged from the Army, and he took a train back home to Tennessee.

Vanderbilt Undergraduate Years, 1948-1951

Bob Sanders entered Vanderbilt University as an undergraduate in the Fall of 1948. He had been home from the U.S. Army since February. Having served the year and a half in the military, he received the GI Bill, which paid his tuition for 4 years. He was told he would never be drafted because he had volunteered for those 18 months.

He did very well, and he made some very good friends at Vanderbilt. He pledged Sigma Chi fraternity, because of Tommy Wiseman and Lester Freeman's urging. Plus Lester and Bob had been in the army together. Also, he joined Sigma Chi because his brother Bill was in Sigma Chi at Georgia Tech a few years earlier. In fact, his uncle Marthame Sanders had founded the chapter at Georgia Tech. So, it was a Sanders legacy to be in the Sigma Chi fraternity. On the other hand, Enfield (Flicky) Ford and Bob had been at Castle Heights together and were football teammates. He was already an upper classman and had wanted Bob to join him in the Beta Theta Pi fraternity. He was very disappointed that Bob joined a different fraternity.

Another influencing factor for joining the Sigma Chi was that they were tee-totalers. There was not any drinking of alcohol in the house. (That changed and was no longer true in later decades.)

Several of Bob's Sigma Chi brothers who were also in pre-med were Gordon Long, Bill Alford, George Burrus, Bill Clark, and Jack Reeves.

Bob played intramural football for the Sigma Chi fraternity. He was also on the Vanderbilt University track team, his track coach being Herc Alley. He did the relays, short distance running, and the broad jump.

By this time, Bob had made the decision to study medicine and become a doctor. During his teenage years however, he had considered going into ministry and becoming a Methodist minister, but he realized that more lives could possibly be saved in the field of medicine.

He studied pre-med courses, and the arts and sciences. He took the scientific German, (not the spoken German), Math, Chemistry, English, and History.

In Chemistry lab, Bill Alford and Bill Clark always got done with their lab experiments earlier than the other Sigma Chi brothers.

His major was Chemistry, and he got a Bachelor of Arts degree. Lamar Field was Bob's faculty advisor and one of his Chemistry professors. Dr. Field recommended that Bob stay on and obtain a Ph.D. in Chemistry, if he didn't go to medical school.

Bob was a pledge trainer for the Sigma Chis his junior year. His room-mate that year was Jack Reeves.

Bob was on overload and was trying to do too much, and he came down with a bad case of mononucleosis. He had to be hospitalized in the infirmary.

Vanderbilt Medical School, 1951-1955

Bob was interviewed more than once for entrance into medical school at Vanderbilt University. The first interview didn't go all that well, and before his second interview, his brother Bill, who really wanted Bob to get in, initiated and rounded up several letters from prominent people of Tullahoma, and they were sent to the admissions committee. Some of the letters were written by older Sigma Chi's. Bob's second interview was with Dr. Sam Clark, (who was actually a cousin on the Smith line). The second interview went a lot better. After all, he had done pretty well in under-graduate school. Bob was accepted.

His senior year in undergraduate school was actually in absentia because it was also his first year in medical school. This was possible only because he stayed at the same school for medical school. If he had gone to any other medical school, he wouldn't have been able to do that.

Several of Bob's Sigma Chi buddies were in that same class, and they continued in medical school at Vanderbilt. During his first year, he roomed again with Jack Reeves.

Vanderbilt Medical School was one of the best medical schools in the country with some prominent, nationally renowned professors and a large complex of state of the art classes, clinics, and the hospital. It also included a school of nursing. Three tightly connected buildings formed the medical school-hospital complex, constructed in the Gothic style and being built of concrete with limestone walls and bricks. There were faculty offices, classes, laboratories, inpatient wards, and outpatient clinics. The layout was engineered so that clinical problems at the bedside could be taken into the research laboratories of the scientists and medical staff, a very well designed medical school.

In addition to its being one of the best medical schools, it was also one of the toughest, with the medical faculty's main goal being to make it difficult for the students, overload them with study material and work, and try to weed them out. They tried to make them fail, but Bob Sanders and his classmates were diligent and studied hard. Only a small percentage of them succumbed to failure.

In their freshman year, the students were loaded up with Gross Anatomy, with a head full of complicated names to memorize and understand in Latin! That was the main course which included labs, and it began with a study of the head and neck, the most complicated parts of the human body. In labs, they dissected cadavers, and there were two professors, Dr. Sam Clark, and Dr. Jim Ward.

Nearly every professor instilled fear in the students, and the professors demanded a lot. They had high expectations of their students, as they wanted them to become knowledgeable and competent doctors. Failure to respect that could result in flunking out of medical school. The motto was to study hard to avoid the faculty's wrath, and endure the hard and rigorous road ahead.

With the addition of Neuroanatomy in the same year, the difficult workload made students have to do priority juggling with their courses of study, get behind in one, catch up on another, let another one slide a day, then catch that up. Group study was a big help with time limits put on each course of study, whether completely finished or not.

The medical students soon learned the truth that in medical practice, there was almost never enough time to get everything done. Doctors in the real world seldom went to bed at night with all their work completely finished.

Gray's Anatomy was the main textbook used at Vanderbilt Medical School. Some of the professors had actually written some of the textbooks used nationwide. For example, Dr. Kampmeier wrote the textbook for Clinical Medicine: Physical Examination in Health and Disease.

The tough curriculum caused many students to feel a kind of de-tachment from the real world. Dating, going to games, and other fun activities basically had to be put aside for more study time to complete the coursework. It was very rigorous. Most doctors feel a sense of emotional detachment, even when they're in practice. It is said in general that it is not a wise practice for doctors to have close relatives or close friends for their patients. It's as if doctors are somewhat set aside, never being meant to be fully a part of the world around them.

In the second year of medical school, they studied Pathology, the study of diseases. Dr. John Shapiro was the professor. Having been a battalion surgeon in Italy during WWII, he was badly injured and was left with a bad knee. He walked with quite a limp, swinging his straight leg around to the side with every step. Dr. Shapiro was a tough professor who demanded performance and hard work. He was devoted and was also determined to teach every medical student everything there was to know about Pathology. He was fair and played no favorites, and he was accurate in what he said. Like other professors, he instilled fear in his students, and he called everyone by last name only.

There was a story that an earlier class experienced, in which two students were washing a slippery intestinal tract, which suddenly slipped right out of their hands and down the drain! Dr. Shapiro, with his limp, came over to them. The two students had their backs to him, but they knew Shapiro was coming straight to them. He glared at them and then said, "So, have you decided which one of you two is going to tell the SOB?"

Once the students were finished with pathology during their second year, Dr. Shapiro would become more friendly and then call them by their first name. He would then be cordial, and he was remarkable with his continuing interest in each medical student. Bob Sanders continued to know Shapiro and his wife for many years into the future.

There were numerous labs in Pathology, and instead of dissecting cadavers like they did in Anatomy, they were now dissecting and analyzing autopsies, recently dead bodies, not yet embalmed. The color was certainly different and more vivid than in cadavers. They would determine what disease the person had and what the person had died from.

Vanderbilt Medical School had a nationally, actually *world* renowned, Pathology professor by the name of Dr. Ernest Goodpasture, who was famous for his chick embryo technique for culturing viruses that led to the developing of vaccines for several diseases, such as: yellow fever, small pox, influenza, and typhus. It was Goodpasture who established the legitimacy of Vanderbilt's Medical School after its reorganization in 1925. He was very famous for his accomplishments and had become quite an icon at Vanderbilt. Dr. Shapiro had high regard for him. Dr. Goodpasture deserved the Nobel Prize for his valuable work and research, but someone else received the prize instead.

At least once a week, Dr. Shapiro had his students attend lectures given by Dr. Goodpasture, and Shapiro *fully* expected his students to know and understand Goodpasture's lecture material. It was also imperative that they show him complete respect. Shapiro told his students, "I'll flunk the first student who ever shows any disrespect for Dr. Goodpasture!" All of the students complied, and Shapiro never had to flunk any of them.

Pathology was a difficult hurdle, but Bob Sanders and most of his classmates made it through. Under Dr. Shapiro, many of the medical students learned that being a doctor was demanding. Medicine and its demands came first, no matter what.

Halfway through the second year in medical school, all students also studied Parasitogy, the study of parasitic diseases. Parasitic diseases, like malaria, hookworm, roundworms, and pellagra were still common in those days, especially in the rural South. Dr. Alvin Keller was the professor. Soon after the mid 1950s, the course disappeared, as parasitic diseases were made rare by modern medicine and better sanitation.

Vanderbilt Medical School's third year courses included Clinical Medicine. Dr. Rudolph Kampmeier was the professor, the best one they could have had, because he had actually written the national textbook on the subject. All medical students had to buy instruments for these courses, and much of their study involved clinical settings, lab work, seeing patients, writing detailed lab reports, and going over the whole check list every time. Paying attention to details, and thoroughness were very important, which taught students how to be thorough and complete. The motto was Look, Feel, Listen, and write detailed descriptions. Also, give the patient a chance to talk. He/she will usually tell a doctor what his/her ailment is, if given the time to talk.

Also during the third year, students took courses in surgery, pediatrics, ward work, and clinical obstetrics. This would give each student a taste of each field of medicine and help steer each one toward the field of his/her choice. Bob was favoring pediatrics. Dr. Amos Christie was the chairman of that department.

During the third and fourth year, students continued as clinical clerks, having assigned tasks, scut work, attending to patients in hospitals, etc. There was lots of lab work, blood work, analysis, etc. The last half of the senior year was easier, with less of a workload. The students were able to start dating again, to do extra activities, and go to ball games. They also put in applications for intern work, some of them out of state, and they travelled by train to interview for the intern positions. Bob Sanders decided to stay on at Vanderbilt and intern there.

Bob felt a closer bond with his medical school classmates than he did with those in undergraduate school. There was a certain comradery among them that was not there before. They had more in common.

There was a funny lab story that happened in the fall of 1951. Bob Sanders, Danny Dolan, Jack Reeves, and Jack Rice were cadaver mates and were the usual serious, overwhelmed, edgy first year med students in the cadaver lab, quite devoid of any humor - until a $20 cash check fell out of Walter Puckett's shirt pocket.

Walter Puckett was one of the brightest and most colorful classmates. He was a handsome, big, strong, red-head, a practical joker, and he especially liked to kid Jack Reeves, a kind and religious soul. Earlier he had pinned a "Jesus" sign on the back of Jack's lab coat.

It was Jack Reeves who deftly retrieved the check and cashed it for two $10 bills. After quiet, even sinister deliberation, Danny Dolan was chosen to cut out a one inch square piece of formaldehyde-laden scalp from their cadaver and boldly asked Puckett what he would take to hold that piece of scalp in his mouth for 30 seconds.

Puckett, never before so challenged, pondered a moment and answered, "Ten dollars!" whereupon Dolan slapped a $10 bill on Puckett's cadaver table. Puckett paused then bravely eased the morsel between his teeth. After 30 seconds were counted out loud by gathering classmates, Puckett spat out the scalp, rushed to the sink, washed out his mouth, and held the $10 high in the air, triumphantly announcing, "Now we'll have a party!"

Jack Reeves stepped forward. "Puckett, since you have been such a good sport, here is a bonus of $10."

Instantly, Puckett put two and two together, and he checked his shirt pocket. The $20 check was no longer there. His face and neck turned red as his hair and he quickly left the lab. He returned some 30 minutes later, having called a law student who discouraged any attempt to recover another $20 from them. After all, they *had* returned the $20 to Puckett, hadn't they? The rest of the afternoon he sat upon his stool looking at them, (so very busy with their cadaver), tapping his metal probe on his cadaver table, even smiling occasionally, repeating the words, "I ate one."

Two years later, Walter and Bob lived in adjoining rooms at the Phi Chi house. One night, Bob had just settled into a hot tub bath with a book when Walter entered the room, leaned over the tub and asked, "What are you reading, old man?" (Bob was one of the oldest in the class and bald-ing.) With no warning he emptied a whole bottle of ink into the tub. Bob tried to wrestle Walter into the tub but he was too quick and considerably stronger. Puckett had the last laugh, and Bob ended up with blue feet.

Even still, Walter Puckett and Bob Sanders became good friends, even shared a bachelor apartment later on (1959-61) when Walter was a cardiology fellow and Bob was on the pediatric staff. Walter went on to become one of Chattanooga's most respected and beloved physicians.

Jack Reeves ended up dropping out of medical school after the first year and going to law school instead. He had started medical school to please his father, but med school wasn't to his liking. Even still, Bob Sanders kept in touch with Reeves for many years.

The only other one who dropped out was Nick Nicopolous, but he came back and finished later. He went on to be Elvis Presley's private physician.

Danny Dolan went on to become a doctor in Asheville, North Carolina. He also kept up with Bob Sanders throughout their lives.

Jack Rice became one of Bob's best friends, and Bob would become Jack's best man in his wedding with Joan Pelot in 1954. Years later, they would become brothers-in-law, when Bob would marry Joan's sister Pat. Jack Rice went on to become a psychiatrist, worked for many years in Boston, Massachusetts, then lived and worked over 20 more years in Nashville, Tennessee before retiring and moving to Philadelphia in 2005.

During his junior year, Bob's roommate was John Collins from Monterey, Tennessee. John was one year behind Bob, and he and John came to know each other very well, and also became lifelong friends.

While Bob was in his last year of medical school, it was Dr. Amos Christie, the chairman of pediatrics, who convinced Bob to go into pediatrics because through pediatrics your patients were "more salvageable," so he said.

Dr. Christie had a special way with babies and young children. While a baby would cry while being examined by most doctors, interns, and nurses, Dr. Christie could keep a baby calm, and it would rarely cry. Most of the time, he examined babies while on their mother's lap.

Bob Sanders took a liking to pediatrics. It was true; the patients were more salvageable. They got over diseases faster and were much quicker on rebounding back to good health. That was especially rewarding. Granted it was harder to diagnose infants and young children because they either couldn't tell you what was wrong with them or could only say that they hurt, not very specific, but even still, there were ways to diagnose and treat those patients.

First Year of Residency, 1955-56

photo by Walden Fabry

As a first year intern at Vanderbilt Hospital and Medical School, Bob Sanders made $25 per month. He got his room and board and laundry for free, with that package. He lived in the intern's quarters, where residents also lived. He still didn't have a car then.

Bob Sanders wrote the following about that year:

My internship was a year of intense responsibility and learning, bolstered by a group of uncommonly compatible fellow interns, a year that molded self confidence and self assurance.

These events and experiences come to mind:

-the guidance of our rather stern but fair Chief Resident, Milton Peeler, who required us to appreciate the virtue of detail in caring for children,

-the physical exhaustion of my first rotation, the "green ward"; I soon learned to take naps while walking down the hall, sliding my finger along the wall.

-sweating on the medical records in the hot, non-air conditioned nurses' station.

-the amazing ability of a certain treatment room nurse's aid to utilitize her buxom anatomy to immobilize any small, wiggling patient; we never thanked her enough.

-on my clinic rotation, my giving the first shot to a child in Randy Batson's pioneer field study of the new SALK vaccine, that is, the new polio vaccine.

-Dr. Christie's breakthrough integration of the infant ward rooms:

One day, Dr. Christie decided to integrate the hospital wards for black and white children, as they were still segregated in those days. One hot summer day, the hospital ward for black children was too hot, as only the white ward had air conditioning. So, he threw them all together in the white ward, quite to the dismay of other faculty members, but since he was the chief of pediatrics and a big man at that, he did it anyway. Actually, there wasn't a whole lot of protest. That was the last day of segregation in the hospital wards, and it was well done to have turned that page in the firm manner in which he did it. It was his right, and it was the fair thing to do.

There were several interesting medical cases that I remember:

-an eleven-month-old that swallowed an open safety pin that punctured the wall of the esophagus and pericardium, causing sepsis and cardiac tamponade.

-a nine-year-old female with a parathyroid disorder whose peculiar signs and symptoms were recognized and a diagnosis made on admission by Tommy Dungan, the Assistant Resident.

-my saving Budge McKee's baby's life. The baby had hyaline membrane disease.

Every rotation had strengths and premier faculty instructors; notable was the nursery with Dr. Mildred Stahlman, and the lab with Dr. Sally Sell.

His Year in San Francisco, 1956-1957

Dr. Bob Sanders decided to go to San Francisco for his first year of residency. Dr. Amos Christie, the chief of pediatrics at Vanderbilt, had grown up in California and recommended that Bob go to the University of California Medical Center at San Francisco, because that was where Dr. Christie had trained. He arranged for Bob to have his residency under a Dr. William Deamer.

So, Bob bought a used 1954 Ford Victoria car and drove out there by himself, visiting Hannibal, Missouri on the way. He had always wanted to see where Mark Twain lived and wrote the Tom Sawyer stories. The trip took around a week, and before crossing the desert in California, the service station sold him a leather pouch to strap to the front bumper of his car to hold extra water. That was a tradition in those days.

He arrived in San Francisco and soon met other pediatric residents, among them Philip G. Strauss, Rainer Arnhold, and Wesley Clapp. His new boss was Dr. William Deamer, the chief of pediatrics. Dr. Deamer was really into and concerned about allergies, and he was a major influence on Bob about allergies. Deamer was very allergic and regularly carried adrenalin and benadryl in case he accidentally ate something he was allergic to, such as crab.

Dr. Deamer invited Bob to play tennis with him one Sunday morning at his tennis club. Bob was doubles partner with him, and the match went well until Bob served a ball and it struck Deamer in the back of the head because Deamer was close to the net at that moment. Deamer fell to the ground. Luckily, Deamer was all right, but he was somewhat stunned. Bob felt badly about it.

One of Bob's classmates, Jean Cortner, had a brother-in-law in San Francisco, Bob Morgan. He invited Bob to go horseback riding one Saturday. Bob let the horse get the bit in the mouth and the horse took off and ran away with it. Bob Morgan skillfully galloped up beside the runaway horse, grabbed him by the reigns, and brought him under control. The next day, they went riding again, and the horse did fine. Bob Sanders was careful to hold the reigns tight this time.

Several times, Bob Sanders went camping with Rainer Arnhold and Phil Strauss. They also went skiing up in the Sierra Nevada Mountains during the winter months. They took several road trips through some of the western states, and they became very good friends.

Phil Strauss, who was in internal medicine, was originally from Brooklyn, New York. His girlfriend was Mary Bruchholz, and she came along on activities sometimes. She later became his wife. Rainer Arnhold was originally from Dresden, Germany, and he never married. Arnhold was a Jewish refugee and came to America at age 16.

San Francisco was a little more unstable than Tennessee, due to the San Andreas Fault, which ran right through the middle of the city. Earthquakes were a regular event, almost commonplace. At times, they would feel the rocking or vibrating in the hospital, residency wards or cafeteria. Lights would sway and dishes would slide on the tables at times. No big earthquakes took place during that year, but one never knew when one might happen. There had been the huge earthquake of 1906 when the city subsequently became ravaged with fire and burned.

After his year in San Francisco, Bob didn't want to return to Tennessee. He had fallen in love with California. However, he knew he had to return to his home state, because that was where his family was.

He drove his Ford car back across the country, stopping by the Reichenbach's house in Lincoln, Nebraska, en route to Tennessee.

Bob wrote the following passage in his diary about his year in California, which also talks about how he decided to go to Sweden for a year of fellowship in research.

In July 1957, I returned home to Middle Tennessee and the Pediatric Department at Vanderbilt University Hospital in Nashville to be Dr. Christie's chief resident. I had a wonderful year in San Francisco. The pediatric programs at U.C. Medical Center and the County Hospital were good, although no better than the training at Vanderbilt. I cannot deny, however, San Francisco, the Bay Area, and northern California had a certain charm that more than compensated for the rather long, solo trek out and back in my little '54 Ford Victoria. In particular do I recall such pleasantries as the Golden Gate Bridge, the fingerlings of fog easing inland over Twin Peaks and under the bridge, covering the deep blue of the bay (the latter often dotted by sails on weekends), the cable cars, Union Square (and how fine and conservatively dressed people were - no one wore white or two-tone shoes), Chinatown (the smell, the clang, the chatter, the way the fogs turn up), the "Top of the Mark," the Honeybucket, Matador, Hungry I, and several other night spots, the four wonderful skiing weekends at Square Valley (2), Reno Ski Bowl and Sugar Bowl, the three trips to Carmel and the Monterey Peninsula, the 10 days of camping out along the Seacoast and in Yosemite, and many other things which make memories rich. Names, too, may soon not be forgotten - such as: Eddie Roberts, Phil Strauss, Rainer Arnhold, Jack Hutchings, Bob Deshbaugh, Samuel Wolfson, Bob Morgan, John Thomas, Herman Wevers, Wesley Clapp. And a few real queens: Loretta Hilfinch, Claire Elder, and Rose Rierden.

I sort of hated to leave; in fact, folks had warned me before that once you go West you may never return. Yet, my roots were pretty deep in Tennessee, and although San Francisco was beautiful, glamorous, unique, that place just didn't seem to have enough real folks. Tennessee did. And I never had any intention but to return home and settle down.

Apparently though, my wanderlust was not quite satisfied. And when I began to think about the future after finishing my residency and the possible rut of a routine practice, I sort of developed a hankering to knock around one more year perhaps. After all, I was still single (but at times, so lonely I could cry). I was without any terrific financial obligation (except to my dear father, whose pockets were empty because of my school costs), and I had never been to Europe. Of particular attraction was the exchange program our pediatric department had with Karolinska Sjukhunt in Stockholm, Sweden. For several years, Rockefeller Foundation had sponsored such an exchange of a Swedish boy to Nashville, and one of our people to Stockholm. I think it all started when Arvid Walgren, the dean of Scandinavian pediatrics at the time, spent several months in Nashville as our Flexner lecturer (around the mid to late 40s). My interest was kindled a tad by talking to Jean Adams and Harold Roberts, both of whom had spent a year in fellowship in Copenhagen. And Millie Stahlman and Bob Stempfil, who had been representatives from VUH, in Stockholm, considered their year in Sweden as perhaps the best of their life. Nor had I ever had a real trial at research, and research was active at Karolinska. A year of research surely would be no detriment to private practice, and moreover would be an asset should academic life lay ahead. And the idea of Europe for a year, perhaps a few cracks at Sweden's slopes, etc. were also appealing.

Due to Drs. Christie and Lind's kindness one obstacle was overcome. Rockefeller Foundation had previously sponsored the program financially with the idea that the individual institutions involved would perhaps continue the program on their own. And therefore as of 1958, there was no Rockefeller aid. Dr. Christie & Dr. John Lind in Stockholm via a few letters arranged matters nicely, however such that Vanderbilt University Hospital would pay my transportation costs while Dr. Lind would pay me a modest salary in Sweden.

Being Chief Resident, 1957-1958

Once back home from San Francisco, Bob became chief resident in pediatrics at Vanderbilt, at Dr. Christie's request. Unlike some other departments, pediatrics was sort of the bottom of the totem pole. It was short on house staff, in other words, understaffed. It was a difficult year for Dr. Sanders, being chief resident and managing the house staff, especially because there were some who didn't want to work. Most of the house staff was an undisciplined bunch, generally had a poor work ethic, and some-times had a belligerent attitude. Often behind his back, Bob was referred to as the "Bald Eagle."

However, there were a few who were very helpful and diligent. They were Eric Chazen, John Fields, Claude Cowan and Bill Doak. They might be considered lifesavers because they were very hard working like Bob, and they lived up to their expectations.

Bob had a routine about checking on patients that was very thorough. There were many sick children to attend to, and the interns had a lot of work to do. He was a man of quiet dignity who taught the staff to always place the patient first, to never leave the hospital until all work and notes were completed, including laboratory work and to always make rounds with the covering house officer, including visiting every patient before leaving the hospital. He ruled by gentle persuasion but also unerring steadfastness. Bob was very kind about giving instructions to his staff. He did not like to be bossy.

One of the faculty members, Robert E. Merrill, noticed Bob Sanders' thoroughness in the written patient histories, and he complimented him by saying, "Pray continue this noble effort."

Bob lived in the intern's quarters, which was the old Victorian house behind the hospital. That house is long gone by now.

One day when he was doing pediatric grand rounds at Vanderbilt in front of the senior med students, he was lecturing about a child in a wheelchair and about the disease the child had. The patient wheeled himself out of the room without Bob realizing it. In a dramatic manner, he quickly exited the lecture room, fetched the child in the wheelchair, and wheeled him back into the room.

Bob didn't get much sleep that year interning. He used to go to sleep, that is, take naps leaning against the wall of the hospital hallways. He and his staff had to learn to get sleep whenever possible, and they also had to learn how to wake up very quickly in needed situations. There wasn't much time to actually sleep in bed. The trend was that it was important to stay up at nights as part of the training, because that would get doctors in private practice used to getting up in the middle of night and driving in to see emergency situation patients, once out there in the real world.

One afternoon, there was a robbery incident. Bob suddenly caught and confronted a strange man rifling through his drawers of things. He asked the man what he was doing, and he insisted that he show him his pocket contents. The man complied, revealing some loose change and his large, red switch blade knife. Bob asked the man to come into the next room and talk to one of the other residents. Suddenly, he bolted and ran out of the house like lightning! The man managed to steal Bob's class ring! He was never apprehended nor was the ring ever recovered. There was theft, even in those days.

Bob wrote the following recollections about his year as chief resident:

This year provided closer association with Vanderbilt's faculty and the chief of pediatrics, Dr. Amos Christie. His very efficient and pleasant secretary was Anne Hudgens. My appreciation and affection for this group of unique individuals and teachers has never diminished.

The year, however, began with difficulty. Our house staff was short-handed, with only two Assistant Residents (Larry Beisel and "Cap" Kaplan). This increased everyone's workload, relieved in part by the mid-year arrival of Claude Cowan and Bill Doak. I always believed and regretted that this initial frustration and fatigue of our house staff dampened morale the entire year. Perhaps I am wrong on this; I would rather hope this difficult experience shored up a resolve to perform well.

Aside from the routine of ward rounds, conferences, and lectures, I also appreciated a new association with Dr. John Shapiro in selecting and preparing a case each month for the Pediatric C.P.C. When we were second year medical students, we had enormous respect for and fear of Dr. Shapiro as a teacher. After completing his Pathology course, we marveled at his cordial and continuing interest in each student. As my senior student faculty advisor, he led me down the hall to Dr. Christie and a Pediatric Internship. Six years later, I was a Virology fellow with Drs. Bill Cheatham, John Shapiro, and Katherine Goodpasture, (Ernest Goodpasture's wife).

As Chief Resident, I routinely visited the Crippled Children's Home. Randy Batson asked me to be a part of studying the seriologic response of these children to the new Asian Flu vaccine. Out of this came the first published medical article that included my name, as Randy's colleague. This was quite a thrill.

I remember a very pleasant weekend when Dr. Christie and I drove down to Huntsville, Alabama to visit Milton and Betty Peeler. Milton was "settling" into his third of many years of practice and service to his hometown children.

I also remember the following:

-fly fishing the Spring of '58 with Pete Riley in the Little Turnbull, followed by a delicious supper prepared by his wife, Peg.

-Cal Woodruff's zest for nutritional statistics and his kindness in loaning me a heavy long black coat that I wore during the dark cold winter months in Stockholm the following year (1958-59),

-the practical approach in teaching clinical Pediatrics by Bob Merrill, fresh from three grueling years of solo practice in Tullahoma, my hometown. In common, we also shared canoe ownership.

Finally, I remember two interesting cases:

1) I was asked by the orthopedic staff to see their patient, a twelve-year-old female, who had become unable to walk. I examined her, talked to her at some length, and persuaded her to get up and walk normally. This was a case of conversion hysteria, later confirmed and treated by the psychiatry staff. The orthopedists were impressed; I never told them I had seen a similar, and my only, case in San Francisco just a few months earlier. This experience

increased my respect for emotional and psychiatric disorders in children.

2) A thirteen-year-old female was admitted with a puzzling hemiparesis, unexplained by the initial history and finding. To our surprise, skull films revealed a golf ball sized abscess containing a piece of nail. Further history documented she had, several days earlier, received a slight peck on her head while her brother was mowing the grass. She recovered from the infection but had notable neurological residue. This experience seeded in me a lasting fear of flying missiles and appreciation for the importance of accident prevention in preventive medicine. My wife, Pat, and I have wondered if this and the safety pin cases influenced our later involvement in encouraging state legislation to prevent road trauma to children.

photo of Dr. Amos Christie

Dr. Christie was very complimentary of Bob Sanders, and he gave him the above autographed photo, telling him, "For Bob Sanders, our chief resident '57-'58, with my sincere appreciation for a job well done."

Dr. Robert Sanders continued to have high praise and appreciation for Vanderbilt Medical School and the hospital. Throughout his life, he would give guest lectures to Dr. Lewis Lefkowitz' class on Preventive Medicine.

He also gave a six week course in Rural Pediatrics, an elective course taken by Vanderbilt freshman medical students. They would come to Murfreesboro once a week for six weeks to attend Bob's lecture. One of the students, John Greer, became one of Bob's doctors later in life.

42

His Stay in Sweden, 1958-1959

NOV 1959

In 1958 after his year as chief resident, Bob Sanders went overseas to Sweden on the Queen Mary, one of the largest ships in the world and one of the Cunard Line ships. He stayed in Sweden for just over a year, and it was an enriching and wonderful experience for him.

Dr. Arvid Walgren of Stockholm, Sweden and Dr. Amos Christie initiated a program for Vanderbilt physicians and pediatricians to go to the Karolinska Institute in Stockholm to study newborn physiology. Dr. Mildred Stahlman was the first Vanderbilt pediatrician to go to Sweden on the exchange program. The second one was Dr. Bob Stempfel, and Bob Sanders was the third one.

Bob studied and did research under Dr. Johnny Lind, and he also worked with Dr. Henry M. Truby, who was a linguistics expert. Bob and Henry (Hank) became good friends, Bob recording the first heartbeat, and Hank recording the first cry.

Dr. Johnny Lind was an art connoisseur, and he liked the fine arts, being a collector of artwork and paintings. Lind was a charming fellow, and everybody liked him. Millie Stahlman had worked under him and she had very high regard for him.

Bob lived six months with the Gribbe family where he began to learn Swedish. The Gribbe family's young children spoke no English. He also went to night school to learn more Swedish. The second half of the year, Bob lived with a Swedish surgeon named Gösta Ehrenborg, and he became good friends with him.

During part of his stay, he went with a team of Swedish physicians to Riksgränsen which was up above the arctic circle, to study the cardio-vascular system. They did a workout regimen where they went cross country skiing, and they measured heart rates with an EKG machine.

Bob Sanders quickly became impressed with Sweden's socialized medicine. The standard of living was very good in Sweden. All medical costs were being covered by their federal government, in other words, the national health system. Not only that, anyone who went to college could go with all expenses paid by the federal government's tax dollars.

Bob enjoyed the festivities during Christmas and dancing around the house and Christmas tree, singing Christmas carols. He spent Christmas with Laird and John Foster in Lund, Sweden. The Fosters were other Americans from Nashville who were also spending a year in Sweden. Winters froze over, and for several months, there was usually around 20 inches of snow on the ground.

Bob also enjoyed the mid summer fest, the longest day of the year. Nights were very long in the summer with sunset being around 11 PM and sunrise being around 2 AM.

While Dr. Sanders was in Sweden in 1959, he noticed that one of the doctors had seat belts in his car. Bob looked at the straps and immediately realized the safety ramifications of such a device in a car and that it was a good idea. These safety straps could save the lives of the driver and passengers, if involved in a car crash. The Swedish doctor was a safety conscious individual and had installed the safety belt (shoulder harness and lap belt) himself. Dr. Sanders was impressed with this doctor's innovative idea, and that's when his interest in seat belts and safety devices began.

After Bob's stay in Sweden, he toured around Europe for a while. He carried a tent and camped in various campgrounds in different countries of Europe. He went down to Wulfsberg, Germany and bought a 1959 VW Bug, which he drove around Europe. He nicknamed the car Akka, after the blue goose in the Adventures of Nils Holgersson.

Before returning to the United States, Bob also toured around Great Britain, seeing mostly England and Scotland. He went to the Isle of Mull and visited the Duart castle, the homeplace of the McLean family.

After his trip, Bob put the car on a boat home, and he returned home to the USA, as well. He arrived at the port in New York, and he drove back to Tennessee from there, stopping by and visiting Bob Reichenbach, now in New Jersey, on the way. He kept his VW Bug until 1970.

When Bob returned from Sweden, he was concerned that Pat Pelot had no seat belts in her 1957 VW Bug. He talked to her about the safety of seat belts and convinced her to have them installed. She took her car to a mechanic's shop where they drilled holes in the floor and bolted in the seat belts.

Dr. Sanders only returned to visit Sweden one time, and that was in the summer of 1977 when he flew over there with his wife for two weeks. It was good to catch up with his old friends while he was there. He had wanted to go back more often, but there were lots of demands and responsibilities, being married and raising two children, not to mention running a farm.

His wife, Patricia Ozburn Pelot

photo by Walden Fabry

Bob Sanders met his future wife, Patricia Ozburn Pelot, via one of his medical school buddies, Jack O. Rice, who was dating and soon married Pat's older sister Joan Pelot. He met Patricia (Pat) at a ball game event at Vanderbilt in Nashville in March 1954.

Pat, who was born December 23, 1937, was the youngest child of Reuben Nisbet Pelot, Jr. ("Bubba" or "R.N.") and Josephine Elizabeth Powell ("Jo"), who were originally from Decatur and Carrollton, Georgia. Pat's sister Joan was born in 1932. Pat had one brother R.N. Pelot, III ("Nib") born in 1935.

45

Pat Pelot, 1939   Pat with Nib and Joan, 1947

R.N. and Josephine had married in 1929 and had moved up to, what was at that time, the small country town of Crossville, Tennessee, which had cattle, chickens, goats, pigs, and dirt streets. R.N. Pelot had received an offer from Oman Construction Company of Nashville, to work for and manage the Crab Orchard Stone Company in Crossville, which is why they moved up there from Georgia. R.N. stayed with the job, apart from his going overseas with the U.S. Navy during WWII, and he eventually bought the company from the Omans. In 1974, he sold the company to Jim Flynn, and it is still owned by that family today.

Believe it or not, Bob's father and Joan and Pat's father knew each other through masonic order meetings. R.N. was a member of the masonic order. William Sanders, having been the Grand Master of the Tennessee Masonic Order with Eastern Star Work, used to travel the whole state and had met R.N. in Crossville back in the late 1930s.

Pat Pelot first learned about Bobby Sanders one day in early 1954 when her sister Joan was talking to her mother in the kitchen. Bobby was one of Jack Rice's good friends, and Joan said she wished there were two of her because she was impressed with Bobby Sanders. Bobby was going to be in Joan and Jack's wedding that August.

Mrs. Pelot said to her daughter, "Is he any relation to Bill (William) Sanders of Tullahoma?"

"Yes, that's his father."

"Well, I'll declare! We've known Mr. Sanders for a long, long time," and she explained to Joan about William's being the Grand Master of the Tennessee Masonic Order, and how he and Mr. Pelot had met back in the late 1930s and had known each other at different meetings.

William had a sort of charismatic way similar to FDR, and he was a good master of ceremonies. He also had a sense of humor, and at one meeting, a John Dooley of Crossville was struggling to remember the text to his part of the ritual, and he was flapping his arms about in frustration.

William therefore asked Mr. Dooley in a joking manner if he was a swimming instructor. Dooley laughed, and then he relaxed and was able to recite the ritual just fine.

So, Mr. Sanders was already a household word in the Pelot family, and Bobby Sanders was like somebody they already knew.

Pat first met Bobby Sanders in March 1954, when she was visiting her sister Joan at Vanderbilt one weekend. They met at the medical school, old section, near the post office, and the three of them walked to Rand Hall cafeteria for supper, then over to the memorial gym to see a basketball game. The gym was brand new, and there were no sidewalks yet, just wooden planks to get across the mud, but it didn't matter to them. It was a nice event.

They saw each other again, of course, at Joan and Jack's wedding in August, 1954, in Crossville.

Pat Pelot with her parents: Jo and Bubba

In January 1955, Pat was attending her senior year of high school at Westminster in Atlanta. She rode a train up to Nashville one weekend to visit Joan and Jack, to visit Vanderbilt, and also to sign up as a student, for next year, at the admissions department.

It happened to be Cadaver Ball weekend, and Joan and Jack mentioned that Bobby had no date. That was unusual, because everyone had dates, and he was already a senior in medical school.

Pat graduated from Westminster, and in the fall of 1955, she entered Vanderbilt University. She put Bobby Sanders and Danny Dolan's names down as people to contact in case of an emergency, because Joan and Jack were no longer there. They were in Winston Salem, North Carolina. Bob was already in his first year of internship at Vanderbilt Hospital and Medical School.

In January 1956, during Pat's freshman year, Bob asked Pat to go to the play, "Tea House of the August Moon," at the Tennessee Theatre. That was their first date. It was a double date, which was commonly done in those days, and Pat and Bobby went along with John and Johnnie Alexander. Bobby still had no car.

Pat didn't see Bobby again for some time because he was very busy during his year of internship at Vanderbilt. Then he went to San Francisco, California, for his second year of residency, 1956-1957.

By the summer of 1957, Bob had returned to Nashville, and was now pediatric chief resident at Vanderbilt Hospital. He asked Pat to fix him up with someone from time to time, which Pat obligingly did. She was sometimes seeing a mutual friend, Joseph C. (Jack) Bailey. Pat fixed up Bobby with Yvonne Couch, and they double dated, going to a drive-in theatre.

Bob and Pat saw each other again in the fall of 1957. Pat fixed him up with Madie Conn, who was Pat's roommate at the AOΠ house. Bob and Madie saw Pat perform in the all student production, "Arsenic and Old Lace," at the Vanderbilt University Theatre.

In February 1958, Pat asked Bob to take her to her AOΠ Rose Ball, which he did. Bob came in the spring of 1958 to see Pat perform in "The Marching Song" at the Nashville Chamber Theatre.

The next time they saw each other was in August 1958 at the Pelot house in Crossville as he was on his way to Sweden.

From mid 1958 through most of 1959, Bob Sanders was in Sweden on a Vanderbilt medical exchange/research program (newborn physiology), and when he returned, it was like he was a whole different person. They had lots to talk about. Pat had already graduated from college and was now a third grade teacher at Parmer School in Nashville.

She became good friends with several of the other teachers, among them Eileen Plummer, Lucy Joslin, who was also a cousin of Bob's, Frances Jones, Frances Kristofferson, Clara Harris, who was the principal, and Nan Teeter.

Bob invited Pat to the engagement party for Bill Alford and Helen Tanley, December 1959. Helen had been a suitemate and a sorority sister of Pat's during her junior year at Vanderbilt.

48

In February 1960, Pat had surgery for a ruptured ovarian cyst and was in terrible pain. Bob sent Pat a dozen roses while she was recovering.

In the fall of 1960, Pat finally met Bob's parents: William and Inez from Tullahoma. They came up to Nashville because William had had a mild stroke, and he was in the hospital. Bob took his older brother Bill and his wife Jean, and their mother Inez to a football game. Pat visited with William at the hospital. She was presently in a production called "The Curious Savage" at Theatre Nashville. Bob sent Pat another dozen roses at that time. Pat was awarded the Best Supporting Actress for that play.

In December 1960, William suffered a massive stroke, which left him like an eagle with his wings clipped. Bob went to Tullahoma and accompanied his father on an ambulance to Nashville, and he was admitted to Vanderbilt Hospital. Robert E. Merrill called Pat on the phone and said to her that there was someone who wanted to talk to her. It was Bobby. He was very sad. What was the situation, and what was going to be done with William?

William was at the hospital until May of 1961, after which he was moved to a nursing home facility in Tullahoma, where he died September 14, 1961. (It needs to be said that long hospital stays were much more common in those days. Nursing home facilities were hard to come by, and hospital care was far cheaper than it is today.)

While William was in Nashville, Pat went to visit him several times. She used to push him around in the wheelchair. She had stopped dating other people by now. Bob was the one. One day, William said to her, "I want you to change your name to Sanders."

On January 21, 1961, William found out the sad news about Inez's brother Dana Smith. He had just died, and William was telling Pat about it. He was very sad. William had a lot of good memories about the Smith farm, and he loved it there.

Bob continued to work on a fellowship in Nashville with Dr. Ernest Goodpasture's wife, Katherine Goodpasture at Vanderbilt in virology until June 1962. It was a very trying year for Bob with his father's illness. Pat was in another play at Theatre Nashville, this time doing "Look Homeward Angel." Bob was uncomfortable with Pat's being in that play, because it was competing with his time with her.

On March 4, 1962, after teaching at Parmer School for three years, Pat filled out applications for teaching in Boston, Massachusetts. Joan and Jack were living there, and Pat wanted to be up there near her sister. Bob was about to move to Chapel Hill, North Carolina, to do virology research on hamsters and guinea pigs with a Dr. Floyd Denny.

Pat had some interviews lined up and was about to fly up there, and when she was telling Bob about her plans, he then said, "You think we ought to go down the drain?" He was asking her to marry him.

photo by Harry Cravens
Pat and Bob at their wedding, 1962

photo by Harry Cravens
Bob Sanders on the day of his wedding,
his mother Inez, brother Bill, Jean, and family

Pat happily accepted Bob's proposal. She called and cancelled her interviews in Boston, and she finished out her year of teaching at Parmer School. As soon as school was out for summer, she and Bob were married in Crossville June 2, 1962.

They had their honeymoon at Gatlinburg, Tennessee, and afterwards, moved to Chapel Hill, North Carolina, for a year, after which they moved back to Tennessee and settled down on the Smith Farm in October 1963. This was due to the fact that his aunt Missie had fallen and broken her hip. Plus his aunt Celene had threatened to auction off the whole farm, if he didn't want to buy out the rest of the family. His heart was attached to the Smith farm, more so than Tullahoma.

Also, Bob decided that he would rather work with human patients instead of continuing with hamsters and guinea pigs, which was another deciding factor for him to move back to Tennessee.

Bank Hangers

When Bob Sanders was at Vanderbilt University and in medical school, he was known to tell some tall tales, one of them being the story of the bank hangers. They were takeoffs of a group of people called the Melungeons, a back woods sort of people, that is, country people of Appalachia, who were barefooted. They lived their lives among the Cumberland and Appalachian Mountains. Their ancestors had come over from a mountainous district of Europe, somewhat near the Mediterranean Sea, and in accordance with their culture, they made a practice of building their houses overhanging banks or cliffs of mountain sides. They would cable the house and firmly anchor it into the ground behind the house on top of the cliff, and the house would precariously hang over the cliff, which afforded them great views.

One of their favorite past times was standing on their back porch or deck and yoyoing down into the valley, and they were experts with their yoyos, using different shapes and sizes. Some of the yoyos measured as much as two feet in diameter. Whenever the bank hangers gathered or had reunions, they would have yoyo contests.

Apart from their past times, most of them worked in the manufacturing of yoyos, and they also made cheese.

Bob first learned of this story at Camp Mountain Lake near Monteagle, Tennessee where he was a summer counselor with Fred Graham and George Reynolds, the latter whose father owned the camp.

Tennessee history relates the story of the settlement of the Melungeons in east Tennessee, and they had similar appearances and characteristics to the bank hangers.

One day in 1961, Bob came to Pat's 3rd grade class and told this tall tale. One of the students raised his hand and said he actually had one of those big yoyos and that it was red. That very much surprised Bob, but then the student was joking!

Bob liked to draw little cartoon images and decorate his notes with them. Below is a sample of one of his cartoon drawings that he used in some of his medical lectures.

Presenting Monocytes

Private Practice Years and Farming, 1963-1966

courtesy: Tom England

When Bob and Pat returned to Tennessee from Chapel Hill, North Carolina in the summer of 1963, Bob decided to set up private practice in Murfreesboro, Tennessee.

Upon arriving back in Tennessee, they managed Dr. Sam Carney's practice near Nashville for three weeks while he went on vacation.

Then they lived at Frances Jones' house on Richland Avenue in Nashville until October, when they moved to the 370 acre Smith Farm southwest of Murfreesboro. Bob had a romantic view of farming, having stayed there every summer growing up, and he thought it would be fun.

Dana Smith, Bob's uncle, had passed away in early 1961, but his sheep were still there. Bob's aunt Missie, for having fallen and broken her hip, was placed in a nursing home in Murfreesboro. When Bob and Pat told Missie they were going to live on the farm and take care of it, she was very pleased and replied, "That's the answer to my prayers."

The farm also had a milk cow, but as Bob didn't have any experience milking cows, he sold it pretty soon.

Bob decided to add to the flock of sheep, and he bought more ewes from Bascom Cooksey's father in Lebanon. Among the flock were South Down rams, Shropshire rams, Suffolk-Rambouillet ewes, and some sheep from Idaho. They did pretty well with the sheep for nine years, except for foot rot, and neighboring dog packs, who would come and kill sheep in the middle of the night. Bob had to have a rifle by the bedside at night and he installed floodlights in the barnyard, as well. Most of the time the dogs were too quick, and he was rarely able to kill a dog.

53

Every year, he and/or the tenants used Uncle Dana's 1949 M Farmall tractor to plow and plant Balboa Rye pasture and Crimson clover. It was expensive, and he would plant it fresh every year. Pat disagreed about planting it so often, but Bob was an idealist and overdid it.

Once every April, Bob's tenants would help him shear the sheep and sell the wool. There was never a big profit gain on the wool sold during sheep shearing. Sometimes he sold some lambs, but they didn't bring much profit either.

All of this Bob was managing during the same time that he was establishing his private practice business in town. Pat helped Bob take phone calls, and he also hired a secretary, Mrs. Buckingham. She was very efficient, and she greeted everyone who entered in a genuine friendly manner, which made people feel welcome, and want to come back.

The standard of living was quite different in Murfreesboro in the 1960s. No one seemed to have any money, especially the patients who came to see Dr. Sanders. Plus, those who were more affluent already had other doctors, and only a very few, one of them Hubert McCullough, brought their newborns to Bob. It was rare that other doctors would refer patients to him. They always wanted the patients for themselves! At any rate, some patients did come, but they were the ones who were not economically affluent, or they had serious medical problems.

As Bob was thorough and complete with his exams and physicals, he spent more time with patients and their mothers than other doctors would, and that wasn't economical. Bob wanted the reputation of having a sense of caring for his patients, but the only way a doctor could make a decent living was to herd the patients through like cattle and have a lot more patients, too. He made a $50 profit his first year and $3,000 the next year.

One night during his few years of private practice, Dr. Sanders got a phone call from Dr. John Cason about Sam Lasseter's daughter Jeanine. She was age 4 and was having convulsions that wouldn't stop. Dr. Cason had done all he could, and Sam Lasseter asked Dr. Cason if there was anyone else. Seemingly as a last resort, Dr. Sanders was called.

He drove straight into town and as soon as he got to her, he administered rectal paraldehyde suppositories. Her seizures soon broke and they hospitalized her at Rutherford Hospital, putting her in an oxygen tent. Bob stayed by her side the whole night and didn't go home. The next morning, she woke up from her coma, looked at Dr. Sanders, and asked, "Who are you?" Tears came to her father's eyes and also to Bob Sanders. He had saved her life.

Sam Lasseter was very grateful and asked Dr. Sanders how much he owed him. He added up the price of the suppositories and shots, medicine, the service call, and the hospital visit . . . a grand total of $75. Mr. Lasseter wrote him a check with a look of gratefulness but also with an expression of, *This is way too cheap. My daughter is worth more than that!* Had Dr. Sanders charged $500, for example, Mr. Lasseter would have paid it on the spot. His daughter's life had been saved! $75 was far less than Mr. Lasseter expected.

But that's the way private practice was in Murfreesboro in the 1960s. There was no money in it. Reviewing his meager earnings and profits in 1966, he thought, "Well, if I work twice as hard, I might make $6,000 next year. The fact is, he was already working very hard, and it wasn't bearing enough fruit. Private practice was very demanding, and very time consuming. It would have been expecting the impossible to double that! Patients that he referred to the hospital only received limited care, and none of the nurses knew how to keep a drip in. They would frequently call Bob in the middle of the night, and he would have to drive back into town, to re-install a drip because the nurses didn't know how! (Nurses know a lot more now than they used to.)

There was never any room for Bob at the Murfreesboro Medical Clinic. They didn't want a third pediatrician in those days. They were afraid there would not be enough patients for themselves. It was as if they would starve to death if they took on a third doctor. Bob had been told by doctors in Nashville that Murfreesboro was a medical jungle. It was very difficult to get patients, and when he got patients, they were usually so sick that he had to send them on to Vanderbilt Hospital. That cut Bob out of making a profit, and he only got $5 per patient for referring them. He was not getting the newborns either. Instead he got the complicated cases.

Dr. Marion Young, a lifelong friend of Pat's family, had recently entered public health, and he recommended that Bob go into that, too. That sounded like a very good idea. After all, public health means public service, responsibility for and accountability for our fellow humans.

1965 was an eventful year with major things changing in his life. He lost his mother Inez April 11, 1965, and his son Robert was born in August of 1965. He didn't even get to spend much time with his son for all the demands of his private practice. Bob seriously considered public health. He applied at the state office for a position in Murfreesboro, and he was awarded the job, to become the physician at Murfreesboro's Rutherford County Health Department in August 1966. It had regular hours, no night calls, no middle of the night trips to the hospital, and with a secure salary of $16,000 per year. Financial problems were solved!

Now with a reasonable salary, Bob would be able to negotiate with his kinfolks to buy out their part of the 370 acre farm. The Federal Land Bank granted him a 35-year loan for $36,000, which he paid to his aunt Celene Smith North in Dallas, Texas. That was in August of 1966.

In May of 1966, Bob Sanders sent out letters to all the parents of his patients, notifying them that he would be closing down his private practice of pediatrics. He closed down his practice in June 1966, and he took July off while he emptied out the office.

In August 1966, Dr. Robert S. Sanders began his job at the Rutherford County Health Department. Now working for the state of Tennessee, he was a state employee. A welcome relief, Bob now had more time to spend with his family, and soon a second child, a daughter, was on the way!

Bob continued to run sheep on the farm for several more years, but it became too much trouble to keep them, especially with roaming dog packs that would kill one or two on several nights each year. The last of the sheep were sold in 1972.

In 1970, Bob started buying cattle, mostly steers that were young calves, and he would sell them the next year. Most years brought little or no profit, but 1978 was an exception, a good year for selling cattle. He finally gave up the cattle business in 1996.

There were several fields that were tillable, and Bob rented the land for crop planting to S.D. Lester up the road. His son Jeff was a little older than Robert, and he used to come and play with Robert and Priscilla in childhood. In 1980, Mr. Lester started slowing down, and Bob started renting to Wendell Jones down the road. Jones still rents from Bob's widow Pat to this day.

Bob always liked to have a vegetable garden, and he grew plenty of tomatoes, corn, beans, squash, pumpkin, and melons. Much of the produce he gave away to friends and relatives.

the Sanders' farmhouse, 1965 (Inez Smith's old homeplace)

57

Bob and Pat Sanders on the front porch, mid 1970s   photo by Benjamin Porter

His son, Robert Smith Sanders, Jr.

Born in August 1965, Robert S. Sanders, Jr. was the first child of Bob and Pat Sanders.

He attended kindergarten at the First Methodist Church kindergarten program, as there was no public school kindergarten in those days. He also attended a summer enrichment program offered by Mrs. Boutwell at the MTSU Campus School. Then he entered MTSU Campus School for 1st grade. Robert recognized some of the children in his class from the enrichment program. However, 1st grade didn't work out so well, and his parents transferred him to Bellwood Elementary School by December, where things went a lot better. Robert stayed at Bellwood School through 6th grade, making friends as he went along.

Robert was age 6 when he learned to ride a bicycle. He was in Crossville at his grandparents' house when he finally learned. His grandfather bought him a Starjet bicycle right away, and Robert rode it many miles up and down the long driveway of his home and to different places around the farm.

Robert enjoyed visiting his grandparents in Crossville, and it was good to have them, as Bob's parents had already passed away by the time Robert was born. The Pelots were good grandparents. They had a boat, and they used to visit Watt's Bar Lake. They had a nice woods behind the house which had a path they called the Bunny Trail. Plus they had a lake house, and everyone used to go swimming and boating in the lake. Even though Bob's parents were already gone, he did have his uncle Brock and aunt Frances, who lived in Murfreesboro, and they visited regularly. They were always considered the Sanders grandparents on Bob's side.

Friends used to come and visit to play with Robert on the farm. There was not much traffic in those days. Life was nice and rural. Robert ventured out on the public roads with his bicycle, going as far as 10 miles away by age ten. One of his favorite places to go was the Versailles Grocery, a country store between Rockvale and Eagleville.

Starting at age 10, Robert enjoyed exploring around and going up into the 90 acre woods on their farm in the afternoons after school, taking his dog with him on most of the excursions. Sometimes, he walked over to the Versailles Hills, which were a few miles to the southwest of the farm, and he explored many stretches of woods over there. At age 12, Robert created a trail up in the woods, which is still there to this day.

He also joined the Boy Scouts and participated in their outings and campouts. By age 15, he became an Eagle Scout. He also attended one of the National Scout Jamborees and enjoyed meeting and trading with people from other regions.

Robert attended 7th and 8th grades at Murfreesboro's Central Middle School. Things went pretty well there, and he made a lot more friends, as the school took in the students from all of the elementary schools in those days. One highlight was a bus trip to Washington, DC and New York City during Spring Break of 7th grade.

Robert took on a project of bicycling every road in the southwest portion of Rutherford County. On some weekends, he went riding on new roads out to the county line beyond Eagleville. In high school, he expanded his project to include every road in the southern half of the county, and he reached and completed his goal at age 15.

Robert attended Riverdale High School for grades 9-12. He did very well there, making all A's and graduating 2nd in his class. In high school, Robert ran on the track team for two years, and he did marching band for one of those years, as well.

Robert began participating in farm chores, cleaning fence rows for his father and feeding hay to the animals. There was bushhogging to be done each summer.

At age 16, Robert built a log cabin in the woods, and it was a nice get-away place for him at times. He also took time to take bicycle rides and visit friends.

Once out of high school, Robert began travelling on his own. He drove his Ford Fairlane station wagon to Canada and visited some friends up there. Plus, he hiked a section of the Appalachian Trail.

In the Fall of 1984, he entered Tennessee Technological University in Cookeville, Tennessee. There he studied Electrical Engineering. During his summers off, Robert drove his station wagon out West several times, where he went exploring and hiking up in the many mountains. He always took his camera and got some really nice photos of the scenery everywhere he went. He took an interest in trees and used to mail them home and plant them in the yard. Rocks and fossils were another thing of interest, and he collected some of those during his travels.

In addition to trips out West, Robert took two separate years off and travelled to Australia and New Zealand both times. He had always wanted to see the homeland of the Eucalyptus trees and of the Koalas. Australia had a lot to offer, and he went hiking and travelling in many different areas.

After graduating in May 1991 with a degree in Electrical Engineering, Robert went over to England and Scotland to travel around on bicycle. He also took his backpack. He was over there for 3 months, and he saw many places during that time. One project was hiking the entire Pennine Way, which took 3 weeks.

There was quite a hiring freeze for engineers at the time Robert graduated, and it took him 2½ years to finally land a job in engineering with a firm in Nashville. Meanwhile, Robert had already begun working for himself, doing carpentry, painting and repairs. The engineering job lasted for 3 months, at which time he was let go. The probationary period was up, and Robert had not fit in well enough for them. The good news was that he received 3 months of severance pay, which he used and travelled over to England and Scotland again.

In 1993 and 1994, Robert took on a big project of compiling the family genealogy and doing family photo albums on all 4 sides of the family. Included in the books were photos of all family members and ancestors, family reunions, and family homes. These books were printed and distributed to all family members at cost.

Also in 1991, Robert took an interest in Mexico and began travelling down there, usually staying in the town of Bustamante, Nuevo León, around 60 miles north of Monterrey and situated at the base of some beautiful mountains. Robert learned and became fluent in Spanish, and he has made many friends along the way. To this day, he still makes a practice of staying there every winter, where he writes novels and other books, and takes photos up in the mountains, in the desert, and up in the canyon.

In 1995, Robert decided not to return to an engineering job. He took a different road in life and began writing novels.

His first 3 books are a science fiction trilogy, which promote peace, friendship, and communication between Earth and other galactic races. They are titled:

1) Mission of the Galactic Salesman, published 1996
2) Mission Beyond the Ice Cave, published 1999
3) Heritage Findings from Atlantis, published 2000

He has also written his "Cliff's Notes" to the trilogy: Galactic Salesman Trilogy Synopsis, published 2003.

The next novel Robert wrote was Walking Between Worlds, a novel of an American in Mexico, by (pen name): Robert Alquzok, published 2001.

Robert went on to write two books about autism and Asperger's syndrome. The books are mostly autobiographical, portraying different experiences of Robert's life. Asperger's syndrome is a high functioning and mild form of autism, but it is not an illness nor a disability. It is merely a different template for living.

The books are:

Overcoming Asperger's: Personal Experience & Insight, (2002)

On My Own Terms: My Journey with Asperger's (2004), which is also available in Spanish.

All of Robert's books are self published through Ingram Book Company's Lightning Source, Inc., and they are available from the author or from www.Amazon.com .

In a way, Robert also pursued the Arts. In 2003, he went through all of his old negatives from his travels and had the best images scanned to CDs. Printing from those CDs, Robert sells 11x17 printouts of his many photos of nature scenery, and he also sells copies of his books that he has written.

Jo and Bubba, Robert and Priscilla's grandparents

His daughter, Priscilla Pelot Sanders

photo by Benjamin Porter

Born in June 1967, Priscilla P. Sanders was the second child of Bob and Pat Sanders.

She attended a play group, then nursery school near MTSU in Murfreesboro and then she attended kindergarten at the First Methodist Church. It would be 1973 before kindergarten would be incorporated into the public school system. Priscilla never touched MTSU Campus School. She began first grade at Bellwood Elementary School. Somehow, she knew how to read long before first grade. She also had the uncanny sense of knowing what her mother was going to say before she said it, and she frequently completed sentences that her mother was telling her.

She also did well in school and made plenty of friends, would have some of them out to the farm to play, or would go visit them also.

Priscilla also enjoyed going and visiting her grandparents, the Pelots. They did things for her and took her places in Crossville. Priscilla always enjoyed making snicker doodles and pound cakes with her grandmother. Brock and Frances Sanders were also special to her, and she visited with them regularly too.

At age 7, Priscilla began taking piano lessons, which she continued right through her school years. She began with Ms. Cary Borthick, and then by high school, she took lessons from Mrs. Linda Gilbert. She continued playing the piano even in college, and she has become an accomplished pianist.

During her early school years, Priscilla took ballet and tap dancing from

Ruth Cordell, and mime from Susan Chreitzberg. Also while in child-hood, Priscilla took several years of horseback riding lessons from Mrs. Judy Sikes on her farm near Murfreesboro.

In childhood, Priscilla wanted to become a movie star. She also liked music and used to watch movies on the TV. Her favorite TV shows were Mr. Rogers and Sesame Street. The late Mr. Rogers is one of her heroes to this day. Her favorite music group was the Beatles, and she collected all of their albums and songs. Her brother, Robert, soon knew the melodies to all of the Beatles' songs, because she played them so much on the stereo.

Priscilla attended seventh and eighth grades at Central Middle School and she also took a bus trip during Spring Break to New York City and Boston.

Like her grandmother, Inez, Priscilla took up tennis as a sport, and she played on Riverdale High School's tennis team, where she did pretty well. Some of Robert's friends also played on the tennis team, and he used to visit with them and watch his sister play tennis on certain afternoons after school.

In addition to tennis, Priscilla played the saxophone and oboe in the band. She also did one year of marching band her freshman year in high school.

During Priscilla's senior year, she travelled to China for three weeks with the U.S.-China People's Friendship Association to study China, its culture, its government, and its school system. It was an enriching trip.

When high school was over, Priscilla essentially moved out. She went away to school at Earlham College in Richmond, Indiana, where she studied Sociology and Anthropology, majoring in that, and she also minored in music. She played tennis there too, and she became number 1. While at Earlham, she studied abroad one quarter in London, England. She graduated in 1989 and moved back to Tennessee.

Priscilla began doing theatre work at the Cumberland County Playhouse in Crossville under Mary Crabtree, Jim and Anne Crabtree. She stayed with her grandmother, Josephine Pelot.

In 1990, Priscilla and her former college roommate, Caroline Roan, from Earlham College decided to move to Boston, Massachusetts, where she worked for Feminist Majority Foundation. She also studied lyric writing, improv acting, acting techniques, and voice.

In December, 1993, she decided to move back to Tennessee. Robert and his mother went up there in his Ford pickup truck and moved her and her belongings back to Tennessee, where she took up residence in Nashville. She worked at the Kennedy Center at Vanderbilt University, and she studied the Arts and other interests on the side. She also taught private piano lessons. She even considered going to graduate school to study music/expressive arts therapy.

In the summer of 1996, Priscilla loaded a U-Haul van and moved to New York City. There, she took up stand-up comedy. Rex Knowles and Sherry Landrum were contacts from Crossville, and she studied improv acting with them.

Three years later, she moved to Los Angeles, where she worked at HBO (Home Box Office) as an archivist. She continued to pursue the Arts.

In 2002, Priscilla took up song writing and became a good singer. She found several people who helped her put together an album of her songs. Her CD album was called "Ride a Wave With Me." In 2005, she launched her CD release and did several performances back in Nashville, and also out West in California. One of her songs, "Josephine" is dedicated to her grandmother. She also wrote a song dedicated to her father called, "My Sweet Daddy."

In the process of promoting her new CD, Priscilla moved around to different states, including California, Hawaii, and Oregon, after which she moved back to Tennessee, where she presently does singing/songwriting.

courtesy: Kathy Ferris
Priscilla singing to an audience, 2005

The Trips to Pawley's Island and Other Places

playing on the beach, early 1970s

Back when Robert and Priscilla were barely more than toddlers, Bob and Pat learned of a nice vacation spot from their friend, Millie Stahlman. She had just stayed for a week at a place called Pawley's Island, a very old and charming beach resort on the coast of South Carolina between Charleston and Myrtle Beach. Actually, it is part of the main coast, but is considered an island because of the tidal marsh that runs behind its 6 miles of length.

Pawley's Island was a place that was bereft of sophistication, otherwise known as arrogantly shabby. Actually, the island was historic and several of the 250-year-old wooden clapboard houses have withstood many hurricanes. There is also a legend of a ghost called the "Gray Man". Some say he can still be seen walking the beach, or appearing in the upstairs windows of certain older houses.

Bob and Pat liked what they heard, and they were told of the Ellerbe Tavern, a down to earth resort of three very old houses converted into a series of rooms with wooden walls and floors where each family would stay. The tradition was to go and stay for a week. A few families would stay as long as two weeks. Dot and Luke Ellerbe stayed in the main house, which also incorporated the dining hall and lobby. Three meals a day were served to the staying guests, cooked by the locals who lived there. The Ellerbe's maids would come each morning and sweep the sand out of each room and make the beds. It was great service.

Bob and Pat made their first trip to Pawley's Island in 1969. Having liked it, they continued the tradition every summer, taking Robert and Priscilla with them. There were some special friends that Bob and Pat had

66

met in Murfreesboro in the mid 1960s. They were known as the Porter family. Ben Porter used to work at Murfreesboro's VA hospital, and his three children were Alex, Marion, and Benjamin. They had moved on to South Carolina by the late 1960s, and as a result, they decided to establish the tradition of staying at the Ellerbes the same week as the Sanders every summer. It was a treat to visit the Porters in Eastover, South Carolina and then convoy with them to Pawley's Island to begin the week's stay. Such an exciting time it was, to arrive and begin the week. Robert would already have on his bathing suit, and as soon as they would park the car at the Ellerbes, Robert would run to the ocean and take a swim.

Sometimes other friends from Nashville and Murfreesboro stayed at the Ellerbes, like Millie Stahlman, Hakan and Julie Sundell, Louise and Virgil LeQuire, Bobby and Sally Thomas, John and Linda Collins, and others. Robert and Priscilla became friends with the children of some of those other families. Also, Robert's Godparents, Phemie and Marion Young from Chattanooga and their family would stay in another house further down the island. Plus Priscilla's Godparents, Fritchie and Sandy Lawton, along with their family and friends, would stay nearby in the Boyle house, one of the oldest houses on the island, and also one of the most noted places for the ghostly Gray Man to appear.

Bob and Pat at the beach   Bob on a raft

The Sanders came to like Pawley's Island very much. Robert went swimming and riding the waves every day, and he went searching for shells, sand dollars, and fossil shark's teeth. Some days he would run and play with friends. Plus, he would walk to the North End of the island every morning and evening, and some days he would walk to the South End. Priscilla enjoyed her swims too, plus good times playing with other friends. Many of them visited and played games in the Ellerbe's lobby, which was open at all hours. Bob and Pat took swims too, but not as often. They used to sit on the beach under huge umbrellas, visiting with their friends, and they would take other outings to the mainland, such as the hammock shop, or different restaurants.

A few years after they began staying at Pawley's Island, someone told them about a magician named Reese Hart. They went to visit him and always enjoyed seeing his magic tricks. Some of them were funny, and his wife Sis would laugh with them. Mr. Hart had quite a collection of shells and fossils displayed in his front foyer, and Robert always marveled at them. Mr. Hart was also a nationally known chemist and made chemical potions used in some movies. He was an interesting man and had lots of stories to tell. There was a sense of unique wonder about him as well, and it was interesting that he was born the very same day that Robert Andrew Smith died while separating a dog fight back in 1916. The Sanders continued to know Reese and Sis Hart into the mid 1990s.

Yes, there were many good memories from Pawley's Island, and at the end of the week, it was always sad to leave. The only consolation was that they knew they would return the next summer for another week of fun and adventure.

In addition to swimming and looking for shells, there were plenty of other activities at Pawley's Island: fishing from the pier, surfcasting, setting crab nets and traps in the marsh between the island and the mainland, flying kites, and particularly lying in Pawley's Island rope hammocks, reading, napping, or just restoring your soul by taking it easy. Most of all, there was a lack of urgency to be busy. Bob always needed the rest away from his hard work at the Health Department.

In the early 1970s, a few years after the Sanders began their tradition of staying at Pawley's Island, there were some modernized condominiums built at the island's pier. Soon Pawley's Island's local government stepped in and prevented any more of that from being done. They didn't want to lose their tradition of wooden style houses and being arrogantly shabby, which was a good thing. So many beach resorts were full of high rise hotel resorts of modern style, such as Myrtle Beach.

By 1980, the Ellerbes closed down their traditional resort. They stayed on there and had rooms for guests, but meals were no longer served. It wasn't the same as before. The Sanders began staying at other places like the Seaview Inn, the Pelican Inn, and Holiday Downs. 1999 was the last year they stayed there.

During one of the first stays at Pawley's Island, a young woman got sick and had an allergic reaction after eating crab meat. She was having trouble breathing. Bob Sanders and Bobby Thomas got right to it, called Georgetown's emergency room on the phone, advised them to be ready to receive her and have adrenalyn and benadryl ready and in hand upon arrival. Bob and Bobby rushed her down there at nearly 100 mph, and they saved her life. There was no time to call an ambulance.

After that incident, Bob decided to obtain an emergency kit to carry in the car at all times. He found one from the EMTs back in Murfreesboro, bought it, and placed it in the back of the red Volvo wagon. It was a grey box nearly the size of a footlocker, a super first aid kit. There was never an occasion to use it, but it was good to have on hand, even though it occupied much needed space for luggage, rafts, and other beach equipment. The next year when the Sanders arrived at the Porter's house in Eastover, on the way to the beach, Bob proudly showed them the entire contents of the kit.

Though Pawley's Island was the main place to visit for vacations, Bob and Pat did take their children to a few other places while their children were growing up. They went to Massachusetts a few times to visit Joan and Jack Rice, usually during Easter holidays. They drove down to Florida a couple of times to visit Hank and Ann Sofi Truby and their family, and they visited Pat's aunt and uncle, Lillian and Lefty Hodges. Many times going or coming from Pawley's Island, they would visit relatives in Atlanta. Both Bob and Pat had several aunts and uncles there, along with plenty of cousins. A few times, they stopped by Chapel Hill, North Carolina, where Bob and Pat had lived for a year, and they visited friends there, including Pete and Jan Reist.

When Robert and Priscilla were in middle school, Bob had a big medical meeting with the American Academy of Pediatrics in San Francisco, and all four of them flew out there to visit for a week. California had a certain charm with its large Redwood trees and Eucalypts. It was an amazing place to visit, almost like being on another world.

Also, when Robert and Priscilla were in high school, Bob and Pat drove them out to Texas, stopping in New Orleans, Louisiana on the way to Houston. They visited relatives there, in Austin, and in Dallas, before returning back to Tennessee through Little Rock and Memphis.

Smaller excursions were made when Bob had medical meetings, in places like Paris Landing State Park, Fall Creek Falls State Park, a trip to Memphis, and several trips to Gatlinburg and even to Mt. LeConte.

In addition to that, Bob and Pat took Robert and Priscilla on regular trips to Crossville to visit Pat's parents, Jo and Bubba, and to Tullahoma to visit Bill and Jean Sanders and family. They also went to Chattanooga to visit their special friends: Phemie and Marion Young, and John and Linda Collins; plus to Birmingham, Alabama to visit Fritchie and Sandy Lawton.

Even though they travelled to other places, Pawley's Island remained their favorite vacation spot.

the Sanders and the Porters, 1977

the Sanders and the Porters at Pawley's Island, 1989   photo by Benjamin Porter

70

Bob and Pat Sanders with their children, Robert, and Priscilla, 1993

Sanders family reunion: all of William and Inez's descendants:
children, grandchildren, and great-grandchildren, including in-laws
Tullahoma, Tennessee, December 2002

Bob enjoyed drawing little cartoon figures on notes he would leave around the house. He used to create his own birthday cards for people and decorate them with cartoon drawings, as well.

His Years at the Rutherford County
Health Department, 1966-1991

courtesy: Bealer Smotherman

In August 1966, Dr. Robert S. Sanders went to work for the state of Tennessee, becoming a state employee. He was now the physician at the Rutherford County Health Department.

The Rutherford County Health Department was a fine structure that was built back during the depression years. In the early 1930s, the Commonwealth Fund of New York's Division of Rural Hospitals appropriated $75,000 to build a modern public health facility in Murfreesboro. Funding for equipment was also provided. It was built on Colonial Revival architecture with large porch columns on the front and rear of the building, and it was designed by New York City architect James Gamble Rogers. Murfreesboro's local hospital was built during the same era and on the same type of architectural style. Roger's Colonial Revival architecture was at the height of its popularity in the early 1930s.

The Health Department played a major role in Tennessee's statewide public health movement in the first half of the 1900s. Dedicated in 1931, the Rutherford County Health Department trained over 400 health officers, nurses, and medical students in its first four years of operation.

Back in those days, the Health Department would go to all the schools in the district to give shots to the children, and they also gave any type of medical exam the children would need. They ran what was called a Blue Ribbon Campaign, and those children who got all their necessary shots and vaccinations would be given a blue ribbon and would therefore be able to march in the Blue Ribbon Parade which was held annually. That was a promotional incentive to make all the kids get their shots, so that they would stand a better chance of being in good health.

Dr. Hollowell was still the director of the health department (health officer) in 1966, and he wasn't yet ready to retire. So, Bob entered as chief physician, and he saw patients. Every week the state had him go to several other county health departments in the district, among them Wilson, Trousdale, Dekalb, and Smith counties. He would run the circuit among those counties, in addition to working some days in Murfreesboro.

Dr. Sanders at his desk   photo by Daily News Journal

In 1969, Dr. Hollowell retired, and Dr. Sanders took his place and became the chief health officer, director of the Rutherford County Health Department. There were certain days called clinic days where he saw patients, most of them being children. The clinics were also divided into several sectors, called prenatal, well baby, and general medical clinics. Most of the days, Bob worked in Murfreesboro. However there were still a few days that he travelled to other counties: Wilson and Trousdale. Those days were irregular, and not every week.

There were other days that he had administrative duties, board of health meetings, and county court meetings, all regarding business at the health department.

Being the director of the health department, Dr. Sanders signed the death certificates for Rutherford County, and he signed some of the birth certificates, as well.

One sector of the health department was the environmental department. A group of environmentalists worked there, and they oversaw soil conditions and ground quality for building sites, and whether or not the soil perked for septic tanks. They were in charge of approving permits for building sites, and they rejected sites that would not perk. Sometimes the realtors didn't like that. One time, it angered some developers in LaVergne. Some were even known to sue the Health Department for the permit on occasion, and win. The Health Hepartment would then issue the permit, but stamped it: "Issued under court order."

Developers wanted to blast with dynamite, but Rutherford County would not allow that. Wilson County did, however.

Bob Sanders making a home visit, 1981   courtesy: Tom England

One of the programs offered by Dr. Sanders at the Health Department was a course given to Vanderbilt freshman medical students. It was an elective course in rural pediatrics that medical students could take. They would come to Murfreesboro once a week for six weeks and attend a lecture given by Bob, and they would make different field trips, as well. For example, they went on rounds with the nurses, making home visits.

75

They went with the environmentalists to check on motel swimming pools and other sanitation matters. Plus they attended clinic sessions there at the Health Department, obtaining first hand experience.

Dr. Sanders worked for a total of 25 years at the Rutherford County Health Department, retiring in December 1991. He always had the same office. In 1983, he also took on the task of being the county medical examiner, which he kept until 1999.

The County Landfill Project, early 1970s

Since Dr. Robert Sanders was director of the county health department and the health officer, he was given a court order by Judge James Threet to find a place in Rutherford County for a sanitary landfill. That was in 1971.

Murfreesboro only had an above-ground city dump, and it was located on what is now the Old Fort Parkway on the west side of town. In fact, there were 150 above-ground burning dumps throughout the county! Residents were complaining because the city sanitary department would simply burn and incinerate the garbage on a regular basis. It was time to begin disposing of the garbage in a more sanitary way, and also to meet new state health guidelines.

Dr. Sanders went down to Alabama with Bill Wilson, the Rutherford County Road Commissioner, to see a sanitary landfill in operation and to find out how it worked and what criteria would have to be met to have one. The main requirement was that a landfill would have to have very deep soil, not clay type nor rocky, but instead be of a rich loamy type.

They returned to Murfreesboro, and Dr. Sanders began searching up in the north part of the county. Near Walter Hill, they found some suitable land. Epps Matthews agreed to lease one of his big hills to the county for the landfill. While Matthews was fine with it, the surrounding neighbors weren't!

There were hearings at Middle Tennessee State University to discuss different suitable locations in the county. Numerous people came, some of them to complain. A Mr. Alsup shouted his complaints about a landfill along with Morgan and Jane Green of Walter Hill.

There were heated discussions and debates. Numerous times, Mrs. Jane Green called Dr. Sanders on the telephone and fussed at him, complaining about the landfill, saying it was going to smell bad, and so on!

Also, an anonymous letter arrived in the mail threatening Dr. Sanders. It read, "You better stay out of that Matthews landfill thing, if you want to live and do good!" That rightly upset Bob, and he reported the threat to the sheriff. Then he contacted Vern Gauby of the TBI, the Tennessee Division of the FBI, and turned the letter over to him for an investigation to be conducted. No one ever found out who the man was that wrote that threatening letter.

One evening Mrs. Green called and was throwing such a fit, that Dr. Sanders called the sheriff and asked him to go out to her house in Walter Hill to talk to her and calm her down. The sheriff obliged and paid her a visit to tell her to knock it off and stop bothering Dr. Sanders with her tirades of abuse!

Anyway, the landfill was opened. Ironically enough, a few years later, Morgan and Jane Green also leased their land when the landfill was expanded. Amazing the change in attitude! Today, the landfill is still in use, busting at the seams with garbage and waste with an unbearable stench to anyone going over there to deliver loads, including construction debris. Rutherford County's landfill even takes in all the garbage from Metropolitan Nashville, and Jefferson Pike is a very busy narrow two-lane road with all the garbage trucks and trailers that go in and out of there daily!

Just in the last year, 2007, it was discovered that the landfill had been accepting low level radioactive waste from California and Michigan for the past 14 years! Quite a dispute was raised by the citizens of the county, and they founded a group called ENDIT. They successfully got the radioactive waste dumping stopped.

Medical Examiner, 1983-1999

In the spring of 1983, Matt Murfree retired from being Rutherford County's Medical Examiner, and the county was having a difficult time finding someone to replace him. None of the doctors in town wanted to be the medical examiner, or that is, coroner. It was a job that didn't pay that well, and by that day and time, doctors were making pretty good salaries in their private practices and clinics. They went this way and that in their search.

One day John Mankin, who was early in his career as a judge, went to Dr. Sanders' office, and he nearly backed him into a corner saying, "Would you, please, do this for a little while, for a few months?" Dr. E.C. Tolbert, who was president of the Medical Society, also begged Dr. Sanders, telling him, "We'll cover for you some of the time, but would you take it on?"

Bob saw that no one really wanted the job. As the director of the Health Department, and the County Health Officer, he was already signing the death certificates. So, he took it on. At least the pay would supplement his income. His son and daughter were essentially grown anyway, and there would be time to do it. After all, he needed the extra boost in income, which might help make up for the meager earnings from buying and selling steers each year.

The pay was $50 per case, and the job of the Medical Examiner was to investigate deaths that were unnatural and untimely, such as car accidents, handgun deaths, drug overdoses, suicides, or other accidents. When he began, he averaged around 50 such cases per year. He dealt regularly with the ambulance service and the Rutherford County Emergency Medical Service (the EMTs). He also dealt with the Rutherford County Sheriff's department and the Murfreesboro Police pertaining to cases. He would write a case history and turn that in to the county.

Many times, Dr. Sanders had to visit the accident site or the home where a homicide had taken place. Sometimes he would have to go to the morgue and examine the body. He was the one who was in charge of ordering an autopsy if he saw it necessary. There was one instance when the hospital was against having an autopsy done on a certain person, and Dr. Sanders thought that an autopsy was necessary. He was persistent, and he steadfastly objected to them, insisting on an autopsy, asking the lady on the phone, "Who's your superior?" and asking to talk to him. Dr. Sanders got his way, and the autopsy was done. It was the right thing, because in that particular case, an unsolved mystery was surprisingly resolved.

With Dr. Sanders' connections as Medical Examiner, he had the right to find out information from the county officials, and from the police, as well. For example, he could even obtain license plate information. It was amazing how he could call the sheriff's department, reach dispatch, and say, "Yes, Dr. Sanders calling here . . . need to find out the name and address for the following tag: QMH-607," for example. In seconds, dispatch was giving Dr. Sanders the name and address of the owner and what make and model the car was, every time and with no conflict.

Robert, his son, never succeeded in getting a name and address from a license plate from the sheriff's department. They always shoved it back in his face that it was confidential, but Dr. Sanders could. On three or four occasions, Dr. Sanders called the sheriff's office and got the license tag information for Robert. There was never any mal intent involved. Dr. Sanders, with his position as medical examiner had certain rights that ordinary people didn't have, and with his gentle persuasion but also his direct nature, the sheriff's officers and police were compelled to give him whatever information he needed, regardless of whether or not it was confidential.

After taking on the job of medical examiner and working it a few months, no one else ever came forth. Dr. Sanders therefore kept the extra job and became permanent. At that time, he requested a raise to $75 per case. The county granted his request, and he worked the job for the next 16 years. Even after retiring from the Health Department in 1991, he kept his medical examiner job until August 1999.

Dr. Bart Warner replaced Dr. Sanders, and he is still the Medical Examiner to this day.

Volvo of Sweden

the Sanders' 1970 red Volvo station wagon

As earlier mentioned, when Bob Sanders returned to the United States from Sweden in 1959, he brought his 1959 VW Bug home with him. He had bought it new in Germany. He kept the car until 1970 when he sold it to a tenant. In that year, partly for being reminiscent of his stay in Sweden, he and his wife bought a red Volvo station wagon, 145 S Model for $4,000. It was a 4 cylinder with a 4 speed on the floor. Volvos were known to be safe cars compared to other models, ranking very high in rollover collisions and crash tests. He had chosen red to try and get a safe color.

It was a great car body-wise, but not so great with its motor. The car broke down on the highway several times and left him and his family stranded until a wrecker would come and tow them home. In retrospect, it would have been better to have bought an American model, say a red Ford Ranch Wagon station wagon with standard shift (manual transmission). It would have had equally as good a crash test rating and would have been much more dependable on the highway. The 1970 Volvo with its dual carburetors only got 20 mpg, and a big Ford station wagon achieved that easily, especially with standard shift and just one carburetor. Besides, the Ford Ranch Wagon would have been more roomy with much more cargo space. 1970 would have been a good year to have bought a Ranch Wagon because that was the last year that Ford offered standard shift in their full size models. Plus shoulder belts and head rests were standard equipment by then in the front seat.

Many years later, in 2006, his son Robert in efforts to rewrite history for the better, found a 1970 Ford Ranch Wagon station wagon, bought it and brought it home from Illinois. It actually came equipped with factory standard shift! When Robert got home to the family farm, he parked the car in exactly the same spot outside the yard gate where the 1970 red Volvo wagon had been parked the first time, so many years before.

Granted, Bob Sanders had safety in mind when buying the Volvo, as Volvos did have a good crash record. There was a Volvo ad attesting to that fact, showing 4 Volvo cars stacked on top of each other, and the bottom car withstanding the weight without buckling.

In 1973, when Robert was age 7, Bob decided to trade in Uncle Dana's old blue 1960 Chevrolet stepside pickup truck. He asked Robert what color he wanted to truck to be. Robert suggested orange. Bob liked Robert's suggested color very much. Not only was it Robert's favorite color, it was a safe color, as well. Orange it was, and Bob ordered the truck from the Chevrolet dealer for $2,900. When he and Robert went to pick up the new truck, the dealer gave $185 cash for the old truck that was traded in. The orange truck certainly stood out on the road and was visible, much more so than the grey, brown, and blue cars out there, and even more so than the red ones. The truck was kept in the family for nearly 30 years, until it was worn out and sold for one tenth of its new price, in 2002.

The Tucker and the Lack of Seat Belts

Seat belts existed before the 1950s because Preston Tucker considered having them as standard equipment in his 1948 Tucker automobiles. Mr. Tucker was a safety conscious individual, and he had safety in mind when designing the car. There were several other safety features that he did include: a padded dashboard, a pop out windshield made of safety glass, a padded crouching area under the dashboard so a front seat passenger could crouch down in the event of an accident, (as if there were time for that)! Instrumentation was grouped around the steering column to ensure that there wouldn't be any protruding buttons or gauges in case of a collision. The Tucker automobiles even had a 3rd headlight that would turn in accordance with the steering wheel and help illuminate the road when making a turn, a commendable safety feature indeed.

However, in the end, it was decided that seat belts would *not* be installed at all, because having seat belts might make consumers think the Tucker was an unsafe car. Amazing the lack of reasoning and common sense on that one! The safest car in the world, for example, could be subject to a collision by some other careless driver on the road, and seat belts increase the person's chance of surviving the crash. It seems that Mr. Tucker forgot that collisions can happen due to the fault of another vehicle and its driver's being careless. Even though the driver of the Tucker automobile may be the best driver in the world, some collisions are unavoidable. In half a century, the understanding and rationale of people and their viewpoint on seat belts has vastly improved, and on this issue, society has taken a step forward and in the right direction.

Even still, back in the 1960s, 70s, and even 80s, passengers riding with Dr. Sanders were sometimes surprised that he always put on his seat belt, even though he was driving. A few would even say they didn't believe in seat belts, that the Lord would protect them.

Dr. Sanders would usually answer, "And if I were the Lord, I would say that I provided your car with seat belts, so that you could *use* them, right? That would make it a lot easier for me to protect you, and thus increase your chances of surviving a crash."

Thankfully, people are a lot more educated in this day and time about seat belts and the benefits of using them, than were the people in the days of Mr. Tucker, and even the people a mere two decades ago.

Dr Sanders' knowledge of the above fact is part of what motivated him to push for better protection for the youngest of passengers: the infants, toddlers, and young children.

Lobbying and the Child Passenger Protection Act, 1975-1977

Bob Sanders holding a child car seat   courtesy: Alan Loveless

Dr. Robert Sanders was a man who had determination, and when he took on a cause he saw as important and also beneficial to the public, he was like a dog with a tire in its mouth. He had tenacity, stuck with it, and saw it through to completion. This sort of traits runs in the family, as is seen in the following passage about his grandfather William Josiah Sanders, DDS., written by his son C. Richard Sanders:

"He worked hardest for a cause which he knew would benefit many other people, although it might not put a cent in his own pocket. Working with other difficulties he would not be defeated. The work for which he is best known, that of founding the Co-operative Creamery and the dairy industry in Rutherford County, could never have been accomplished if he had lacked this trait. He knew that the farmers with whom he had to work at the beginning had had almost no experience in the ways of cooperation and that they were extremely individualistic, somewhat suspicious of one another and afraid that someone would try to sell them a gold brick. When only a few came to the first meeting that had been called and these were far from enthusiastic, one or two of the leaders said, "It's no use; they don't want it." He said, "We haven't gone at it right." And soon he called another meeting, at which the idea began to take root. He knew how important it was that people have faith in one another. He also knew that he had to be patient,

82

determined, and resourceful. During the long, hard months in which the movement gradually gained strength, he had many little talks with individual farmers. I can remember overhearing some of these. He read all he could find on the subject, and he wrote many articles on it, which his friend Louis Burgdorf, editor of the Murfreesboro Home Journal, (a weekly), willingly published. These articles were filled with quotations from the best authorities on dairying, creameries, and enriching the land. At last the combination of facts and faith did the job, and Rutherford County became a land of green pastures and alfalfa, growing more fertile each year and no longer dependent on soil depleting cotton in its economy."

It is interesting the parallel of activities that his grandson Dr. Robert Sanders undertook in 1975, 1976 and 1977 in terms of calling and visiting many people and writing letters about the need for a child passenger restraint law, in addition to his lobbying efforts. One can note the similarity in family traits, both of them for good causes.

Even though Bob Sanders served in the U.S. Army from 1946 to early 1948, he was not a believer in war, nor did he support it. It was a blessing for him that WWII was over by the time he enlisted for 18 months. (His brother Bill had not been so lucky, who fought right during WWII on a destroyer in the Pacific Ocean. Nevertheless, Bill was very fortunate because he returned home uninjured.) Even still, Bob Sanders has far more peaceful and good memories of his days in the Army than his brother Bill, without a doubt.

Perhaps Bob's grandfather's philosophy about war had rubbed off on him. William Josiah Sanders, DDS wrote some memoirs about his life, and in them, he talks about his philosophy on war. His father Drury had fought in the Civil War of the early 1860s. WJ (Joe) as a boy used to frequently hear his father chat with his old comrades about their experiences in the Civil War.

WJ Sanders wrote:
"The horrors of war were indelibly impressed upon me to such an extent that I believe I would have suffered death rather than enlist in anybody's army. I have not changed. I have no respect for war and less than no respect for any man or set of men who would advocate war. War is born in brains fixed with the principles of evil darkness. Its horribleness is beyond description and is only known by those who have participated in it. This is one place where imagination cannot be as vivid as reality, where words fail of meaning and participation in, is to visualize the tortures of the very evil."

youngest of citizens who cannot protect themselves. Casey pointed out that the biblical basis for the concept of a child passenger protection law was that in Deuteronomy 22:8, Moses, the prophet is conveying God's requirement to Israel for their new life in the Promised Land of Canaan. He states, "When you build a new house, you shall make a parapet for your roof, that you may not bring the guilt of blood upon your house if any fall from it." Casey thought of the parapet, or low wall or railing around the edges of a roof, as being analogous to a child restraint device itself, including its anchorage inside the car. Like the parapet which passively keeps someone from falling off the roof, the child restraint system keeps the child, in the event of a crash, from being ejected or thrown against the interior of the car.

Soon, Ed Casey and Mike Ellis met with someone from the National Highway Traffic Safety Administration (NHTSA), and they drew up a six-page bill. That was in the autumn of 1975. It was a long bill.

None of them at that time had ever done any lobbying, nor were they experienced at it. How did one go about it or who approached whom? What did one need to give the legislators, as far as literature or whatever? No matter what, they made the decision to start working on a state law. It seemed timely. In other words, it was high time, and it would indeed save lives.

So, when the Tennessee Pediatric Society had their annual meeting at Fall Creek Falls State Park, with pediatricians gathering from all over Tennessee, Dr. Sanders presented the Child Restraint Law proposal to all of them. As chairman of the Accident Prevention Committee of Tennessee, he could do so. He pointed out the unnecessary deaths to babies, toddlers, and young children that could be largely prevented by the use of child safety seats in automobiles, even more so prevented if there were a state law. He also showed a movie called, "Where Have All the People Gone?" put out by the National Safety Belt Council in 1974, and featuring Dr. Gordon Trinca, a surgeon from Melbourne, Victoria, Australia, where their federal seat belt law, in place since 1967, had greatly reduced traffic accident deaths.

The movie opened with a football stadium full of spectators, cheering, yelling, activity normal to a big event. Then the next scene shows the stadium empty, all silent now. They asked the viewers where have all the people gone, and then pointed out that *that* many people, 50,000, die in car crashes each year (that is, per year) just in the United States!

There were three Es: education, engineering, and enforcement. As far as educating the people, there were a few small national organizations in the mid 1970s who were focusing on child passenger safety: Physicians for Automotive Safety (PAS) and its parent-based nurse-based spinoff, Action for Child Transportation Safety (ACTS). These and some local child passenger safety associations and women's clubs had only raised the child passenger safety seat usage very slightly. It was far from enough, and Dr. Sanders realized that.

One of the earliest child passenger safety seats was engineered and designed by Quinten MacDonald, of New York state. The seat was called the "Bobby Mac", named after his son Bobby MacDonald. As time went on, improvements would be done and engineering design changes would make even better seats.

The "E" representing enforcement by law of using child passenger safety seats in cars, was what Dr. Sanders realized would be the most effective method of significantly increasing usage rates, (which at that time was only 9% and very low). Higher usage rates would significantly decrease deaths from crashes.

Bob Sanders set out to investigate how to bring about such a law. The movie, "Where Have All the People Gone?" had a story about the mayor of Brooklyn, Ohio, who decided to make it a city ordinance to wear seat belts. He managed to get it passed, and Brooklyn, Ohio was the first town in the United States to have such a law. Dr. Sanders spoke with the mayor several times by telephone to find out how they succeeded in passing such a safety law. The mayor of Brooklyn sent some literature and information about their unique law. Also included was a video showing a city police officer in Brooklyn, Ohio kindly telling a lady driver that there was a city ordinance and for her to put on her seat belt. The car was a mid 1960s Ford Galaxie 500, which only had lap belts, and the video showed her putting it on (not too safe by today's standards, lacking a shoulder strap, especially with the steering wheel in front of her). 1968 was the first year that American cars carried factory installed shoulder belts for the front seat.

One of the first local medical groups that Dr. Sanders met with was the Rutherford County and Stones River Academy of Medicine. Ed Casey came too, and he brought a car seat. Together they made a presentation, and the medical group bought the seat, but not without some discussion and dissent, questioning individual liberties and personal rights and that sort of thing. There was opposition to such a law. Dr. Sanders was realizing that he was indeed a pioneer in child passenger safety.

Early on, Bob also called Dr. Eugene Fowinkle, the state commissioner of public health for Tennessee, and he explained what he was trying to do. Fowinkle gave Bob the green light to work on the bill and lobby for it, and that he could do it on state employee time, but not to expect much help from the department of public health nor from the public health sector in general. Fowinkle also wrote a nice letter in favor of such a law. Bob took the reigns and carried the project through to completion.

courtesy: Tom England

l-r: Bob Sanders, Commissioner Gene Roberts, Ed Caldwell, Sam Carney, Senator Douglas Henry, and Representative John Bragg on the capitol steps

To go before the legislature in Nashville, Bob and the other pediatricians would have to find a sponsor. His local state representative John Bragg of Murfreesboro was a possibility. Bragg was also the Budget and Finance Committee Chairman for the House. Bob also considered and called two local pediatricians: Charles W. Lewis, MD and R. James Garrison, MD. Together, they met with John Bragg and presented him a copy of an article that had recently appeared in Pediatrics Magazine in September 1975, and written by Seymour Charles and Annemarie

Shelness. It was titled: "Children as Passengers in Automobiles: The Neglected Minority on the Nation's Highways."

(transcript is in the Appendix of this book, pp. 176-187)

John Bragg had never seen the article, and he was intrigued by it as he read it. Bragg decided to sponsor the bill. He knew it was a great idea. Also, the Tennessee Medical Association lined up Senators Douglas Henry and Ed Blank to be sponsors of the bill.

There were several committees the Child Restraint Bill had to go through before arriving to the floor of the legislature (House of Representatives). Dr. Sanders had to do everything he could to impress and to educate the legislators, who had so many other things on their minds. He went to the newspapers. Articles were written about the proposed bill.

Bob Sanders spoke with and had interviews with the newspapers, and he even got an endorsement for the bill from Nashville's major newspaper, the *Nashville Tennessean*. As it turned out, the chief editorial writer, Lloyd Armour, was a friend of Ed Casey's father. Ed pulled some strings there, and one of his relatives from West Tennessee set up an appointment for Dr. Sanders with Lloyd Armour, which they happily accepted.

The meeting went well, and Bob took some literature, including the recent article by Seymour Charles and Annemarie Shelness. He also took an actual child safety car seat. Mr. Armour looked over the literature, and after examining the seat, he told Bob, "I think we can go with this, but what I'll need from you is a bunch of letters to come in right now."

Bob answered and said he'd try to get some. That was done successfully, and the *Nashville Tennessean* endorsed the bill that first year and editorialized for it. This was also helped along by the influence of John Seigenthaler, the publisher of the *Nashville Tennessean*. He was also in favor of the bill.

In the spring of 1976, the bill was brought up and passed both transportation committees, after which it advanced to the Calendar and Rules Committee. They oversee whether a particular bill has enough merit to be presented to the floor of the House and Senate in the legislature. The Calendar and Rules Committee killed it, and the bill failed for the year 1976. Therefore, it never even got introduced onto the Senate floor that year. Individual liberties were encroached upon, many people thought. Some of the legislators had been against it, among them Roscoe Pickering, and Senator John Ford. Pickering suddenly shouted out, "Get that Ralph Nader out of here!" He personally didn't like Ralph Nader and was putting Dr. Sanders in the same category with his derogatory comment! A friend from college, Bob Taylor, who was a lobbyist for banking and insurance, said to Dr. Sanders, "Don't be discouraged. Come on back down here next year, but you are going to need more than one newspaper endorsement."

After the bill failed to pass in 1976, Bob realized that he and his comrades needed more help. Pat could tell that Bob really wanted to go back and lobby for it again. He was like a dog with a tire in its mouth, and he didn't want to let it go. She hadn't done much with him the first year, but the second year she did. Bob and his comrades regrouped, and Pat joined in on the effort. What else did they need to do? They had really wanted to pass that legislation that first year. One might compare Bob's being at the legislature to an innocent in the lion's den. To pass legislation, one really had to educate the legislators on what the issues were and to prove the bill's merit.

There had been pros and cons, and some of the cons were that people who live out in the countryside have pickup trucks and they just like to have children ride in the back. Another point was that mothers with little babies like to hold them, very dangerous indeed, if a crash occurs. Some mothers felt very strongly about holding their babies instead of using the child safety car seat, regardless of the risks. Plus, a child riding in a safety seat all by its lonesome might feel neglected and could cry and be quite disrupting.

Ned Ray McWherter, who was then the Speaker of the House of Representatives, (and later served as Governor 1987-1993), reacted with some surprise that Dr. Sanders was going to come back to the legislature again to lobby for the Child Restraint Bill. He said to one of his fellow legislators, John Bragg, "You mean Dr. Seat Belt is going to come back down here again?" That was the beginning of Bob's nickname, "Dr. Seat Belt." It was Ned Ray McWherter who had started it.

They would need a grassroots movement with more people to speak up in favor of this bill. Pat was right there with Bob every day calling more people on the phone, writing letters, going to offices personally with literature (fact sheets) in hand, and an actual child safety seat to show them. At the legislature, they went up and down the hallways and knocked on every door to talk to the representatives and senators in their offices, plus committee members. It took that type of coalition effort to succeed.

The year before, a lot of representatives and senators had been too busy to talk to Bob, but this year, his wife Pat was with him, and she would stick her head in the door and ask to talk to them. Most of them would say, "Yeah, come on in for just a moment." Then Bob would enter on Pat's coat tail. The tactic worked and they succeeded in visiting and talking to just about all of the state representatives and senators.

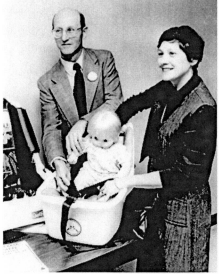

Bob and Pat Sanders with a child car seat

Bob and Pat went to see Senator Ed Blank, from Columbia. He was one of the bill's sponsors for the Senate floor. When they entered his office, Blank was reading the newspaper and hardly looked up at them. Bob and Pat wanted to talk about the bill, and Ed Blank told them point blank, "This year, I am working on ten bills. Most of them are Tennessee Medical Association bills, and this bill is not one of them." Bob and Pat were speechless and also very disheartened. Blank went on to say, "Do you have someone to second the motion in the Senate?"

Bob and Pat said, "No," and they got up and left.

"You've got to have somebody to second the motion," Blank called out to them.

They walked straight over to Senator Douglas Henry's office for advice. Henry took them into his office and sat them down. He asked Bob and Pat, "What pediatrician do you know in Memphis who can get Curtis Person to second the motion?"

Bob thought of Dr. George Lovejoy, told Bragg, and they called him right then and there from the legislature's WATS line. Lovejoy agreed to talk to Senator Person right away.

91

Senator Henry then advised Bob and Pat on how to get some grass-roots support and also how to lobby.

Senator Curtis Person agreed with Lovejoy and obliged, and he said he would be happy to second the motion on the senate floor. Some of the other legislators were also impressed by this bill. Person believed that doctors should be listened to. The Child Restraint bill was not self-serving either. Some thought it might be self-serving for the car seat manufacturers, and Dr. Sanders did his best to make sure that he wasn't making any money on this project, nor that he was receiving any commissions from car seat manufacturers. In every letter that Bob wrote, he made it clear that the bill was not self-serving. He also spoke personally with a number of the legislators before certain committee meetings. Instead of being self-serving, this bill was in the interest of safety for babies and young children.

How Senator Ed Blank was chosen to be a sponsor for the bill remained a wonder to Bob and Pat, especially since the Child Restraint Bill was not one of the ten bills that Blank was working on. Blank had almost no interest in the bill and was unwilling to do any footwork on it before it would arrive on the senate floor for discussion.

Rep. John Bragg was the sponsor of the bill for the House. He was determined to see this bill pass and become law this year.

He noticed that the Speaker of the House, Ned Ray McWherter, was not very enthusiastic about this bill. Bragg soon found out that McWherter had recently attended a TMA (Tennessee Medical Association) meeting where they had discussed different bills that were slated to go through the legislature that year. The child restraint bill wasn't on the list of the bills that the TMA was going to work on. In other words, their lobbyist was not really going to support it. It was just going to be lip service on the part of the TMA. Dr. Morse Kochtitzky, who was the president of the TMA, did not favor this bill, and thus he didn't want the lobbyists working on it. It was like Fowinkle had said. Don't expect much help from the public health sector.

Dr. Joseph Bailey, a personal friend of the Sanders and a Murfreesboro ophthalmologist and contact physician for the TMA, was actually at that meeting. He promptly called Bob on the phone and expressed his concern.

Bragg also got very concerned after learning of the TMA's lack of interest in this bill. So, he set out to find people to come and testify. Several people came, among them a married university student who told his story about driving a VW Bug along East Main Street. At the intersection with Baird Lane, he lost control and ran off the road and into a fence. His child, who was 2½ years old, was standing in the back seat and was thrown forward. His head hit the window crank handle and was gashed. They had to go the emergency room in Murfreesboro, and the boy was rushed to Vanderbilt hospital where he was operated on by a neurosurgeon, Dr. Cully Cobb. The hospital and surgery cost was $13,000, which was quite expensive in the mid 1970s. When the father and little boy entered the House floor to testify, the boy walked over to the stage where some of the senators were seated, and he climbed up on the lap of one of them. The scar on the head was visible, and it was an emotionally touching scene for some of the legislators. Their testimony was very persuasive to the legislators and also to the Senate Transportation Committee. They realized how important a law like this would be. This was just one case of many out there in the state, which could have been prevented if a child safety seat had been utilized.

The bill, once again, was presented to the committees for voting in 1977. Both of Bob and Pat's children, Robert and Priscilla, were present and witnessed the committees as they discussed the pros and cons. Then they voted it through. It went on to the legislative floor. The bill did better this year with more help from more people, especially legislators, Senators Douglas Henry and Ed Blank, Representatives John Bragg, Robb Robinson, and Mike Murphy. There were several Nashville pediatricians and doctors who also helped. Among them were Sam Carney, Eric Chazen, Amos Christie, Ed Caldwell, Walton Harrison, Lewis Lefkowitz, George Lovejoy, Bob Quinn, and David Thombs.

There was a Vanderbilt medical student, Bruce Dan, who also helped. He was extraordinary and was really excited to be in on the ground floor of such a bill. Bruce rounded up people, students, whoever at the hospital, issued them lab coats, brought them to the state legislature where they sat on the front row of the calendar and rules committee, and posed as doctors.

On the floor of the legislature, there were many discussions concerning the bill. Some of them were heated discussions. One senator was concerned about the cost of each seat, which was between $50 and $75. Sam Carney pointed out that it was a small price to pay to protect a small child in a crash, much better than $13,000. Without a seat, death or an emergency room visit, or much worse a funeral, would carry a much higher price tag than a mere $50 to $75 for a child safety car seat.

After considerable arguing and debate, the bill was passed and became law, but not without Roscoe Pickering's sliding in a nice little amendment, which was quite *disagreeable* to Bob and Pat Sanders. Pickering said, "The happiest day of my daughter's life was the day that she brought her newborn baby home in her arms. I've been against this thing, but I'll compromise here. I submit, I'll make an amendment that these children need to be in a car seat or required to be, or be in the lap of an older person." A mother or even a person age 12 or older would be allowed to hold the baby or young child in his or her arms. It was known as the "Babes in Arms Amendment." Bob and Pat had another name for it: the "Child Crusher Amendment." Roscoe Pickering really did resent that nickname for his amendment. No matter what, the legislators settled on adopting that amendment to improve the chances of the bill's passing at all. John Bragg explained to Bob and Pat that this is the way a lot of laws get passed, and then later on, they get beefed up and improved upon. Bragg said, "Don't worry. This is a compromise. It is passed. You can come back later to clean up the bill and take the amendment out."

Bob and Pat knew that several kids would be killed, due to that amendment, or crushed against the dashboard.

Annemarie Shelness was grief stricken by the amendment. Why did they allow that awful amendment to pass?

One must keep in mind that the governor might not have signed that bill into law, had it not carried that "Babes in Arms Amendment."

Four years later, 1981, the amendment would be gotten rid of.

It needs to be said that Dr. Sam Carney was one of the members on the Accident Prevention Committee, and he was very good at politics. Having grown up in Tullahoma, he was a lifelong friend of Bob Sanders, and he was very helpful at some of the most crucial moments. He happened to be the private pediatrician for Governor Ray Blanton's grandchildren. Also, one of Sam's friends was George Barrett, who was Ray Blanton's attorney. Gov. Blanton was planning to veto the Child Passenger Protection Act, despite all the hard work that Dr. and Mrs. Sanders had put into it, along with so many other people who got that bill passed through the legislature.

Sam Carney and George Barrett talked with each other. Sam was quite upset to hear that Gov. Ray Blanton was planning to veto it, and he called Blanton's daughter on the phone. "Look, I see your children. You *see* to it that your father *doesn't* veto that bill." Sam was very direct and adamant about it, and he went on to explain to her the benefits of the bill, especially concerning safety and that many lives would be saved.

George Barrett called the governor on the phone and said to him, "I don't know what kind of words to use, but this is like apple pie, more than apple pie. Don't make a fool of yourself."

Blanton's daughter also went to have a talk with her father, telling him "Please do *not* veto that bill. It's important."

Thankfully the governor listened to his daughter, and to Barrett, and he signed the bill. The law went into effect January 1, 1978, and Tennessee was the first state in the nation to have such a law. In fact it was the first such child passenger restraint law in the world, because Australia only had their seat belt law, nothing for infants. Tennessee's Child Passenger Protection Act required children under age 4 to be in a child passenger safety car seat, (except for babes in arms.)

PUBLIC CHAPTER NO. 114

HOUSE BILL NO. 300
By Bragg, Murphy (Davidson)

Substituted for: Senate Bill No. 382
By Blank

AN ACT to amend Tennessee Code Annotated, Section 59-930, requiring that children under the age of four (4) years use passenger restraint system

BE IT ENACTED BY THE GENERAL ASSEMBLY OF THE STATE OF TENNESSEE:

SECTION 1. Tennessee Code Annotated, Section 59-930, is amended by inserting after the first paragraph of such section and before the second paragraph, the following additional paragraph:

(b) Every parent or legal guardian of a child under the age of four (4) years residing in this state shall be responsible, when transporting his child in a motor vehicle owned by that parent or guardian operated on the roadways, streets or highways of this state, for providing for the protection of his child and properly using a child passenger restraint system meeting federal motor vehicle safety standards, or assuring that such child is held in the arms of an older person riding as a passenger in the motor vehicle. Provided that the term "motor vehicle" as used in this paragraph shall not apply to recreational vehicles of the truck or van type. Provided further that the term "motor vehicle" as used in this paragraph shall not apply to trucks having a tonnage rating of one ton or more. Provided that in no event shall failure to wear a child passenger restraint system be considered as contributory negligence, nor shall such failure to wear said child passenger restraint system be admissible as evidence in the trial of any civil action.

SECTION 2. Tennessee Code Annotated, Section 59-930, is further amended by designating the first paragraph of the section to be subsection (a) and by deleting the period at the end of the last paragraph of the section and adding the following:

of subsection (a) of this section and not less than two dollars ($2.00) nor more than ten dollars ($10.00) for each violation of subsection (b) of this section.

SECTION 3. This Act shall take effect on January 1, 1978, the public welfare requiring it.

PASSED April 13, 1977
Approved the 27th day of April, 1977
Speaker of the House of Representatives: Ned R. McWherter
Speaker of the Senate: John Wilder
Governor of Tennessee: Ray Blanton

One might note that according to the text of the law, it doesn't state a minimum age requirement for the older person holding the babe in arms. It was understood by everybody that the older person had to be at least age 12, but it wasn't written in the law. Plus, trucks and vans were exempt! The law was very much watered down during its first few years on the books, but later on, those exemptions got eliminated, making it a better law.

Once the law went into effect beginning in 1978, lives began to be saved, that otherwise wouldn't have been, across the state of Tennessee. One such person who benefited from the law was Sharri Chappell, whose son Chaz was saved by the child car safety seat in a horrible crash.

Dr. Sanders started getting invitations to be on television. There were many TV and radio interviews across the state, which soon led to his being interviewed even on national news. In November 1978, he was interviewed by David Hartman on ABC's "Good Morning America." It was really quite an accomplishment and milestone to have caused the Child Restraint Law to become a reality. He appeared on Walter Cronkite's CBS Evening News June 30, 1980. He was also covered in People Magazine in the summer of 1981.

The father of one of Robert's Bellwood classmates wrote Dr. Sanders a nice letter, praising him for his efforts and commending him for his accomplishments. Some other complimentary letters arrived, as well.

Even with all the press coverage that took place, it was three entire years before another state in the union passed a child passenger restraint law. The next state was Rhode Island in 1980. During such a lapse of time from 1977 to 1980, Dr. Sanders and others were concerned that Tennessee might repeal their Child Restraint Law, but fortunately they never did.

After Rhode Island, the good idea began to take hold. Albert Gore, Jr., who was a U.S. Representative and represented parts of Middle Tennessee, including the district where Dr. Sanders lived, wanted some incentive grants to go to the states who would pass the same law as Tennessee. At Al

Gore's request, Bob Sanders went to Washington, DC, accompanied by a Tennessee Highway Patrol officer, and they went before a congressional committee to speak in favor of such a law nationwide. The National Accident Prevention Committee also asked Dr. and Mrs. Sanders to come up to New York City and talk, which was in November 1977. Thomas Reichelderfer, MD was committee chairman then of the National Accident Prevention Committee for the American Academy of Pediatrics. The Academy presented Dr. Sanders a special award. Reichelderfer wrote a nice letter endorsing the law. Dr. Sanders was pleased, because he wanted to get the other states hopping.

Things got moving a lot faster after the incentive grants were in place, plus the American Academy of Pediatrics got more involved. They got behind the effort along with the automotive safety groups. Its importance was realized, and by 1985, every state in the union had child passenger restraint laws. When you've got something good, one can see how quickly it moves along.

The Babes in Arms Removal

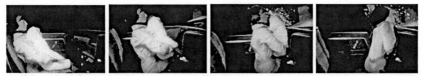

4 slides, showing what happens to a baby in its mother's arms during a car crash
courtesy: Insurance Institute of Highway Safety

Due to the "Babes in Arms Amendment" being added to the Child Passenger Protection Act of 1977 in Tennessee, there had been a number of infant and toddler deaths in crashes because they had been smashed or crushed against the dashboard and/or windshield by the mother or another passenger holding the baby in his/her arms. There had been a total of 12 deaths like this in Tennessee during the past three years.

Bob and Pat Sanders called John Bragg and Douglas Henry, told them what was happening, and they went down to the legislature to inform them that several children had been crushed against the dashboard in the arms of another passenger. Bob and Pat had nicknamed the loophole the "Child Crusher Amendment." John Bragg, Douglas Henry, and Robb Robinson and Mike Murphy worked very hard to convince the legislature of the practicality of removing that loophole.

John Bragg worked to find several people to testify. In front of the Transportation Committee, Sharri Chappell testified about how her son

Chaz was recently saved in a car safety seat. Also a James Davis went and testified for his wife. He hadn't been so lucky because his wife was holding her baby during a crash, and it had been crushed and killed against the dashboard! The mother was not killed, not seat belted either, and therefore the baby was in essence, a human air bag! (Most cars didn't have air bags in those days.) The repeal of the bad and dangerous amendment barely made it through the Transportation Committee with a passing vote. It would now proceed to the Calendar and Rules Committee.

Larry Daughtrey wrote up the testimony about what happened in the House Transportation Committee meeting. The *Nashville Tennessean* article showed the words "lucky" and "unlucky" with corresponding photos.

During the Calendar and Rules Committee meeting, they discussed whether or not to remove the "Babes in Arms Amendment," Both Roscoe Pickering and Shelby Rhinehart were adamantly against removing it! They discussed it and argued about it, but they weren't getting very far with it. Somewhere during the discussion, Shelby Rhinehart got up and went to the bathroom. Without waiting for Rhinehart to return from his nature break, the committee suddenly and sneakily decided to vote on it, to hurry and get that done without Rhinehart's being there. It received a passing vote. Success! It could now go on to the House floor. Rhinehart came back into the committee session after his bathroom break, and when he found out they'd voted on it without his being there, he sure was fuming mad!

The "Child Crusher Amendment" removal became a major discussion on the House floor. There, Robb Robinson, chairman of the House Transportation Committee, had a long roll of paper, which he dramatically unrolled and displayed before the representatives. It had the names of all the babies and young children that had been crushed against the dashboard in their mothers' arms and/or unrestrained. "These are the names of all the children that have been crushed and killed against the dashboard during crashes because they were in the arms of their mother and not restrained in car seats." Robinson was also a funeral home director in Madison, Tennessee. He didn't like being the undertaker for unnecessary deaths of babies and young children. The House listened to him. Pickering had the audacity to say, "How can Dr. Sanders be down here doing this, and why isn't he back home in Murfreesboro doing his job as the director of the Rutherford County Health Department?" Pickering didn't know that the commissioner of public health, Dr. Eugene Fowinkle, had given Dr. Sanders the green light to work on this whole bill, which also included working on the removal of that awful "Child Crusher Amendment" four years later.

Rep. Jim McKinney came to Sanders' defense, and he responded to Pickering's derogatory question, explaining that this is what Dr. Sanders ought to be doing. After all, it was an effort to save babies' lives and was considered preventive medicine. Child car safety seats were like vaccines against the highway epidemic, more specifically, against car crashes.

Tennessee state gov't photo
Gov. Lamar Alexander signing the approval for the Babes in Arms removal, 1981

Tennessee state gov't photo
Sen. Douglas Henry, Gov. Lamar Alexander, and Rep. John Bragg holding a child car safety seat, with others, in recognition of the law

Tennessee's Department of Safety developed a loaner program with child restraint seats with the motto: "Don't punish parents; protect children." State troopers would issue a violator with a ticket and also issue them a child safety seat on loan. If they bought their own seat and returned the loaner seat on the day of court with proof of purchase, the ticket and charges would be erased. That loaner program really helped and boosted usage rates considerably.

Commissioner of Safety Gene Roberts said that that one program was enough to make a major change and that it was the best public service program that the Tennessee Department of Safety had ever had.

Dr. Sanders continued to be interviewed nationwide, actually more than that, and he frequently travelled to different states to speak in favor of child passenger protection and the benefits of such a law. On the next page is a transcript of one of his many interviews. It was from a radio station in western Canada.

at Commissioner Gene Roberts' office, 1978; l-r: Ed Caldwell, George Lovejoy, Sam Carney, Walton Harrison, Gene Roberts, David Thombs, Bob Sanders, Luthur Beazley, and Eric Chazen

CJOR interview, September 1981

I'm in public health. Our central theme in public health is in preventive medicine. I'm also a pediatrician and was chairman of the Accident Prevention Committee in this state, so it was sort of a natural that when the idea came about to have a task force here several years ago that I was to be a part of that. We knew that this sort of protection for a child would be equivalent really to immunization. That seems to be the central theme here is that this particular kind of illness, this particular kind of death and destruction is essentially preventable then why not, why not as we do with other immunizations, require our children to be in those little car seats.

Quite controversial, we understand that, but I believe it is beginning to pay off even as seat belt laws in the rest of the industrialized world, including your own province there, must be paying off, these laws must be paying off, so it's time that we look at what's really killing children and try to get a handle on it.

Statistical evidence is really irrefutable. An ongoing study in the state of Washington state from 1970 was that a child under say 5 is in one of these child seats and a significant crash occurs, that the chances of death are reduced by 90 percent, injuries by 80 percent. That's evidence enough that we can thus have a handle on what happens to these children if we could just get the kids into these seats.

Question: Is there any specific brand of children's car seats that you'd recommend?

No, there are so many good ones on the market and it should be clear to your listeners that some dozen, or dozen and a half companies make some 20-25 very fine models, and be sure and follow the manufacturer's instructions that require a tether strap to be worn on the back. That should be done and the strap should be secured firmly and tightly, and the lap belt should secure the seat.

Question: Have you ever been called upon as a pediatrician to take care of a child who was in a car seat at the time of an accident?

Well, I guess not—I am a pediatrician but most of those cases in the hospital setting are taken care of by surgeons. But in my unique position now as a public health officer and as a county register, all the death certificates that come through this office are signed by me and it's very dismaying and disheartening to sign one on an innocent, unprotected, dependant child whose death was caused by being crushed against the dash, or a trooper had to peal him off the dash or unstick him from the windshield.

101

Question: I had a police officer tell me once, "If you want to talk about safety, you take the best quarterback playing pro football and you give him a metal box—a rectangular box about the size of a football and throw a bullet pass as hard as you can against a stone wall and if you believe the egg is gonna be intact on the inside, then you'd believe that your child would be intact in a car crash."

That's the size of it, and the way human nature is. We buy a dozen eggs, do we not, in a carefully packaged carton so that if you bump it around a bit, they don't break and we package our expensive vases and lamps and even our television sets, do we not, but the most valuable thing in a family, a young family, is that *baby*, which many of us carry in our arms or in our laps or on the seat of the car, and that is what kills them nowadays. Much more so than the usual childhood diseases, polio, diphtheria, or all those things that used to kill them, for which we have immunizations that are required by the state, so we think it is timely that legislators assert themselves responsibly by requiring such immunizing protection for these helpless little ones, as we do for those other infectious diseases.

We have a lot to learn in the United States now—a lot to learn from your people and three other provinces in Canada and most of Western Europe, Australia and New Zealand in that somewhere along the way we must encourage our legislators to enact laws to protect adults and older children, even as you do. Your usage rates may not be as high as you wish, but there's no doubt that those laws are cutting in half, in all likelihood, death and injury and saving all sorts of tax dollars. We've got to come to that eventually someday and we are way behind you, so we do appreciate the good example you are giving.

*   *   *

Seat Belts an Influence

Having grown up in a safety conscious household, and realizing the safety of seat belts, Dr. Sanders' son Robert personally added rear shoulder belts to their family car in 1986. Robert had travelled to Australia the year before and was very much, and also pleasantly surprised, to see cars with rear shoulder belts, even in a 1968 Ford Fairlane and a 1971 Holden Kingswood, for example. Shoulder belt laws and seat belt laws had been in effect since 1967 in Australia, and that included the back seat too! Why was the United States behind Australia on that one? No American nor Japanese cars back in the mid to late 1980s had rear shoulder belts, just lap belts, and it was worse in Europe and Great Britain . . . no seat belts in the back seat at all, except Sweden. Thus, when Robert returned home, he made the situation right in their family car. Robert even went on to install rear shoulder belts in the first car he bought back in high school, a 1970 Ford Fairlane station wagon. Classmates at college were surprised and noticed. They asked Robert why he went to the trouble to install them. He answered that he was bringing his car up to Australia's standards, and also it was the safe thing to do.

Seat belts were an influence in another way too. School busses never had seat belts, and neither did public transport busses such as Greyhound and Trailways. One day in the 1980s, Robert decided to remedy that situation. He bought a lap belt out of a junk car, attached two rappelling loops to the ends, and whenever he rides a bus, he passes the seat belt straps between the seats and attaches them to the foot rack behind him. He has received comments from other passengers, most of them of surprise, but also positive, telling him they think he is wise.

For example, in Great Britain, their National Express busses had seat belts in the front seats in 1994, and by 1996, their new busses had seat belts in *every* seat on the bus. They are to be commended for being safety conscious.

To this day, busses in the United States still don't have seat belts! But Robert wears his seat belt on every bus he rides, because he carries it with him.   *   *   *

In the mid 1980s, seat belt laws for adults were being passed in many states around the country. New York was the first state in the country with a seat belt law, passing theirs in 1984. In 1986, Tennessee's legislature discussed the possibility of having a seat belt law, and Bob and Pat Sanders went down to Nashville to help lobby for it. A lot of people were against it, and some of them were strongly criticizing Bob and Pat, who weren't being paid any money. A lot of seat belt opponents didn't like a seat belt law being shoved down their throats, one might say.

Bob and Pat soon discovered that there were two attorneys, hired by General Motors Co., to lobby for the seat belt law. One of the legislators told Bob and Pat that the two attorneys were being paid very well at $100,000 each, per state. Their names were Frank Gorrell and Bill Leach. They were very good attorneys and effective too. They worked the miracle of getting the *Nashville Banner* newspaper to endorse and support the law.

When Bob and Pat saw how well the two powerful GM hired attorneys were doing, they went back home. Why suffer such strong criticism from seat belt opponents and not be paid any money? If the attorneys hadn't been there, Bob and Pat would have stuck with it and pushed hard for it, but they left the reins with the much more effective attorneys, grateful that they were there lobbying so hard for the law.

Rep. John Bragg sponsored the seat belt bill, and Rep. Robb Robinson co-sponsored it. Sen. Douglas Henry did not support it because of infringement of liberties and that sort of thing. The only reason Henry had supported the child passenger restraint law was that children have no say so, and they need protection. Adults have their own say so and are old enough to make their own decisions and take their own responsibilities.

Granted adults need to be protected in automobiles too, and the majority of the legislators saw it that way, and thanks to those two GM attorneys, the seat belt law passed the first time it was presented. It became law in January 1987, but as one might guess, it was watered down. There were many exemptions, like being permissible to ride in the back of a pickup truck. Plus, no one could be stopped for not wearing a seat belt. It was only a secondary offense, in that one could not be ticketed for not wearing a seat belt unless he/she were stopped by a patrol car for some other primary moving violation.

The seat belt law became popular as the years went on, and by the 1990s, nearly every state in the nation had some sort of a seat belt law. Today, 2008, New Hampshire is the only state in the nation without a seat belt law, living under the motto, "Live Free or Die." Tennessee's seat belt law is now a primary offense law, but many states today still have secondary offense laws.

The Family Life Curriculum, 1987

Several years after Bob Sanders and his wife Pat managed to get the "Child Crusher Amendment" successfully removed from the Child Restraint Law, Bob took on another project, the Family Life Curriculum, for schools. Back in 1965, family planning had come out in all health departments across the state of Tennessee. It was now 1986, 21 years later, and the state board of health came out with a family life curriculum, basically having to do with pregnancy prevention. No, it was not endorsing abortion, built it had more to do with sex education. It would be beneficial to teach this in the schools, with the appropriate teachers and appropriate interests.

As it turned out, and it was not surprising, it was a very controversial topic. Many parents of school children simply did not want sex education discussed in the schools! Some were very outspoken about that, as well, including some members of the Rutherford County Board of Education.

Jerry Gaither was the school superintendent, and he was against it, too. Dr. Sanders went before the Board of Education, and as the health officer for the county, he presented his case and made his argument about why the family life curriculum should be taught and incorporated in the school system. A lot of people were against it, because these were considered private issues that were taught in the homes. However, at the same time, it was a public health issue. There were a lot of teenage pregnancies, and apart from that, there were venereal diseases, like gonorrhea, syphilis, and now AIDS. Some sort of program was needed to help put a control on those diseases, so they wouldn't reach epidemic proportions. Still, it was very controversial.

Jerry Gaither talked to Bob Sanders and fussed at him; he was rude actually! That upset Bob. After all, Gaither believed the whole family life curriculum belonged more in the home than in the schools. The fact was that in many homes, it was not discussed, and there had been a lot of unwanted pregnancies. Bob was worried about the whole thing.

On April 30, 1987, Bob suffered a mild heart attack in the middle of the night. He kept feeling a tightness in his neck. His wife Pat drove him to Nashville and placed him in St. Thomas Hospital. Bob remained there all week, and the Family Life Curriculum was scheduled for a hearing the first week of May.

Frieda Wadley, who was with the Metro Health Department, came to Murfreesboro and went before the school board with Bob's wife, Pat, and spoke in favor of the curriculum. They pointed out that it's not like it was a generation ago, in the days of "Leave it to Beaver" or "Ozzie and Harriett's World." They handed literature to every school board member at the hearing. They needed that information.

Jerry Gaither came over to Pat after the hearing and asked her where Bob was. Pat answered him directly and said that he was in St. Thomas Hospital recovering from a mild heart attack. Jerry was a little taken aback. With a look of worry, he then came forth with, "I hope you didn't think I caused it." Jerry knew he had been cross with Bob on the phone a little more than a week ago.

Over time, the Family Life Curriculum never got adopted into the schools as a whole piece. Part of it did. It was just such a large issue that it didn't go over very well.

The Stupid Collider, 1987-1988

When Bob came home from the hospital just a few days after the hearing, he was greeted with a big, front page newspaper article about a Super Conducting Super Collider, which was soon to be nicknamed the "Stupid Collider." It announced Tennessee's plans to have a 52-mile tunnel built in Rutherford County, with a campus and research facility of several hundred acres. Looking at the map in the newspaper, the campus was shown to be right smack on top of the Sanders' 370 acre farm, plus the neighboring farms on both sides! The tunnel would have had a huge particle accelerator, similar to Illinois' Fermi Lab, but much larger.

Originally, it was called the Desertron, and the plans had been to put it out in Arizona in the desert and away from populated areas, but politics had gotten involved and had changed that.

That very much distressed Bob and Pat along with their son and daughter. There were many states in competition for it at that time, so it would likely go to another state anyway. However, it was still a considerable worry. Bob and Pat talked to their congressman, Bart Gordon, and also to their U.S. Senator Jim Sasser. Sasser said to them, "Don't worry, it's not going to be funded anyway." True, but what if it got partially funded. The land would still be condemned, jerked away from its owners, ruined, and then *never* returned no matter what! Never mind that a man's home is his castle!

As Bob and Pat checked into it and talked with neighbors, officials, scientists, and others, they came to realize that a project like this had no business being built in Tennessee, nor in any populated area, nor in a place with hydrology (underground water and streams). A project like the Super Collider belonged in a desert out West, say Arizona, in a place with sparse population. Being a project of particle physics, there were risks of contaminating the underground streams and wells with atom smashed particles, radioactivity as a result, and tritium (heavy water) which is toxic.

Plus, the excavating involved to create a 52-mile tunnel would create a colossal amount of rock, all of it limestone. Every mile or so, there would be a vertical mine shaft to access the tunnel below. There would be a lot of lime dust in the air and atmosphere, not to mention lime slurry from the tunneling, all of which would flow into underground streams and contaminate fish and caves. It was simply not going to be a harmless tunnel like many people thought. It belonged in the desert where hydrology and underground streams wouldn't be a problem. In other words, it was stupid to have the Super Collider in Tennessee, thus the nickname it deserved, the "Stupid Collider."

The limestone bedrock under Middle Tennessee's Central Basin was sort of like Swiss cheese. One didn't know if the tunneling would pierce a stream, flooding out the whole tunnel, or even after being built, there might be a collapse of rock above, at which time water would be released into the tunnel, ruining the whole project! It just wasn't convenient for Tennessee to have it.

Activist groups were formed, including the spelunking society, and they spoke out against it.

A month or two after the project was first announced, survey crews went out and spray painted marks and set out stakes on roads, showing where the tunnel would run. They put a stake right on the Sanders' driveway. Robert saw them doing it, and he tried to chase them down, but they left before he could reach them. When he reached the entrance and saw the stake, he angrily pulled it up and broke it in two! The Sanders took the broken stake to Bart Gordon's office and complained. Those officials had trespassed on the Sanders' private property to put that stake in, and the Sanders didn't take kindly to that.

By August 1987, they had some hearings over at MTSU (Middle Tennessee State University). Many of the states had been dropped from the list, and it was down to just a few states now. Tennessee and Texas were still on the list, along with Illinois and Arizona. Tennessee planned to condemn the land, buy it under eminent domain liberties they granted themselves, at low prices, jerk the land away from its owners, and then give it to the DOE (Department of Energy) who was manning the whole project.

For Gov. Ned Ray McWherter, this would make a nice plum, which would make him, as governor, and also make the state of Tennessee look really good.

Pat and Bob and their family were somewhat suspicious that some of the Tennessee state officials were upset about the Child Restraint Law ten years earlier, and that they chose to put the Collider's campus right on the Sanders farm as a means of vindication or retaliation. It made them wonder. None of them were even willing to move the site to another area of the state nor shift it over, despite Dr. Sanders' plea that they do so.

So, Bob and Pat increased their opposition and activism. They began to organize a petition that pointed out all of the dangers and demanding to the DOE that the project be placed elsewhere, and *not* in Tennessee. Bob,

Rutherford County's health officer, felt an obligation to speak out against it and to point out its dangers to fellow residents of Rutherford County.

It wasn't long before Bob received a phone call from one of the directors of the state health department, Doris Spain. She said she had gotten a complaint from the governor's office and Gov. McWherter. In short order, she paid Dr. Sanders a personal visit to his office and ordered Sanders to cool it, which actually was quite out of order on her part. She sat across from his desk and said, "You know, the governor thinks that you as a state employee are welcome to do whatever you like on private time, but to take a position against the Super Collider representing the state since you're a state employee, is objectionable to the governor. Don't do that anymore."

That upset Bob, and he objected to her mandate handed down from the state. He explained his position as health officer and his obligations and duties that he had in that position and that construction of the Stupid Collider would pose health problems and dangers to the residents in the area. She didn't care. That was the mandate from the state, and that was it. An article ran in the newspaper, "State Asks Sanders to Cool It."

Bob resented the squelching tactics, and he didn't like Doris Spain much either. She enjoyed her power and considered herself upper level material. There was an unrelated visit later on where she relaxed in the chair across from his desk and casually propped her feet up on his desk! Bob got angry and told her, "Get your feet off my desk right now, or I'll report you to the state commissioner of public health!" She obliged on that one, but she was not a pleasure to be acquainted with. Her position as a partial state level boss helped lead Bob to make his decision to take retirement just a few years later in 1991.

Fighting the Stupid Collider was a long battle, and it was a lot of hard work, organizing more than 4,000 petition signatures. Bob and Pat were not alone. The cave groups were working and getting petition signatures, too. Some of the neighbors were also helping.

New York had succeeded in getting their state taken off the list. A Jim Alexander and Bill Herbert had managed to get 20,000 signatures and got Gov. Mario Cuomo to take it off the list. In April 1988, they came and gave a lecture to Rutherford County citizens about how to petition and help get Tennessee taken off the list also. They had some good pointers and good suggestions, and their visit to Tennessee was greatly appreciated.

As the Sanders went around to their friends and relatives, some of them didn't want to sign the petition. Some said point blank, "I don't sign petitions." Some others said they were for the Collider, and even said, "Well, somebody's got to go." Those were insensitive statements with lack of compassion and feeling for others! Most of the friends and relatives did sign it, but there were some who never did. The Sanders found out who their friends were, and who weren't! A real friend out of respect would have signed the petition against the Collider, even if he/she had been for it.

By June of 1988, the list had been narrowed to only two states, Texas and Tennessee. Never mind the practical location of Arizona's desert! That was very disconcerting. The campus had never been shifted to miss the Sanders farm either. Bob and Pat were almost certain that some of the state and/or government officials were angry about the Child Restraint Law.

The heat increased in more ways than one. It was a hot, dry summer to boot. More and more petition signatures were obtained. Some of the residents spoke out at meetings. The DOE came down to tour the countryside in their federal cars. Residents followed them like a motorcade. One retired fellow, Bob Ragland, put two large banner signs on the sides of his truck: NO SSC IN TENNESSEE! and followed the federal DOE officials all over the county. It's a wonder they didn't get the police to stop him, but then he did have freedom of expression, the First Amendment.

1988 was also a presidential election year. George H.W. Bush from Texas was the Republican candidate, and Mike Dukakis from Massachusetts was the Democratic candidate. No decision had been made about the Stupid Collider. There were more meetings and hearings. Bob couldn't speak on a state level, but Pat went and spoke, even gave lectures at the meetings, speaking out against it. There were newspaper interviews, articles, radio and even TV interviews.

November 6, 1988 was election day. George H.W. Bush won by a landslide. Dukakis lost.

The very next day, the DOE announced on television that TEXAS had been chosen as the state for the Stupid Collider. It was a major relief to the Sanders. However, they felt sorry for residents in and around Waxahachie, Texas, south of Dallas. Ideally, the Collider, or better said Desertron (its original name), should have gone to Arizona to an uninhabited area of federal land.

That presidential election was definitely the deciding factor. Indirectly, the Sanders were grateful to George H.W. Bush for winning that election, if nothing else to get the Stupid Collider away from Tennessee. Ross Perot, a Texas billionaire, was also a major influencing factor toward getting Texas chosen for that project.

Life began to get back to normal after November, 1988. They could let bygones be bygones. The drama was over, and they would get to stay home and continue their lives on the farm. There was one farming family up the road who hadn't signed the petition. Robert went to visit them to let bygones be bygones. He also let bygones be bygones with a select few of his friends who hadn't signed the petition either. One of them said he was glad in the end that the Stupid Collider hadn't come to Tennessee after all. In some ways, it was good to make amends and let the resentment fall by the wayside.

The Sanders were glad that Tennessee did NOT get the SSC.

One of the state officials later saw Pat and Bob, came over to them, and kindly asked if they were still mad at him. Pat answered no, that they could forgive and forget. He later became one of Tennessee's governors.

Out in Texas, people were run off of their land, and Texas acquired the land. The project began, but the funding was cut in mid stream because it was costing many billions of dollars more than estimated. The DOE, having acquired the land, certainly never offered the land back to the residents like they should have done! It was a lamentable situation for the people in and around Waxahachie.

Retirement Years

Bob and Pat, 2002

Even though he kept his medical examiner job until August of 1999, Bob enjoyed his retirement years after retiring from the Health Department in December 1991. There was a big retirement party in the upstairs lobby, and plenty of friends and relatives came for the event.

Cleaning out the office was a major project, as it turned out, with lots of literature collected on various subjects, especially on child passenger safety. Some of the books and medical journals were donated to Vanderbilt University's medical school library.

Pat's mother Josephine Powell Pelot passed away the same month that Bob retired, and they had to clean out her house in Crossville at the same time in early 1992. That was a major project, as well.

In the Spring of 1992, Betty Bumpers from Maryland called Bob and Pat and invited them to come to the Carter Center in Atlanta, Georgia to attend conferences to do with immunizations for all children by age 2. The program was called *Every Child by Two*. Betty Bumpers and Rosalynn Carter had a mission to have all children immunized nationwide, and they visited the governors of all 50 states to have the *Every Child by Two* program adopted. Many states were lacking on immunization requirements, and they needed to be standardized. During the years 1992, 1993, and 1994, Bob and Pat made several trips to Atlanta. Rosalynn and Betty wanted Bob's ideas on the subject. The mission was successful, and all 50 states adopted the program.

During his retirement years, Bob enjoyed life on the farm, and he continued managing cattle, buying and selling steers every year. He always had a garden every summer, growing different vegetables and giving some of them away to local friends and relatives.

There were family reunions and class reunions from time to time, and it was nice to visit different cousins, friends and relatives. Bob and Pat visited regularly with Bill and Jean Sanders and their family in Tullahoma, and they also visited with Joan and Jack Rice in Nashville. They visited Nib and Barbara Pelot in Knoxville, but not as often, since they were further away. In addition to relatives, many of their friends celebrated 50th anniversaries, and it was nice to visit and catch up with so many friends at those events.

Bob became involved in the autism field, taking an interest in it after an article came out in late 1993. It was called "An Anthropologist On Mars" written by Oliver Sacks. Bob and Pat then realized that their son Robert had some of the traits described in that article, traits mostly known as Asperger's Syndrome, the mild form but also the high functioning type of autism. As Bob researched the subject, he found out about Future Horizons, Inc. and contacted them. They were holding conferences all over the country, and when they came to Nashville, they attended the conference. It was very informative and interesting.

As time went on, Robert went on to write his two books on Asperger's Syndrome, and they are listed in Future Horizons' bookstore online. More and more came out on the subject, and they became involved with Vanderbilt University's Kennedy Center, and with TRIAD (Treatment Research Institute for Autism Spectrum Disorders), which was also at Vanderbilt. TRIAD had conferences, as well. There were local autism society chapters formed and even a support group that meets once a month in Murfreesboro.

Bob was also involved in other projects. He always wanted a Single Pay program for health care, in other words, a national health care program similar to what Canada and Sweden have. He wrote letters to the editor about that, and also about other subjects related to health issues, saving lives and injury prevention.

Even when Bob was working, he was given several weeks vacation per year, but now there was more time to travel, and with the children grown, it was easier. They continued to go to Pawley's Island once a year to stay on the beach, and they made other out of state trips to attend weddings for different friends and relatives.

There were a few health problems that Bob had to contend with. He had to have heart bypass surgery in 1995. One of Bob's medical school classmates and also one of his better friends, Bill Alford, did the operation. Bill used to come and attend some of Bob's lectures through the years, always being interested and wanting to keep in touch with him as a friend.

Also Bob had some minor knee surgery in 1996, to repair an old high school football injury.

Bob had never been to Canada. So, they drove up to northeastern Canada and visited Quebec in 1997. They stayed in Montreal.

Bob had also never been to Oregon. So, they flew out there in 1998 and visited David and Jane Maynard. They visited Fort Clatsup National Monument at the mouth of the Columbia River, where Lewis and Clark finished their journey across the country and reached the Pacific Coast.

They travelled to New York City to visit their daughter Priscilla, and once she moved out to Los Angeles, they also went and visited her out there. On their trips to California, they also went to San Francisco and visited with friends of theirs, like Phil and Mary Strauss.

Robert graduated from university the same year that his father retired, and he began staying in Mexico in the small town of Bustamante, Nuevo León part of every winter. He had hoped that his parents would come to Mexico and visit Bustamante, but they never did.

Travel became more difficult after 2000, because Bob was diagnosed with a blood disease called Lymphoma. By 2002, there were times of sickness, and he had to be hospitalized a few times (on average once a year) to be given treatments.

Bob's brother Bill also became ill with prostate cancer in 2002, and he passed away in September 2003. That was very sad for Bob, losing his only brother.

Still, Bob and Pat managed some travelling, the last trip being to Houston, Texas to attend the wedding of his brother Bill's oldest grand-child in July 2004, a very important event to Bob. He had trouble walking, but he was determined to go to that wedding, and he did. After all, neither Robert nor Priscilla had ever gotten married, and the wedding event of his brother's oldest grandson would suffice as a substitute in that respect.

In early 2004, the shingles got Bob down, which resulted in several mini strokes, making him more and more feeble until he couldn't walk anymore. The strokes were shingles related because it attacked the right front part of the brain and forehead, and the left side of the body was affected. Treatments and physical therapy were given, and he spent several months in a nursing home facility. Pat was there visiting him every day. Several friends and relatives came by to visit, including Bill Alford, Lewis

Lefkowitz, and other classmates. Some of Bob's cousins came up from Atlanta, and some other friends came from as far away as California.

In 2005, Pat brought him home and faithfully took care of him for the last year of his life. It was a difficult year. She took him everywhere she went and even managed to take him to important events, like class reunions, which they enjoyed. Bob attended a major autism conference where Robert displayed his books and photographs, and he also attended a major CD release party in Nashville, where Priscilla sang her songs.

Still, Bob slowly continued to go downhill. He was not improving, and he was hospitalized at Vanderbilt Hospital in December of 2005. The doctors and nurses did what they could, but he didn't make it. He passed away January 19, 2006 at the age of 78. He was buried in the Sims Cemetery, a small, private family cemetery started by his great-great grandfather, southwest of Murfreesboro

*   *   *

Bob and Pat, 2003   photo by Benjamin Porter

Bob Sanders giving a lecture at the United Nations,
International Year of the Child, 1979

American Academy of Pediatrics booth at the 1982 Worlds Fair
l-r: George Zirkle, Martha Bushore, Frank Boyer,
Pat & Bob Sanders, and Jim Holroyd

Annemarie Shelness, Bob Sanders, and Bob Vinetz, 1979

Paul Hletko, Annemarie Shelness, and Bob Sanders
Physicians for Automotive Safety conference, 1983

Bob and Pat with the plaque naming the clinic the
Robert Smith Sanders Public Health Clinic, 1995

Bob Sanders lecturing at the World Traffic Safety Symposium, NYC, 1998

Pat with Bob Sanders receiving an award at the symposium, NYC, 1998

Safe Kids Day on the Hill, Nashville, Tennessee, April 2007
Row 1: Susan Helms, Rep. Lowe Finney, Pat Sanders, Sen. Douglas Henry, Becky Campbell, Janet Howerton, row 2: Sharyn Thompson, Mary Kate Mouser, William Booker, and Sharon Patten

Bob (Dr. Seat Belt) Sanders exhibit at the Rutherford County Archives, 2007

Dr. Sanders on a typical morning, leaving for the office

Tributes to Dr. Sanders

I, John Frederick Leditschke, a Paediatric Surgeon in Brisbane, Queensland in Australia with a long involvement with measures to reduce the death and injury rate to infants and children in Motor Vehicle crashes, had the pleasure of visiting Dr. Bob Sanders in Murfreesboro, Tennessee in 1981. Bob Sanders, who was a Public Health Medical Officer, was the driving force in the Legislation, that made Tennessee the first state in the United States to introduce child occupant restraint laws. Highway patrol officers carried a car seat in their vehicle. If a parent was found with an unrestrained child, they were issued with an infringement notice and asked to show cause why they should not be fined for the offence. However, they were also given a child restraint seat on loan. When summoned to court, if they could prove and show that they had purchased a car seat to restrain their child, all charges were dropped and no charge or conviction was recorded. This proved a very satisfactory method to increase child restraint usage. However, once it ceased, and enforcement by the police once again became lax, the restraint usage rate fell markedly. Bob told me that even at the peak, the rate of usage was however only 25% of children.

Bob Sanders was a passionate person for the safe transport of infants and children, and it distressed him to see the cavalier manner in which parents and care givers transported their supposed precious cargo. He lobbied the Legislature for change and would be delighted to see that after all the campaigning, laws are now in place to ensure the safe transport of children. The battle is on-going with the constant arrival of new parents and their almost entrenched attitude that what was acceptable in the past, should be accepted today. Bob Sanders, you fought hard and very long for the welfare of those unable to voice their concerns and demand their right to life. May you now rest in peace that your struggle was not in vain. To your family saddened and shattered by your passing, we send our sincere sympathies and know that the memories you will treasure are those of a caring compassionate husband, father, and wonderful human being.   Rest in Peace.

Dr. Fred Leditschke, Consultant Paediatric Surgeon, Royal Children's Hospital Brisbane: Chairman of CREST (Child Restraint Education & Safe Travel Committee) a sub committee of the Queensland branch of the Royal Australasian College of Surgeons Trauma Committee: former National President of Kidsafe-SafeKids Australia.

Dr. Robert Sanders and I did not know each other when he called me one day to express his interest in an article published in *Pediatrics*, the official journal of the American Academy of Pediatrics. Co-authored by Dr. Seymour Charles, founder and president of Physicians for Automotive Safety and myself and published in 1975, the article drew attention to the dearth of information in books and other publications dealing with child care on the protection of children in cars. Following extensive research the authors found that not only was there very little information, but what was available was either incorrect, inadequate, or out of date.

The article, "Children As Passengers in Automobiles: The Neglected Minority on the Nations Highways," became the starting point for a crusade launched by Bob Sanders which culminated in the enactment in 1978 in Tennessee of the very first child restraint law in the nation. This was a significant step and led the way to similar laws being adopted in other states over the next few years. But enactment of laws was insufficient. It was also necessary to word the legislation in such a way that protection was adequate. Often, clauses including exemptions from the laws were "tending to the 'needs' of the child." Such "needs" included breast feeding, changing diapers, and comforting a disgruntled child – all while the child was riding unprotected. But due to efforts by innovators such as Dr. Sanders, this soon changed. While laws are by no means uniform even today, especially when it comes to use of booster seats, they are consistent in not allowing the child to be removed from the restraint while the vehicle is in motion.

Dr. Sanders was a quiet, mild-mannered man who brought about changes in the field of injury prevention at a time that few people–including legislators–could relate to it or understand the issues. What was so remarkable is that he accomplished this without alienating anyone.

The field of child auto safety owes him a great debt and so, no doubt, do the children who might not have survived an automotive crash had it not been for Dr. Sanders' efforts ensuring that they were riding appropriately protected.
Annemarie Shelness, Greensboro, North Carolina

Dr. Robert Sanders, a tireless fighter for child passenger safety, died in Nashville, Tennessee, on January 19, 2006, after a long illness. He was 78.

Sanders, a pediatrician, was the director of the Rutherford County Health Department from 1969 to 1991. In 1976, with the active support of his wife, Pat, and other Tennessee pediatricians and their spouses, he spearheaded the adoption of a law requiring parents to restrain small children riding in cars, a radical idea at that time. The soft-spoken physician, then chair of the state chapter of the American Academy of Pediatrics (AAP) and a member of Physicians for Automotive Safety, proved to be a tough, persuasive lobbyist.

The bill passed by a close vote in the state legislature in 1977, effective in January 1978. Tennessee paved the way for child restraint use laws in all other states.

The struggle continued until 1981, however, when the last-minute amendment that got the original bill through was eliminated. Dubbed the "child crusher amendment," it had exempted children riding in the arms of an older person, and at least twelve child passengers had been killed that way, as "human air bags," Dr. Sanders argued persuasively.

Following the upgrading of the law, he turned his efforts to helping county health and police departments establish child restraint loan programs for low-income families. He became county medical examiner in 1983 and retired in 1999. In 1998, at the Second National Child Passenger Safety Seminar in Cleveland, Ohio, Dr. Sanders was honored with the Annemarie Shelness Award for Lifetime Service in Child Passenger Safety. In 2004, the AAP published an oral history of his remarkable life and accomplishments.

Gisela Moriarty, California

Dr. Robert Sanders' passing brings me great sadness but provides an opportunity to reflect on his inspiring, revolutionary work.

Of the "Three E"s (education, engineering, and enforcement) of public health, only the first two were being tackled at all in 1976, when Dr. Sanders began his legislative effort. Only very small national organizations were focusing on child passenger safety: Physicians for Automotive Safety (PAS) and its parent and nurse based spin-off, Action for Child Transportation Safety (ACTS). Educational efforts during the 1970s by members of PAS, ACTS, and some small local child passenger safety associations and women's clubs had raised usage rates only slightly. These groups also pushed for engineering improvements, especially the upgrading of FMVSS 213 to require dynamic testing. (Such testing was being done only voluntarily for some CR models in the 1970s.) Dr. Sanders had the insight to see that the third "E", enforcement, was the only hope for saving many lives. He also had the persuasiveness and perseverance to push that through the legislative process.

His idea proved the most effective solution by far. It inspired not only child restraint laws - passed in all states by 1985 - but also safety belt laws for adults. And the presence of state laws demanded that NHTSA, the states, major organizations, and institutions become involved in education, provision of child restraints to low-income people, and eventually training of advocates. Of course, all three "E"s are necessary, but the Tennessee child restraint law was the catalyst and foundation of what we do today.

Dr. Sanders truly has saved countless lives.

Deborah D. Stewart, editor of *Safe Ride News*, Seattle, Washington

A Tribute to "Our Dr. Seat Belt": Dr. Robert Sanders

Safe Kids Tennessee hosted Safe Kids Day on the Hill in the Legislative Plaza, Nashville, Tennessee in April of 2006 in tribute to one or our nation's most important voices for child safety, Dr. Robert Sanders.

Dr. Sanders was a steadfast, determined, and genuine leader for children's safety. His work was truly revolutionary and inspirational.

He had seen what happens to children in automobile crashes when they were not restrained. He knew that so many of those injuries and deaths were preventable. And so he decided that someone had to speak out on behalf of children and their safety. Starting with the Tennessee General Assembly, he and his wife Pat spent countless hours presenting medical data. That perspective and their passion overcame initial doubts. In 1977, thanks to the vision and determination shown by Dr. and Mrs. Sanders, Tennessee became the first state to adopt a law mandating that all children under the age of 4 must ride in a child safety seat. State by state, the rest of the nation and the District of Columbia followed. Today, all 50 states require this protection for young children.

Dr. Sanders died on January 19, 2006 after a long illness. He leaves behind a legacy of fighting for the needs of others. Even after he fought the battle for child safety seats, he continued to speak out on issues such as the need for seat belt laws, health care reform and environmental protection. His work earned him the love and appreciation of citizens across Tennessee.

Dr. Sanders believed that every citizen has a responsibility to help others. He lived his life doing that every day. In addition to his public policy work, he was chief physician and director of the Rutherford County Health Department from 1969 until his retirement in 1991.

Dr. Robert Sanders, our "Dr. Seat Belt," will be missed by all who were fortunate to know him as a family man, neighbor, friend and an inspiration. Safe Kids Tennessee will continue to be a voice for children that Dr. Sanders so brilliantly echoed.

submitted by Susan A. Helms R.N.,M.A.L.S., Memphis, Tennessee
Executive Director, Safe Kids Tennessee

When I remember Bob Sanders, I always think of the word restraint, but not just in the seat belt sense. I was always impressed by his restraint when his admiring colleagues accolades heaped upon him. His humility made the rest of us feel that we, too, could accomplish great things.

Bob was a true activist. When he found a cause he believed in, nothing could stand in his way. As a pediatrician, he was concerned about protecting children. When Bob dedicated himself to auto safety, it was only a matter of time before his presence was known. That one pediatrician could contribute so much is astounding.

Sanders was a member of Physicians for Automotive Safety. PAS worked on a wide range of automotive safety issues, calling for safer passenger vehicles, safer school buses, and safer child restraints. The members issued press releases calling for safer transportation practices. They developed relationships with automobile manufacturers, even sharing an exhibit with General Motors. They were instrumental in promoting air bags and combination lap/shoulder belts in rear seats. PAS members worked to develop the 1981 dynamic testing standard for child restraints, testified before Congress, and submitted petitions. They staffed exhibits at meetings of the American Medical Association and the American Academy of Pediatrics.

In 1989, at the closing of PAS, Dr. Seymour Charles, co-founder and president, wrote a farewell letter to his colleagues who shared an interest in the organization he had begun. As he summed up some of the accomplishments of PAS, he said, "My feeling of sadness and frustration at the demise of PAS is tempered by the fact that we accomplished a great deal at a time when few others spoke out, and the need for activism and trailblazing PAS engaged in during the sixties, seventies, and even the early eighties is no longer as pressing today as it was then. Not that all the problems inherent in auto safety have been resolved - not by any means - but several organizations are in place whose resources are far greater than ours have ever been."

In his remarks, Charles singled out a few of the physicians and organizations that played vital roles in furthering child passenger protection. When he listed Sanders, he said, "Robert Sanders, M.D., of Murfreesboro, TN, without whom child auto safety might never have made the headlines; his dogged efforts in his state led to the nation's first Child Restraint Law, effective in 1978. Nothing before or since has had a greater impact than this event. Today, every state in the nation has a law requiring small children to ride protected."

Bob Sanders has rightly earned a position on the Mount Rushmore of child transportation safety. I am proud to say I worked with him.

Paul J. Hletko, M.D., F.A.A.P., Georgetown, South Carolina

The recent death of Dr. Robert Sanders, "Dr. Seat Belt," reminds me of another goal which he supported and which has been accomplished in all developed countries except the United States: universal health care. Dr. Sanders, along with many other U.S. health professionals and world leaders, thought the best approach to be a single payer plan (such as standard Medicare for everyone). As market approaches to health care continue to leave 43 million Americans without insurance and many more underinsured, I am beginning to think that Dr. Sanders was right.

Our present hodge-podge "system" spends more than 30 percent of health-care dollars on administrative costs, creating a lot of jobs and income (and vested interests) in health administration, but making health insurance unobtainable or unaffordable for many individuals and businesses. Insurance company executives got tens of millions in bonuses while their companies deny coverage to sick people and limit services for those who are covered. Much of my time as a physician and my staff's time is diverted from promoting health to dealing with the idiosyncrasies of differing insurance plans and formularies. Some experts think that the administrative cost savings of a single-payer plan would be enough to cover all of the uninsured.

Piece-meal attempts to improve health-care delivery tend to create new problems and often benefit other constituencies more than average patients/health-care consumers. The Medicare Part D Prescription Drug Plan, with its market-based approach, is too complicated for most people to understand and appears to benefit pharmaceutical and insurance companies more than patients. While Health Savings Accounts (HSAs) will help the bankers who administer them and some consumers who are relatively healthy and wealthy, they add another layer of bureaucracy/ administrative costs, and it is hard to imagine people who are living from month to month putting money into HSAs, much less spending that money on wise preventive health care.

One of Dr. Sanders' eulogies said, "When Bob saw an injustice, he tried to correct it." If a market approach to universal health care, such as what Gov. Mitt Romney has proposed for Massachusetts, turns out to be feasible, let's give it a try. If not, I hope we can find the will to set aside vested interests, look at the overall good, and put everyone on a single insurance plan. While this approach will be a difficult pill to swallow for many people, it is a more bitter pill for me that a country of our wealth, ingenuity, and compassion fails to make basic health care available to all of its citizens.   Frank Carter, M.D., Murfreesboro, Tennessee

The term "lobbying" is not in good repute right now because of scandals in the Tennessee General Assembly and in Congress. There are lobbyists for virtually every aspect of our society and one we hear little about is the "public interest lobbyist." A prime example of such a lobbyist recently passed away and will be memorialized Saturday, February 4 at Murfreesboro's First Presbyterian Church at 2 PM. Dr. Robert Sanders was from a rural part of Rutherford County, and he became a pediatrician and a public health official. He became a lobbyist when he decided something had to be done about the incredible number of deaths of children under the age of four in automobile accidents. Statistics showed that was the major cause of death in that age group.

As a public interest lobbyist, he received no pay, made no lavish contributions to legislators' campaign coffers, spent little if anything on meals for legislators, nor those things for which lobbyists are well known. Instead, he depended on facts and reason to convince legislators to pass a law requiring child restraint seats in all vehicles for children under the age of four.

Though Bob Sanders was a quiet-spoken gentleman, he could take on opposition with skill and tenacity. A legislator managed to amend the bill to allow an exemption in cases where an adult held the babe in arms. After the bill passed, a new bill was drawn up four years later to eliminate the "Child Crusher Amendment". The exemption was crushed.

When we hear of abuses by lobbyists and legislators, remember there are people trying to help the public with no gain for themselves. These are public interest lobbyists, and they deserve our respect. Bob and his wife Pat can legitimately take credit for saving tens of thousands of infant lives in the past and many more in the future. What they began in Rutherford County quickly spread across the country. Tennessee led the way.

David Grubbs, Murfreesboro, Tennessee

While most people will remember Dr. Robert Sanders as "Dr. Seat Belt," there is a small group of us who will remember him for his dedication and concern for families affected by autism spectrum disorders. I vividly remember meeting Bob and his enthusiastic wife, Pat, at the first Rutherford County Autism Support Group Meeting about five years ago. They were an invaluable resource to our group. How fortunate we were to have a pediatrician in those meetings! And no ordinary pediatrician at that- Dr. Sanders had walked the walk. Though in retirement, they came to meetings faithfully, usually armed with news articles and other literature about research and treatment of autism. They attended autism conferences and kept up-to-date on events at Vanderbilt's TRIAD Center so they could share with parents who, like myself, lacked the time or resources to do these things themselves.

Of the two, Pat did most of the talking. Dr. Sanders was a listener. When necessary, he would interject softly, gently making his point but he could say more with a nod or a smile of sympathy than most people can say in an entire paragraph. Whether discussing the neurology of brain disorders or green beans, Dr. Sanders had a way of making you feel that what you were saying was the most interesting thing he had ever heard. He never left a meeting without asking me how my son was doing. His concern was genuine. I cherish the memory of an evening, when frustrated by my son's seemingly slow progress, Dr. Sanders shared with me how long he had waited for his own son to talk and how precious those first words were when he finally did hear them. It was encouragement like that that kept me going during really tough times.

Dr. Sanders attended his last support group meeting late last summer. Cancer and a series of strokes had left him frail. It was a great effort for him to get out of his car. It was an even greater effort for Pat to get him through the doors of Belle Aire Baptist Church, down the hallway to the elevator and finally to the room where our group meets but effort never was something the two of them were lacking. They were always ready to exert themselves for the benefit of others. They raised a child with autism during a time when there was little if any awareness of the disorder and certainly no support. They weren't about to let us do the same. I'm sorry Dr. Sanders is gone, but I am so glad he was my friend when he was here.

Jo Ver Mulm, printed in the Daily News Journal, Murfreesboro, TN, January 20, 2006.

Sympathy Notes, Reminiscences

Dear Pat,

Please excuse the informality of this stationary but the new order has not arrived. On the eve of Bob's memorial service, I want to offer a few memories and possibly some solace of a wonderful friend and mentor. When Barbara and I arrived in Nashville in June 1957, we didn't know what we would find in the city or at Vanderbilt. I did know and was prepared to work hard and see little of her, all of which came true. We house staff were an undisciplined bunch and had generally a poor work ethic and sometimes a belligerent attitude. Enter Bob Sanders—chief resident, army veteran, often behind his back referred to as the "Bald Eagle." Here was a man of quiet dignity who taught me to always place the patient first, to never leave the hospital until all work and notes were completed, including laboratory work and to always make rounds with the covering house officer, including visiting every patient before leaving the hospital. If I ever became a competent physician, I owe most of it to Bob. He ruled by gentle persuasion but also unerring steadfastness. Later the two of you honored me by choosing me as pediatrician to Robert, and Priscilla.

He will always be loved and admired by all of us who knew him and in that I hope our love provides some solace.
Sincerely,
Eric Chazen, M.D. FAAP, Nashville, Tennessee

Dear Pat,

I just wanted you to know that we are thinking of you, Robert, and Priscilla. There are thousands of people like us who considered Bob to be one of God's angels on earth. He would not have been able to accomplish so much without your strong support and commitment to his career and causes.

This morning I was talking to Doris Mills Windham and she related one of her experiences with Bob. She was a nurse at the old Rutherford Hospital during the time Bob was a pediatrician. She said he would check on his patients shortly after she began her shift at 3:30 p.m. and then return later that evening. Frequently you would be with him and wait at the nurses' station for him to make his rounds. He always made it clear that he was to be called if there was any change in the condition of one of his patients.

I remember Bob wearing many "hats" but mainly that of a loving, considerate father and as someone always seeking knowledge and patiently listening to what you had on your mind. The many tributes that continue to celebrate his life speak of the various ways he affected those who personally knew him and those who benefited from his life spent caring and doing what was right and needed--someone willing to champion the cause.

Our thoughts and prayers are with you as you grieve the loss of your life companion.

Love,

Emily and Ron Messier, Lascassas, Tennessee

Thoughts About and Memories of Bobby Sanders

I met Bobby in 1946 during Corps of Engineers basic training at Ft. Belvoir, Virginia. Those of us who have known him for 60 years or longer have difficulty thinking about him as, or calling him anything other than, Bobby, so that is how I will refer to him here.

Bobby definitely was one of a kind. Capable of accomplishing impresssive, even towering feats. He was, at the same time, the most humble, self-effacing person imaginable.

We always knew he would become a physician. Throughout our time together in the service, Bobby maintained a stock of pharmaceutical supplies capable of staving off or curing any ill that might conceivably accost him and even supplies to ward off some ills that hadn't even been discovered at the time. We sometimes referred to him as a walking drug store. Bobby was perhaps the most health conscious person we ever had met, certainly in the Army.

He began his career of service to the health of children early on. While we all were stationed on Okinawa, Bobby was with a group working on an island in the Ryukus chain. During that period, a young island child was bitten by a deadly snake and would have expired had not Bobby stepped in and expeditiously taken the actions necessary to save her life. Bobby became an instant hero in the girl's village and a major celebration was held in his honor. At this event, Bobby, a firm non-imbiber, was introduced to a Japanese rice wine called sake (sahkee). Feeling that he could hardly refuse the salutary sake proffered without offending, Bobby consumed a cup or two, making the event more of an ordeal than a celebration for him. Subsequent reports that Bobby narrowly escaped another celebratory award, marriage to the head man's daughter, may have been exaggerated slightly.

What Bobby accomplished, along with Pat, in pushing through child restraint legislation in Tennessee, and later across the nation, is well known. His fellow pediatricians were fully aware of the magnitude of what he had done. Some years back, Bobby, one of five, was nominated to be considered for an award as the pediatrician in the United States who had contributed the most to healthy lives for children. The event took place at the Waldorf-Astoria in New York. Bobby did not win. But when the woman who did, approached a group of us chatting with Bobby afterward, she said, in response to his congratulations, "I may have won the award, but every physician in this room knows that you are responsible for saving the lives of more children than all of the rest of us combined." But you never would have suspected it from the way he carried himself. Even in the face of such accolades from his peers, he was humble in the extreme.

And Bobby greatly treasured personal relationships, as Lester, Laddie, Willie, I, and many others know and appreciate. Once, when Pat and Bobby were visiting us, we took them to a local Indian Pow-Pow, along with our three grandchildren. To minimize the risk of a lost child, we assigned the two younger boys, one to Pat and one to Bobby, for safe-keeping. While we all were sitting on the ground watching an Indian dance, our grandson Andy idly tied a knot in one of the laces of Bobby's sneaker. Years later, long after we had forgotten this little incident, Pat and Bobby were visiting again. Bobby, wearing the same sneakers, proudly pointed out that the knot Andy had tied in his lace was still there.

Most of us, I believe, who knew Bobby can safely say that we have never known anyone quite like him. Nor are we likely to meet anyone like him in the future. It may be a cliché but I really do feel that they broke the mold when Bobby was created. As it always does whenever we lose one of the really, really good ones, the world seems an emptier place without Bobby.

Rest in peace, old friend; you've earned it.

Robert R. (Bob) Reichenbach, Basking Ridge, New Jersey

I first met Pat and Bob at a farewell party for Dr. Robert Merrill at Dr. Amos Christie's home a few weeks after I arrived in Nashville to start my Neonatology fellowship with Dr. Mildred Stahlman in 1966. In their usual friendly way they inquired thoroughly about my Swedish background, which Bob found of special interest because of the year he had spent in

Stockholm himself. This brief encounter started a long friendship and Bob became like an older brother to me. Julie, our children and I visited their farm often and it was especially good for us city people to get out into the country once in a while. Our Christmas preparations traditionally started there by cutting down a Cedar to be used as our Christmas tree and gathering of mosses for our advent candle holder and creche set. Our families also enjoyed several visits to Pawley's Island together. I always admired Bob for his great humor, persistence and patience. His pioneering work with seat belt legislation is a good example of the traits that served him well throughout his life.

Hakan Sundell, M.D., Nashville, Tennessee

Dear Pat,

I was so sad when I heard that Bob had passed away. I had been following his illness through my parents with a heavy heart. What a wonderful man he was. I have so many fond memories of him at your home and farm. He was always so kind, gentle, and patient with us as children.

He also took an interest in my studies in medicine and shared his experiences in medicine with me. I was also so proud to know the man who saved so many lives with the child car seat laws. I am really going to miss him.

I hope you are hanging in there. I cannot imagine the sadness and loss. Please know that Jenny and I are thinking of you in our prayers.
Love,
Erik Sundell, M.D. E.R. physician, New Orleans, Louisiana

Dear Pat,

Judy and I want you to know that you have been in our thoughts these past weeks that we have been away, but I wanted to write something personal for myself, too.

The hours we spent together, as a threesome in those long days in the isolation room at Vanderbilt were reminders of what Bob has meant to me as a friend and colleague, and those thoughts kept coming back to me in the six weeks we were away from Nashville, regretting that we could not have been with you when he died and later when his life was celebrated by so many. The respects that would have been shared with those many others who treasured Bob, we will have to show more privately in the years to come.

You recall that each year from my first year in Nashville, I invited Bob to speak to our Preventive Medicine class, when your crusade for the safety of children was in its own infancy. I (and my students) have followed with awe and admiration your long road to a success that has saved more lives than all the cardiac surgeons in Tennessee and countless other states, here and abroad.

Next Monday, at 10 AM, Mike Decker will return to Nashville to lecture to our class on the subject of unintentional injury, as he has each year since Bob retired from giving his annual presentation. There will be a presence in the room for me, and I will share it with the class when I introduce Mike as our substitute teacher.

The Sanders' example of patient persistence in doing the right thing is one that needs to be reiterated and actively promoted in this contentious and self-centered era. Public Health means public service, responsibility for and accountability to our fellow humans.

Judy and the boys join me in love to you, Robert, and Priscilla.
Sincerely,
Lewis Lefkowitz, M.D., Nashville, Tennessee

Pat,
Laddie's call last evening casts a darkness over us, a feeling of loss that we should have been prepared for, but were not.

Since then, I have lifted much of the pallor by pursuing memories and flashbacks, reaffirming the fact of the enormously powerful and rich influence that good, good man was on my life.

It was my great fortune to have him in my life virtually from the beginning...Miss Carol Bean's first grade in 1934. Even then his strength of character, unbendable integrity and quiet leadership were beacons for us all.

Artist to athlete, farmer to physician, father to friend, intellectual to comic, he was truly a factor that was so positive I am convinced that influence had a major effect on the good aspects of my life.

Bobby was unique, yes, but real in the best friend sense that you have realized from all of us through the years. And he would now admit that you, Pat, have been the strength that even he has needed at the same time.

The Sermon on the Mount comes to my mind as I reflect on Bobby Sanders. He showed us all how to apply it every day.

132

Blessings on you, Pat, as you sadly navigate these trying days. Our best wishes are with you.
Fondly,
Lester Freeman, Cashiers, North Carolina

I just wanted to tell her how much I appreciated your comments and those of Gisela's about Bob (and Pat) Sanders. Steve O'Toole sent me a copy of their columns. He was a genuinely nice human being who accomplished extraordinary things without regard to personal credit. Literally thousands of families owe their well being to him and will never know his name. He was always careful to give great credit to Pat as well. Deborah was exactly right about the impact of Bob's work going beyond even CPS to other areas of belt use and beyond. Please thank her for properly honoring one of my heroes.
Chuck Hurley, chief executive officer, Mothers Against Drunk Driving

Dear Bob and Pat: (written in 2003)
What a wonderful happenstance to run into you at IHOP at 20th Street in Los Angeles. You both look terrific - I am sure because you are living life to the fullest.

Thank you so much also for the pictures. I see both Bob and I have some gray in our hair these days!

You both are such unsung heroes for your incredible work in passing the first state child passenger law in Tennessee twenty-six years ago. This law, and all the others that followed, have not only saved so many children's lives but was also the precursor to acceptance of the idea of adult belt restraint use laws. And now, of course, we are on the track of passing booster seat laws since children's bodies are not strong enough for an adult belt until at least age 8.

If you ever come to Washington, I hope you will give us a call. I would love to see you, and you can learn more about Public Citizen and the incredible work we do. I am enclosing a few of our materials which you might find interesting.
With every best wish,
Joan Claybrook, Public Citizen, Washington, DC

Dear Pat,
Hope you are surviving OK. With such a big hole in your life with Bob gone, it must be hard. We loved the material you sent about his life.

Dale especially enjoyed the Super Collider fight. He had just gotten a book from Herman Wouk called "A Big Hole in Texas." It's about the one you and Bob helped send to Texas. Get it—you will love it. I have such good memories of Dr. Bob.

From over the years, his wonderful help to the Russian doctors from Estonia and other places, it helped change their and their patients' lives. His friendship and counsel and yours, on many issues have been invaluable to me. I treasure all! I know you, Robert, and Priscilla will be sustained by all his life's accomplishments. Stay in touch.
Yours sincerely,
Betty Bumpers, Bethesda, Maryland

These words do not fill the emptiness we feel from the loss of a loved one, but they do help in giving us a better understanding of death in comparing it to life on earth... Oftentimes those who die young have contributed so much to the lives of others....I do believe God has a plan for all of our lives. We may not be in control when a death occurs, but we can be supportive of those who are left behind.
Sincerely,
Frances S. Kristofferson, Nashville, Tennessee

Pat,
I wish I could be there for the Memorial Service next week. Unfortunately, I am going to be out of town, but I wanted to let you know that I was thinking about you and the family. You should take comfort in knowing that Dr. Sanders has had a major and positive impact, not only on lives here in Rutherford County, but throughout the nation. Every time I buckle my daughter's seat belt, I think about Dr. Sanders and thank him for his efforts. Through this letter, please allow me to extend to you my most sincere condolences at this very difficult time.
Sincerely,
Bart Gordon, 6th District, Tennessee, U.S. Congress, Washington, DC

Dear Pat,
What a terrific loss we are all suffering--you most especially because Bob was a great husband--but all of us because he was such a great doctor, not only to his patients, but to the state and nation. He was such a great public health leader and we always need such leadership. Think how many infants and children you two have saved! What a legacy! What an example

134

for the rest of us to follow!

You and Joan, the fabulous Pelot girls, have always been an inspiration to your families and to us all. You will get through this.

We love you,

Jim Cooper, 4th District, Tennessee, U.S. Congress, Washington, DC

Dear Pat,

Bobby was one of the finest men I have known. He truly did our profession proud and managed to help more people than anyone I know. Aside from these great achievements, Bobby was still very special. He was a warm and gentle spirit of light all around, and many people will remember him with much love.

Sincerely,

Joe Allen, MD, Nashville, Tennessee

Dear Pat:

Allison and I had meant to be with you at Bobby's memorial service Saturday, but I came down with fever on Thursday and only today am up with most of a Z-Pac behind me. I had had both knees replaced before Christmas, and the caution against having infection lodge there caused us to be unusually careful.

Bobby was my cherished classmate and pledge brother. I esteemed him as I have esteemed few others, and a day with him in it was almost a Holy day. As a physician, he cared for our firstborn until you left for other regions, and we were grateful that he gave our son such a good start. He-- both of you--did great things for the children of Tennessee and the rest of the nation, but it was those personal qualities of gentleness and humor and consideration that endeared him so to all of us who loved him.

Allison and I hope the worst days will soon be over for you, and that happy memories will begin to replace the loss you must feel now. If ever there were anything we could do for you, we would do it with such a joyful heart. Allison sends her love along with mine.

Yours most sincerely,

John S. Beasley, II

Dear Pat,

I was very sorry to hear from Murphy Thomas about Bob's death. It brought back memories of having met over the years at the Carter Center and Public Health meetings. I have continued to tell about the role the two of you played in making child restraint seats the standard for our country.

It is a great legacy. I hope in this time of sadness that you recall the years together with great happiness.
With Sympathy
Bill(Wm. H.) Foege, M.D

Dear Pat,

I am distressed for you and your family with Bob's long illness and death. The years have passed so quickly, I remember Bob as a bright young medical resident—such a nice guy, smart and friendly at the same time. In the many years since, he has achieved much. As I think of his remarkable achievement of seat belts for children, I join so many parents and grandparents who are indebted to him always. Please know that Charlie and I are thinking of you and your family with deepest sympathy.
Very sincerely,
Ann Harwell Wells, Nashville, Tennessee

Dear Mrs. Sanders:

I was deeply saddened to learn of Bob's death. He was a professional colleague whose friendship I valued deeply. The late Dr. Ed Caldwell, Chair of Pediatrics at Meharry and I, then chair of OB/GYN at Meharry, worked with Bob as advocates to help ultimately implement the passage of his Child Restraint legislation. This creative program and so much more that Bob did with his life have truly left the world a better place.

May these and other lifetime memories help comfort you and your family in this time of your bereavement. My prayers and thoughts are with you. Sincerely,
Henry W. Foster, Jr., M.D., Meharry Medical College, Nashville, Tennessee

Dearest Pat, Robert, and Priscilla,

We are so grateful to have personally known Bob. He had so many marvelous qualities and left a record of improvements for mankind. Not many people have had such a great life. He will be truly missed. Written accounts of him, including news articles, are good to keep his life remembered. Robert, perhaps you may write about him some day. Our hearts go out to you. Please call whenever you want to talk. Also, our welcome mat is standing ready for you.
With all our love,
Charlotte and Mike Bachler, Athens, Georgia

Pat,

I want to personally thank God for Bob and his life of service to mankind. He was the absolute perfection of a pediatrician. I can always hear the soft, caring voice as he thought about the deep issues of children's health. His passionate commitment to the seat belt laws for children and the tenacity he had to get laws changed had repercussions throughout the country and the world. And it all came from proven science. I have a deep respect for both of you and your commitment to children with special needs. There too, we have a common bond.

Blessings,

Andy Spickard, M.D., Nashville, Tennessee

Dear Pat,

Bob's memorial service was so well orchestrated, a real tribute to such a saltwart individual. Bob will be a great loss to this community. His contributions were made with class and magnanimity. Truly, in his interest and by his untiring service, it appears that the original Health Department edifice will endure. This building is unique and one which Bob tended for so long.

Barbara and I hope that you find comfort in the recollection of your lives together and the happiness this union afforded you. He certainly was a wonderful husband, father, and care-giver to this community. I cherish my relationship with Bob and his support of me over the years. Hopefully, you will soon be able to rejoin us in our meetings at the Historical Society. Your input is always thought-provoking and informative.

Thinking of you at this difficult time,

Sincerely,

E. C. Tolbert, M.D., Murfreesboro, Tennessee

Dear Pat,

I was so sorry to hear about Bob's death. He was a fine person with a cool humorous outlook who was a delight to be with.

My best wishes to you.

Sincerely,

Samuel H. Paplanus, Tucson, Arizona

Dear Pat,

I was so saddened to hear of Bob's passing last week. Bob Rietz called me, and we reminisced about Bob and the pivotal role he played in encouraging all of pediatricians to be stronger advocates for the safety of children. I remember Bob's gentle manner and strong persistence in advocating for kids. My thoughts are with you and your family,

Sincerely,

Mark Widome, MD, FAAP, Hershey, PA

Dear Pat,

I was very sad to hear the news that Bob had lost his brave struggle. He was a wonderful advocate for children and a great friend to TRIAD, and his loss will be felt widely and deeply.

Please accept my most sincere expression of sympathy, and know that my thoughts are with you and your family. Please give my best to Robert. Thank you for thinking of TRIAD (Treatment Research Institute for Autism Spectrum Disorders) during this time.

I will call you soon to talk more about how to direct the donations.

Warm Regards,

Wendy Stone, Ph.D., Nashville, Tennessee

Dear Pat,

Betty and I send our sincerest condolences on your loss of Bob. It must be very reassuring and comforting for you to look back on his exemplary life.

From star football player to stalwart protector of young lives with a whole lot in between, his life was one that all of us young and old would do well to emulate.

I know that the fact you had such a wonderful partnership in marriage (it was impossible to think of Bob without thinking of you and vice versa) will make it most difficult in the near future but in the long run will give you great joy and fond memories.

You are in our thoughts and prayers.

Sincerely,

John Dixon, M.D., Murfreesboro, Tennessee

Dear Pat,

Anne and I learned of Bob's death with immense sorrow. He was truly a remarkable combination of excellence, wit, and amiability.

We all, of course, regret his protracted period of declining health and will miss him enormously. The consolations are that his great work—especially on the seat belt legislation—is unforgotten and one memory that he was attended by you with such love and fidelity. Please accept our condolences.

Sincerely,

Bob Taylor, Ph.D., Murfreesboro, Tennessee

Dear Patricia,

Francoise and I would like to extend our deepest sympathy to you and your family. It was with great sadness that we learned of Bobby's passing. I am so glad that we got to visit briefly with you and Bobby at the medical schools' 50th reunion (November 2005). Bobby and I were fraternity brothers in Sigma Chi for 3 years at Vanderbilt and then classmates in medical school for 4 more years.

I don't believe I ever met a kinder or more gentle person than he was. I always enjoyed his company and valued his friendship.

I know you will find comfort and satisfaction in the important work that both of you did in enacting laws to prevent childhood injuries in automobile accidents. I am sure these efforts have saved countless lives of children.

Our thoughts and best wishes are with you.

Fondly,

Francoise and Gordon Long, M.D., Dallas, Texas

Dear Pat, Robert, and Priscilla,

Bob Sanders was a gracious giant, an improbable and powerful combination of traits. He was gracious to all of us who knew him and a giant to all who never knew him yet owe their lives to his life's work. Pat and Bob worked unselfishly to improve the safety of young children. How many lives have they saved? How many more will they save? How many families know to thank Pat and Bob when their children survive injury or death in a car crash? Very few, and that's just what a gracious giant would want. But I know every time a child is saved, the stars wink silently in gratitude.

Love,

Linda Thomas Collins, professor of Biology at UTC, Chattanooga, Tenn.

Pat,

Dr. Sanders was our daughter's first pediatrician after Jim's time in the Army. When he left private practice and entered public health, Robin sadly switched to another physician. In grade 7, Robin had a mysterious illness. After two blood tests revealed no mono, I phoned Bob and you on a Saturday seeking another opinion. Dr. Sanders responded saying these symptoms sound like encephalitis. He called a neurologist at Vanderbilt University Medical Center for Sunday, and it was diagnosed just as Dr. Sanders had thought.

With thanks,

Marietta and Jim Bishop, DDS, Murfreesboro, Tennessee

Dear Pat,

I know there is nothing I can say about your Husband that you don't already know. No one but you knew him best and loved him the best. I just wanted you to know others loved him too...not as you did but as someone we looked up to and respected. As I have gone through my life there has been many people I admired but none as much as your husband. He was one of the greatest if not the greatest person I ever had the pleasure of working under. I do consider myself lucky not to have ever been stuck in a clinic room helping him though. The tales those nurses could tell you now... he tried to make everyone's job a little easier with his humor. Dr. Sanders was always willing to see any one when you asked them how sick they were... not how much money or what kind of insurance did they have? I remember one Friday after closing time I stayed with him to finish checking out a patient because I asked him to see them because the mom was so upset about her baby. .He was so kind to her and never worried about staying late to help someone. He told me to go on home he would finish up... His words were you have small children waiting on you to get home and Pat will understand. Thank you Pat for helping him help others... you have a heart of gold to match his and that is why so many admire what you gave up to support his work for the sick people of Rutherford County.

I have so many memories of the kind and funny things Dr. Sanders did I don't think I could remember them all. The only time I could have kicked him was one time he asked me to get up in front of an auditorium full of doctors from Vanderbilt and explain the WIC program to them. Not only had I just gotten up out of the Dentist chair, but I had never spoken in front of any group!! He wasn't worried one bit and told me to look at him and keep talking . . . he knew I had no problem talking! So I stood up there and never took my eyes off of him as he nodded his head at me through the whole speech. When they started firing questions at me he came and stood by my side and helped me answer them. He thanked me and I gave him a look that could kill....But... He made up for it on Fridays...that's when I always like him best...He would come out of a clinic room and see all of us staring at the clock...it might have been 4:15 or 4:20 and he would say, "Go on home, I will answer the phones until 4:30." You would have thought it was an hour early not ten minutes!! We would run out that door so fast and never look back (at him laughing)....

The first year we tried to do Secret Pals at the Health Department he drew my name. That was an interesting year...I never knew whether you or Barbara would remember or if it was really him! At Christmas when we were to tell who our Secret Pal was, he drew me a picture of himself...It looked like finding Waldo with a stocking cap on! He knew how to make fun of himself and that's what made him such a dear man.

This world is a better place for having people like Dr. Sanders in it. You have lost a dear husband and the rest of us have lost knowing a Great Man...I know the pain of losing a husband and I will always remember how kind you and Dr. Sanders treated me and my girls.

He will be missed by so many, but the wonderful things he did will live on in that little child he made well or by the child he saved with a car seat...And he will especially be missed by the employees of the Rutherford County Health Department who would have followed him anywhere. We loved our leader and how many employees can say that about a boss.

There are so many important people that Dr. Sanders knew and helped...I am honored to say that I knew such a great man. I know you and your children shared a great man with all of us and I thank you for that. May he be in peace and out of pain...And the day will come when you and your children's pain will be easier to bear. Until then I hope you find comfort in the words of the people who cared about him and know we care about you and your loss...

With Love...

Lisa Kilgore, Murfreesboro, Tennessee

Dear Pat,

I learned about your husband's passing early this year. I just wanted to say that I am sorry about your loss, and hope that you, Robert, Jr., and Priscilla are doing OK.

Bob was a humanitarian who used his talent and compassion to help the most vulnerable people. We are all better off for the good work he did. I think about you and your family from time to time, and I wish you the best.

Fondly,

Chris Heard, Nashville, Tennessee

Pat,

As I reminisce about Bob's life and his many achievements, it is obvious that he was a great physician and truly a real asset to this community as a public servant. I remember meeting Bob years ago when he visited his uncle Brock Sanders. Our daughter Beth was one of his first patients in Murfreesboro. His concern and compassion certainly showed in his very meticulous care.

Joseph C. Knight, MD, Murfreesboro, Tennessee

Dear Pat,

A dear friend of 45 plus years, the great twinkle in his eyes, the wonderful sense of humor and his caring and love of his little patients and friends will all be missed. Most of all, we shall miss our dear friend.

Sally and Larry Wolfe, MD, Nashville, Tennessee

To lose a man of intelligence, integrity, and compassion makes it doubly hard. Our son Bob Kilts, now 42, was one of Dr. Sanders' first patients.

Craigie and Ralph Kilts, Tullahoma, Tennessee

Dear Pat,

I was sorry to hear of Bob's illness a few years ago and again to hear of his death recently. I always said to anyone who would listen that he deserved the Nobel Prize for the original Child Restraint Law. If someone ever makes the tally, I'm confident that he saved more lives and disability than the rest of the V.U. 1950-1960 grads combined. I know you have a lot of responsibility and toil in managing the farm. Hope you have a chance to get a little time off.

your friend,

John Collins, M.D., Chattanooga, Tennessee

Dear Pat,

You have been very much on my mind today, knowing that the memorial service for Bobby was happening. My heart was there. I can imagine that there were many eloquent tributes to this great and good man, whose life touched so many people in a very positive way. I don't have to tell you what a unique person he was—you know very well, but I must tell you that he was one of the best friends I ever had. When I visited in Tullahoma, I was probably about 12 or 13 years old. We liked each other. We had this correspondence for years and his funny letters were illustrated by his crazy drawings. We kept in touch off and on while our lives took different paths. I always knew I could count on Bobby for truth. I'm so glad we got together at Sewanee while John and Harriet were there because then I got to know you truly his better half. Together you were able to accomplish so much good and you obviously made each other very happy. Having loved and lost twice, I know your sorrow, but I also know the strength and comfort that comes with the love and concern of friends and faith in God.

Sincerely,

Myra Ann Kelso, Memphis, Tennessee

Pat,

Judy and I appreciate your note, copy of the Celebration program and the notice of the forthcoming book. I didn't think I would know someone for whom a book would be written.

Bobby was a super guy at all the places we were together. He was quiet, concerned about his fellow man, and a good student and athlete.

We appreciate the offer of a complementary copy, but we'd rather buy our copy; I'm enclosing our check.

Bobby was a good man. You will have wonderful memories.

With kind regards,

Judy and Dick Reeves, Florida

Pat,

Dr. Sanders reminded me so much of my father in the virtues he exemplified in his everyday life. I was struck by his humility and his ability to relate to others on their level.

With sincerity,

Bill Harrell, Murfreesboro, Tennessee

Dear Pat,

Bob took the basic public health principle of immunization and applied it to injury, and he did it when no one else was talking about it. He was an important role model for pediatricians all over the country who were uncomfortable with the role of lobbyists. He showed them that they had to be persistent child advocates, that they couldn't simply go to the legislature with a proposal and expect it was just going to happen. From Bob's example, doctors learned how to keep out of the realm of partisan politics and just apply public health principles to a modern problem.

Mark Widome, Pennsylvania, former chair of the AAP's committee on injury and poison prevention

Pat,

Bob helped in getting our car safety seat law under way. His talk to our rotary club made an important impression on our state representative, who later became state speaker of the house, and recently became ambassador to Canada. And the long term effect of this effort for car seat use had prompted a volunteer group to extend it to develop a Safe Kids program that won national and international awards. I wish he could have seen all they have done, and I feel it all started with the safety seat effort.

Bill DeLoache, MD, Greeneville, South Carolina

Pat,

I still remember your both visiting my late wife Pat and me in Rhode Island in 1987 and will always treasure the inspiration Bob gave me in child restraint legislative advocacy. His work in Tennessee was number one. Mine in Rhode Island was number two. What a leader he was!

John O'Shea, MD, Atlanta, GA

"Dr. Sanders' recognition as a pediatrician that he could help protect children from death and injury in car crashes with a child restraint use law resulted in saving countless lives not only in the US but worldwide."

Joan Claybrook, president of Public Citizen periodical, formerly the administrator of the National Highway Traffic Safety Administration (NHTSA) where she spurred the passage of state child restraint use laws, which were approved in all 50 states by 1985.

Dr. Robert S. Sanders Memorial Service, February 4, 2006

Rev. David Garth: Let us pray together:

God who gave us birth, you are always more ready to hear than we are to pray. You know our needs before we ask and our ignorance in asking. Show us now your grace that as we face the mystery of death that we may see the light of eternity. Help us to believe where we have not seen, trusting you to lead us through all our years. Bring us at last with all your saints into the joy of your home, for we make this prayer in your blessed name, Amen.

Song by Carol Ponder:

We come today to say goodbye to one who held us close, to tell the stories of his life that moved in us the most. These memories of a life well lived and of a death well faced are now a part of every life that crosses in this place. No circle has been broken here. No one who stands alone. The threads of life so lately broken are woven through our own. He hoped to see us all again who gather here today, but now we will not meet again. We'll meet again some day. In work we do, in songs we sing, in courage and in pain. In Bibles that we find as one, we'll see his face again. No circle has been broken here. No one who stands alone. The threads of life so lately broke are woven through our own.

John Greer, M.D.:

I knew Bob at the extremes of our professional careers. I was a pupil in 1972 and he showed me things I had only read about, and then he became a patient in the year 2000. He taught me a lot at both extremes, but I learned that there was so much more about Bob in between those times.

When Bob saw injustice, he tried to correct it. We all know the story about Bob's crusade for child safety seats. I almost think that Bob would have been a little - he would have frowned upon the word "crusade," but the Tennessean also said he was a gentle warrior and I think most of us think of him in those terms. When Bob saw illness, he tried to prevent it, and I think everyone in medicine knows that the pediatricians are the best of the lot. Their strategy of prevention has much greater impact than anything else that any of us do. Bob was not only a premier pediatrician - he was a pioneer in public health. And I think in Hurricane Katrina and in the impending bird flue epidemic, we all realize how important public health can be.

When Bob saw goodness, he embraced it. When he saw Pat, he married her and each was a very courageous, caring warrior in their own life, but together they were an army that could move mountains. They had Robert, and Priscilla, and they allowed each one of them to carry on that courageous, compassionate spirit in their own endeavors. Bob and Pat would share Priscilla's music and they enjoyed sharing Robert's writings and photography. They kept me and my wife up to date about Bill Sanders and his wife Debbie in Tullahoma, their children and their exploits.

The last few years of Bob's life were difficult, but he had an angel by his side—a tenacious angel. She truly kept him aloft. You could always see how much Bob loved Pat and enjoyed life. Even though he was ill at the time, he had a sparkle in his eye that you could see how much he cared about his family, his country, his community, his school, and the State of Tennessee.

Knowing Bob has been a privilege. We will all miss him, but his spirit will live on through Pat, Robert, and Priscilla, and all the lives he touched while on this earth and that he will continue to touch through his work. His impact on health care, child safety, Vanderbilt, and Tennessee, is indeed permanent.

When Bob saw injustice, he tried to correct it, when he saw illness, he tried to prevent it. When Bob saw goodness, he embraced it. We are all Bob's pupils and he is our hero.

The Rev. David M. Maynard

He would be touched that you are all here today--a bit embarrassed, but very touched. My connection with the family is that I was minister of a congregation in Nashville, Tennessee for quite a number of years--I say Tennessee because I live in Oregon--you're in Tennessee. I used to speak to the Unitarian Fellowship down here in Murfreesboro, and when we moved back to the West Coast, we maintained our friendship and we saw them frequently on the West Coast up in our house and down in California.

Part of me doesn't of course want to be here, and I wish this day were not necessary. Yet in thinking about Bob, or Bobby to many of you, I realize that one of the things he has done for me over the years, and I suspect for you, is to redefine some common words that are part of our everyday language and yet with him acquired a different depth of meaning. One of those words is "family"--a popular word, even politicians are known to use it, but Bobby (Bob) gave "family" a depth, an importance, a sense of depth and continuity that was truly remarkable. And "family" could be relatives, could be people who were in school with him, could be friends who have been acquired over the years. You knew they mattered, you knew there was never any question of the importance they played in his life. And of course, he lived out his life in the family home where his mother was born and raised. He is ending his life in the family cemetery off Kimbro Road--a mound of dirt in a very old location.

Another word to which he gave great depth is "profession." His grandfather was a physician and then decided to do a little better and became a dentist. One colleague from the military times wrote that in their Corp of Engineers basic training in Ft. Belvoir, Virginia, they knew right off that he was going to be a physician. Bobby was by far, he said, the healthiest of all the other soldiers because he was a walking drugstore. Bobby maintained a stock of pharmaceutical supplies capable of staving or curing any ill that might conceivably accost him and even supplies to ward off ills that had not even been discovered yet. While stationed in Okinawa, a young island child was bitten by a deadly snake, and she would have expired had not Bobby stepped in and taken the actions necessary to save her life. He became an instant hero in the girl's village and then later went on to describe how he had to drink a little bit of alcohol to accept their accolades even though he was a confirmed "tee totaler."

He did all the things that are a part of the history of this land and this people. He kept track of it. I remember we went to visit Ft. Clatsup, the end point of the Lewis and Clark Expedition just south of Astoria, Oregon, and they were so excited to meet him because he was the first relative of Meriwether Lewis they had met in many years. William Clark had many children. Meriwether Lewis had none. And Bob was a direct descendant of that family.

He had a sense of humor. He loved jokes. He loved little cartoons that he would draw for people. He always had a chuckle ready but never at anyone's expense, or in my experience, never hurtful. Of course, you've already heard and will hear more mentioned of the child seat safety law. You will hear some words of his public health work here in Rutherford County as well as its effect on the whole nation. But I have never forgotten his incredible sentence in describing the experience of children being killed in car wrecks when he knew it wasn't necessary.

Another word he gave great depth to was "history." He was a history buff in his way. Roots were vital to him. He, of course, lived on a land grant from the early 1800s. There was blue blood on both sides, and lineage mattered to him. He kept track of the farm--he farmed the farm, or made sure somebody else was doing it. He didn't want to waste good farmland. He raised sheep and cattle. He raised children. He brought new meaning to the word, "kindness" also. Perhaps we can also say "respect." Even if distraught, even if convinced that someone was very wrong, the kindness and respect for the other person's humanity was always there. He was unselfish and open--not only to new learning, but to the reality of the possibility that you could change because if you were wrong, you might want to grow into the right. He brought new meaning to the word, "enthusiasm." Every day--every trip, every life-long friend, every relative, every good story was appreciated and remembered, and you knew that it affected his life. Enthusiasm of course is a word that means to be full of God to be full of that spirit that is given to all of us, but some treasure it and share it willingly and Bob was such a person.

And lastly, he loved life. He simply liked being here--being a part of this world even in his latter days. Even when his illness took a toll on his physical abilities and his ability to get around, he was very cooperative. He wanted to get better. He lived a technicolor life rooted in Tennessee history and thriving in each changing era that he experienced.

So those are some of the words that I believe that Bob gave to us that have a different meaning because he said hello and was in our lives, and while we do not necessarily want to say goodbye, we must, for his passing is a natural part of the land, the plants and the animals and the people--as natural a part as any other part of life. Thank you, Bob, for redefining ourselves with deeper meanings. Thank you Bob for a life well lived indeed.

Toward the end of this service you will have the opportunity to share thoughts and memories briefly of Bob Sanders, and I will have the microphone and will be inviting you to share at that time.

The Rev. Dan Rosemergy

Pat, Robert, and Priscilla, I bring warm wishes, love, and hugs from the congregation of the Greater Nashville Unitarian Universalist Congregation and I also want to thank you for the invitation to be part of the celebration of Bob's life--a celebration which has been an ongoing part of his life and continues as his spirit, work, and commitment lives on in our lives. It's been a gift to know and to be included in the Sanders' circle of friends and to share with the many occasions and moments which gave meaning to his life and to ours.

I recall on many occasions and moments when my wife, Jan, and I would go to a benefit dinner, a justice peace event, a university celebration or a cultural event, there would be Bob and Pat, and often a few days later pictures would arrive in the mail to help us remember the occasion and sharing together. Well, those pictures and memories live on for all of us in many different ways. I remember Bob in all these times as a gracious, warm, unassuming and gentle person with a wonderful smile and underneath all that was a deep love and passion for his life, his profession, his family, the community, and his and their commitments to making all of society a better place.

He gave to us in so many different ways. To those he knew and loved but also to those he didn't know but also cared for. His was a life of caring--a giving and nurturing life--his own and ours. So in that spirit I want to share this meditative verse by Patrick Mervin. It's entitled "Some Tend the Tree of Life."

Some water the tree of life, nurturing its enveloping branches which cast a cool and welcoming shade when a blazing sun threatens to scorch and seer our souls. Some gather the audacious blossoms of lavender and crimson, azure and vermillion whose bare souls have known nothing but thorns and stones. Some glean the windfall fruit bruised and neglected and broken and being alchemy of love, bring us tarts and pies, fritters, and puddings, jams, and nectar beyond our very imagination. Some take the inevitable autumn drop, melancholy, awkward, tumbling, and foreboding gales and do not smudge the sky with their funeral pyres and tend mulch to hummace and nourishment for another season. Yes, some tend the Tree of Life and we are their grateful heirs.

All of us gathered here today and many throughout this community and nation are grateful that Bob tended our trees of life. For that we are deeply thankful, for that we feel the love of this celebration. For that we enter the spirit that arrives on the spirit of work and love and commitments of Bob Sanders.

Paulette Albert

First of all, let me thank Robert, Priscilla, and Mrs. Sanders for thinking enough of me to have me say something about Dr. Sanders. I started to work with Dr. Sanders as my boss in 1972. He was a hard worker, he was a boss and a friend, and he cared about all of us. He talked to us about our families and he would see our children, aunt, uncle, mother, whoever, if they were sick and they needed help in the clinic and he was also seeing patients in the clinic and we knew when he was at work because he always drove this big orange truck and he would pull in the parking lot, and we would always say, "Dr. Sanders, that is the brightest truck." He'd say, "Well, I don't think anybody could miss me, do you?"

When he wasn't in clinic, he was in the old Health Department building. It was really cold, and we could find him sitting in his office with this big hat pulled down over his ears, his jacket on, (his white jacket), and sometimes his suit coat because it was so cold because you know he didn't have any hair up there, so he would always have that hat on and he would be drinking a hot cup of tea and be eating an oatmeal cookie.

Each of us worked with him--he was always smiling, he was always fair, he was always calm. I don't think I ever saw a day when he was angry, and if he was, we didn't know about it. But the most important thing that we remember about him was the love and understanding that he had for each of us that worked under him. He believed in helping others who needed help--medically, physically, however. He always had time and it was a joy knowing him along with Mrs. Sanders, Robert, and Priscilla. We all grew together as a family and we will never forget him because after all we will buckle up. We have a presentation--Mrs. Ellen Gray will do that.

Mrs. Ellen Gray, R.N.

Yes, I'm happy to represent others from the health department, and we want to give to the family in memory of Dr. Sanders this plaque which is a duplicate of a large heavy plaque that used to hang on the old health department addition. We took it down before the building was destroyed and it now has a place of honor in our library. The plaque says, "The Robert Smith Sanders Public Health Clinic, Dr. Bob Sanders, Rutherford County Public County Health Officer, 1969-1991, initiated, crusaded, and brought to reality in 1977 the first Child Restraint Law in the United States, thus earning the appropriate nickname of "Dr. Seat Belt." So this is for you, and we will keep the plaque in its place of honor in our library.

Sharri Chappell

"Men are of two kinds and he was of the kind I would like to be. Some preach their virtues and a few express their lives by what they do. That sort was he. No flowery phrase or glibly spoken words of praise won friends for him. He wasn't cheap or shallow, but his course ran deep and it was pure. You know the kind--not many in a life you'll find. Whose deeds outrun their words so far that more than what they seem they are."

I learned that poem when I was in seventh grade for some extra credit in a poetry class. And in seventh grade, I thought I knew everything, but I didn't know what that poem meant, but I do now, and I believe it was nestled in my heart all these years for this day.

I was 13 years old and the year was 1963, the year that the Sanders moved to Murfreesboro. This was before Murfreesboro was a Mecca, so we probably passed at one time or another--we just didn't know it.

We were doing different things. I spent the remainder of the 60s doing things like cheering at football games, having slumber parties, getting my ears pierced, having my first date, surviving my first broken heart. He was doing more important things. He was rescuing the family farm, celebrating his first wedding anniversary, opening his pediatric practice, welcoming his son, welcoming his daughter, travelling into town late at night to take care of somebody's sick children and becoming the Health Department Director for Rutherford County.

In the 70s I buried my father, became an air force wife, lived in four states in three years, lost two friends in Vietnam, owned my first house, had my first child. He was doing things like working with the Accident Prevention Committee, learning the ropes of lobbying, lobbying a lot, knocking on hundreds of doors, having hundreds of doors slammed in his face, mailing stacks of letters, surviving lots of ridicule, answering hundreds of questions and celebrating with pride when the world's first child passenger protection law was signed in 1977.

And little did I know that I would put it to the test before the ink was dry. My second child was born in the summer of 1980 and thankfully we were living in a time where good news was not always smothered out by horror. And I knew what he'd been up to. I was not a seat belt user--I had never been one. I even went through a windshield when I was a junior in high school on the way to a New Years Eve party--brought in the New Year in the emergency room. That was a long time ago, so not very many people talked about what could have been, a thing that might have made a difference. And that would have been my seat belt. My daughter travelled the 20 miles home from the hospital three days old and less than 5 pounds in my lap and she took many trips to her grandparents' in the bottom of a laundry basket in the back seat of our car. But we didn't know any better.

I shudder to think what not knowing any better could have meant for my son on October 7, 1980, when our car was hit in the middle of an intersection and thrown into a tree--a car that never slowed down because the driver was asleep. Despite the fact that my car was totaled, the outcome was good. Cars can be replaced, baby boys cannot be. There were many voices that day that led me to buckling him into the child restraint device, but Dr. Sanders' voice was the one I heard, the one I believed, the one I understood.

Not long after our accident, he called me one night and said he would like to meet me (we didn't know one another). He wanted to talk with me about testifying in front of the legislature to close the loophole in the law that allowed us to hold children in our laps in the car, a position that would have killed my son the day of my accident. I agreed. We met together. I testified. We celebrated. The law was changed. The loophole was removed, and we were great friends. Over the next years we worked together numerous times, did numerous presentations together.

He brought me into the fold. One of my finest hours was introducing him at a conference in front of about 200 people. In 1985 he and I worked on establishing the First Offenders Class for the state. And I taught that class in the upstairs auditorium of the health department for years. We kept our car seats in an attic that scared me to death every time I went in it. You know what I'm talking about.

Sometimes after class I'd stop by and see him and we'd talk about the class and how it was going and talk a little politics, tell a few jokes. He always wanted to know about my kids and I loved that. And here I have to tell you we've got this brilliant doctor who knows everything, wears a dozen hats, clean-cut as they come, impeccably dressed--but try to find a pencil on his desk. I teased him about it one day and he got up from his desk and came around to where I was sitting and moved some papers around, some books around, chased some paperclips and some tongue depressors, and showed me a little plaque about this big on the corner of the desk and it said something like, "A clean desk is the sign of a sick mind." We never talked about that desk any more. He had anything but a sick mind.

I believe it was around 1990 when he and I met with the Red Cross and moved the offenders class to that building, and we weren't together much after that. We didn't see each other much but he helped me put on a big surprise for Reeves Rogers Elementary School when my son was a fourth grader. We had 250 elementary school age children come in the auditorium and sit down Indian style on the floor and we had a blast. We thought we were really doing a great job. They didn't move, they listened to everything we said, and then we realized that Vince and Larry, the crash test dummies were standing behind us and that's what they were looking at--not us.

There are a lot more stories like that--he was a great friend, a role model, his influence in my life has been inescapable. I recently read that there is an estimated number of 7,000 saved by child restraint devices since Tennessee passed the first law. We talked about this a while ago and I think it is kind of low, but it sounds great anyway. However, I would prefer to say 6,999 and my son.

This past August, Candace and I met Bob and Pat and Priscilla at Borders Book Store for some wonderful music presented by Priscilla and her band and we had a wonderful reunion--lots of laughs, lots of pictures that I got later--always. They always made me feel like the important one. That night as I listened to some beautiful music, I feared that this may be the last time we would all be together. It was obvious that Dr. Sanders was up against a tough opponent and this was not about votes and vetoes and loopholes. Sitting across the room looking at him as Priscilla sang, I was looking at a man who had among many things been a boy scout, captain of his football team in high school--that's always cool. He had worked in a lumber yard. He had graduated from Vanderbilt Medical School, had studied medicine in Sweden, had been director of the health department, medical examiner, a published writer, my favorite had been a good American and was key in the passage of the world's very first children's passenger protection law. That's what I was looking at. But at that moment, I was seeing my good, good friend, real life hero, a devoted husband and somebody's sweet, sweet daddy.

Marilyn Bull, M.D.

I'm Marilyn Bull, and I'm a pediatrician from Indiana, and honored to be here today to celebrate the life of a devoted public servant and friend. For me Dr. Robert Sanders was a role model and a mentor of great proportions. As you have heard many times today, Bob took the basic principles of public health and immunization and applied it to injury prevention and as stated by one of my colleagues, he did it when no one else was talking about it. He was innovative in his approach and effective in his perseverance and diplomacy. He motivated in a way that places me in awe.

We are all familiar with his campaign to introduce car seat usage legislation in an attempt to prevent avoidable deaths in babies and young children, and that Tennessee led the way for the nation in this regard.

153

When Indiana was concerned with initiating our efforts, I called Dr. Sanders for advice, guidance, and assistance. But I was disappointed because he couldn't come and help me out because it was at that critical moment that your anti-baby crusher legislation was coming through and his primary responsibility was to Tennessee and to make that happen. His words to me, though, ring in my ears: "I can tell that you can do this, too," he said on the phone and that incentive plus his sage advice indeed led us forward in our cause and me to many further challenges in child passenger safety and injury prevention. Dr. Sanders is a dedicated and insightful pediatrician with a vision who has inspired countless physicians and who provided an example for advocacy training programs across the country.

A wise philosopher once said there are four things you can do with your hands: You can wring them in despair. You can clinch them in anger. You can fold them in resignation, or you can use them to lift up a child. Dr. Sanders made that choice in his life and has the respect of his many colleagues for his wisdom and contributions. I speak today representing the 60,000 pediatrician members of the American Academy of Pediatrics in expressing our condolences to the family and our appreciation for the life of Dr. Sanders. He was the recipient of many awards: 1991 Pediatrician of the Year by the Tennessee Pediatric Society, 1992 National Association of Women Highway Safety Leaders, 1997 National Safe Kids Champion, and in 2004 he received the Fellow Achievement Award from the American Academy of Pediatric Section on Injury and Violence Prevention.

I think Bob and Pat would think however that nothing is as great as the satisfaction of knowing that the national highway traffic safety administration says that 7,472 lives have been saved between 1975 and 2004 due to use of child safety seats. Thank you, Dr. Sanders.

Mildred Stahlman, M.D.

When Pat asked me to say a few words about my admiration and affection and long-time association with Bob and with his family, I thought maybe that I would talk to you and to them about one of the things which we had in common over the years. We had many things in common besides being pediatricians. Bob and I both were farmers. We both dealt with sheep. One of our long-standing affections was for our sheep.

But what I really wanted to talk about to you, to Pat, and the family was to remind them of the times which we shared at Pawley's Island.

That was the place where so many of us spent our holidays together sometimes and at various times we couldn't everybody be there at the same time, but over the past--many years--40 years or so--we have all enjoyed the wonderful atmosphere which Pawley's Island afforded us. They spent time on the beach between 1969 and 1999. I started a little bit earlier and was more intermittent than they, but I have never lost my almost mystical affection for Pawley's Island. For those of you who are not familiar with Pawley's Island, it's a sandbar--that's all it is--on the coast of South Carolina or about 50 miles north of Charleston. Why is it special, why was it so special to us and to so many people? First is its lack of pretension and sophistication, it prides itself on being arrogantly shabby. I always felt that if I had on shoes, I was overdressed. What were its activities?

Obviously swimming in the ocean, fishing from the pier, surf casting, setting crab traps in the marsh between the island and the mainland, flying kites, and particularly lying in Pawley's Island rope hammocks, reading, napping, or just restoring your soul with gentle movements and a lack of urgency to be busy. The island is historic and several of its 250-year-old houses have withstood many hurricanes. Before such disasters, the Gray Man, their local ghost, is seen walking upon the beach to warn you.

Of course, looking for archaic shark's teeth and gathering seashells at low tide are almost daily procedures. Particularly after a blow the shell population tossed on the beach is greater and multiplied in its quality and enhanced with all the visitors when they return home carrying these bright reminders.

I have chosen a poem for Bob which is an allegory of one of these castles in which a remarkable sea animal that had the ability to grow, to adapt, to expand its world and its influence on the world around it, just as some humans, like Bob Sanders, was able to change the outcome of countless disasters and preserve untold precious children's lives. This is entitled "The Chambered Nautilus," written by Oliver Wendell Holmes.

"This is the ship of pearl, which, poets feign, sails the unshadowed main. The venturous bark that flings on sweet summer wind its purpled wings in gulfs enchanted, where the siren sings, and coral reefs lie bare, where the cold sea maids rise to sun their streaming hair.

Its webs of living gauze no more unfurl, wrecked is the ship of pearl. And every chambered cell, where its dim dreaming life was wont to dwell, as the frail tenant shaped his growing shell, before thee lies revealed. Its irised ceiling rent, its sunless crypt unsealed!

Year after year beheld the silent toil that spread his lustrous coil. Still, as the spiral grew he left the past year's dwelling for the new, stole with soft steps its shining archways through, built up its idle door, stretched in his last-found home, and knew the old no more.

Thanks for the heavenly message brought by thee, child of the wandering sea, cast from her lap, forlorn. From thy dead lips a clearer note is born than ever Triton blew from wreathed horn. While on mine ears it rings, through the deep caves of thought I hear a voice that sings. Build thee more stately mansions. O my soul, as the swift seasons roll. Leave thy low-vaulted past. Let each new temple, nobler than the last. Shut thee from heaven with a dome more vast, till thou at length art free leaving thou outgrown shell by life's unresting sea."

Song: "What a Wonderful World" sung by Rick and Carol Bennett
words and music originally written by George David Weiss & Bob Thiele
originally recorded by Louis Armstrong

I see trees of green, red roses too. I see them bloom for me and you.
And I say to myself what a wonderful world.
I see skies of blue and clouds of white,
The bright blessed day, the dark sacred night.
And I say to myself what a wonderful world.
The colors of a rainbow so pretty in the sky
Are also on the faces of people goin' by.
I see friends shakin' hands sayin', "How do you do!"
They're really saying, "I love you!"
I hear babies cry. I watch them grow.
They'll learn much more than I'll ever know.
And I think to myself what a wonderful world.
Yes, I think to myself what a wonderful world.

Benjamin Porter
That was beautiful . . . and Carol's song also. Fantastic music here today. My name is Benjamin Porter. I'm an old family friend--old enough to say I feel more like family than just a friend, and one advantage of coming up here after so many interesting comments have been made about Bob is there are definitely recurring themes that you hear. These interesting pictures that Pat would mail out immediately. Did yours have captions on them? I didn't know if you got the edited version or not. The funny hats he would wear, Pawley's Island, and humor, and I think I was

156

asked to talk a little bit about his humor. Because when I was with Bob I could not help but laugh, and we would both have creative laughing sessions.

My family moved here when my dad was employed at the Veterans Hospital in the late 60s, and the Sanders were among the first people we met and one of the chores--you see, my sister and I were in high school at the time and we were going to help with their lambs--the baby lambs that were born and not cared for, so we took a couple home and we'd nurse them and give them bottles. We would wake up a couple of hours every night not knowing what a task had been given to us. But as we got to know Bob Sanders, he was a kind of country doctor--soft-spoken, understated, a perfect gentleman. He had the perfect counterpoint of a wife with Pat--the effervescent Pat who had the razor-sharp memory. If you would like to know what color socks were worn in 1971 on February 4, Pat would know. Or maybe even the Thanksgiving dinner that was served in the Carter administration. I don't know, but Pat has an incredible photographic memory.

My senior year in college I spend part of my time in Europe, and part of the time I was going to Sweden. Bob had spent time in Sweden, and he was very excited and we got together so he could share some of his thoughts about Sweden and give some connection and contacts. He also wanted to teach me a little bit of Swedish and the only thing I really remember is the words "tack sa mycket" which if you say it correctly means "thank you very much," but he didn't tell me that if you mispronounce it, that it would actually come out saying "Can I kiss you on the lips?" Bob must have known that would have been a great ice breaker. I wish he would have told me how to avoid the black eye.

I happened to be visiting the Sanders farm on a day—a fateful day that another famous person in Tennessee died. Of course, you know who I mean. That was Elvis Presley. You didn't know that Bob was an Elvis fan? Actually, I don't know that he was, but I am. But actually, as I thought about this, Bob Sanders and Elvis Presley have quite a few things in common. Well, they are both very unique. We have to admit that they both were very famous for their careers and the contributions they made in their fields. Both received national media attention. Both were quite athletic-- Elvis on stage and Bob as a track and football star. They both had a Priscilla who was close to them. They both had female admirers, and, Pat, I'm sure you heard there was even a Sanders female fan club in Sweden for Bob. Well, it might be news to you now, but . . . better late than never, but my memory of Bob just like yours will always be indelibly linked to the fun times shared by our families at Pawley's Island, South Carolina.

We'd spend a week together--and this tradition goes back some 35 plus years. One of the highlights was that we would gather in the ocean and bodysurf. We would wade out there and wait for the waves to come in and carry us into the beach, patiently waiting for the Big One--the big wave, and Bob would be out there yelling "Catch the big one! Get that big one." That would be the signal for all of us to start swimming and catch that wave. I think it was at that time Bob gave us the monitor: "Real men don't use surfboards."

Bob was also a student of style and fashion. One year he arrived at Pawley's Island sporting a funny pullover cap which tied under his chin and he would wear it only on the beach and we giggled at it until he told us it was actually an original Australian lifeguard hat. As the years passed both Bob and Pat would protect themselves from the sun's ultraviolet rays so much that they would be covered head to toe in white, no sun would hit their skin but they would be out there with us nonetheless. An adamant student of anatomy, Bob would go out of his way to point out to me some of the finer specimens of the human species on the beach and taught me the medical term "gams" which refers to your legs.

"Tack sa mycket," Bob. In the end, talking about what made Bob so funny is a bit like trying to define the word beauty. It means something different to each of us. Bob touched and made richer so many of us in our lives. And I know that here we are all of us, we're kind of still in that ocean waiting for that big one, but Bob has caught it and I can hear him and I see him clearly. He is smiling and content, has that silly little Australian lifeguard hat on his head, and I say, "Tack sa mycket," Bob.

Walter Puckett, M.D.

I was one of Bob's classmates and several of his other classmates are in the audience –Danny Dolan, Ben Moore, Gene Regen, Bill Alford. We were all just terribly fond of Bob and you've heard all the good things about Bob, and I'll not reiterate those, but Pat, I would really like to thank you for asking me to say a few words and I'm serious--it'll just be a few-- but I really am touched and honored that I can say a few things about Bob. I guess first I want to say something a little serious. Sir William Osler was the very famous professor of medicine at Johns Hopkins University who later went to Oxford and prior to coming to Hopkins, he was at the

University of Pennsylvania and he gave a final address there and it is very famous--many of you have heard of it--Aequanimatas.

Dr. Osler quoted an Etruscan ruler, Antonius Pilas, who on his deathbed summed up his philosophy of life in the word Aequanimatas. I think Sir William Olsler thought that calm aequanimity was probably the superior virtue of all and when displayed in both success and adversity, it exemplified Bob's life, and that is my serious note.

Now, everyone has talked about Bob's humor. He was jovial all the time, and I can still hear him chuckling at life's absurdities. In 1960 I had just gotten out of the Navy and Bob had just returned from Sweden, and we shared an apartment and to describe this apartment--you won't believe it. The entry way was a fire escape and we went up to the second floor and it was a remodeled attic. I don't think we paid very much for it, but it probably wasn't worth whatever we paid, but that was life. We were the odd couple. I was very boisterous and loud as Bob was quiet and calm, but we did get along well. It might have been likely you might have suspected maybe oil and water, but we mixed very well together. Now Bob had some idiosyncrasies and one of them is wearing a hat and probably something Pat may know and maybe Bob didn't need it once he married Pat, but Bob took an afternoon nap and he never missed a day without taking an afternoon nap--and he always wore a nightcap. So Bob was--I think when Paulette Albert was talking about how Bob was always cold. Bob was *always* cold. We kept the apartment at about 92. The other idiosyncrasy that Bob had, and he acquired this is Sweden--and I guess it was a separate endeavor than with his girlfriends . . . he acquired the taste of

Lingon berries, and there's a down side to Lingon berries. Lingon berries are the Swedish answer to our cranberries, but the downside of Lingon berries is that they're imported and they're very expensive, so we decided that we would have a money pot, and each week one of us would take the pot and go to the grocery store. Well, the first week it was Bob's time. So, he took all our money, he went to the grocery store, and he came back with a sack full of jars of Lingon berries. No, that's not all--and a second sack--it was full of Swedish Rye crackers. So for a week we had Lingon berries on Swedish Rye crackers for breakfast and for supper we had minute rice with Lingon berries. I bought the groceries for the rest of the year.

Now during that year our paths really didn't cross much because I was doing some research that was not original, but I was sort of a flunky and I had to work at night because that was the only time the voltage was stable enough at Vanderbilt Hospital to use this machine I was using, so I spent my nights at Vanderbilt with my current girlfriend, Linda, at my side during the year and so I didn't see much of Bobby after he went down for his nap and then I took off to the hospital, so we didn't pass much through the night but I think that we were very pre-occupied with our work that year and the most important thing that went on that year was that we were courting our future wives. We both won the favor of two wonderful women who've been a source of strength and awesome companions, and Pat, I cannot imagine Bobby without you.

I could say many other things, many of which have already been said, and I think Bobby's life is best captured in the words of Robert Frost, "He took the road less travelled by," and that made all the difference.

Original Poem by Trudy Sanders Guinee

I feel honored that Bob was my cousin and my friend, our fathers were brothers, and we were born just about a year apart. This was written just about a week ago in Houston where I live.

A Walk in the Woods

You would like it here, Bob--this 18 acres of wooded trails away from the buzz and rush of the city where the dog and I walk most days. Each age brings its losses. I need this solace, the crunch of dry leaves, wildlife; we never stray far from our roots. So many memories of your jumping marmots, slow growing boxwoods now grow tall above us, family reunions, walking the fields down to the cave and later our fathers, aunts and uncles performing, music, a flea circus, recitations, horse impressions. Little changed year to year. In that large family we were blessed. The cartoons you drew on the backs of envelopes, a phone message in Swedish, barn owls in the hayloft. One spring night you drove friends to Murfreesboro for the cotillion. Finding your cousin dateless, you whisked me off to the dance and made sure all your friends gave me a whirl, rooting out the wildflower I had planted in my head. It's a long time since Castle Heights and Central High. So many memories, but never enough. I've been trying to describe you to friends--your dedication to what you believed, the gentle performance as your impact saved untold lives by insuring the passage of child restraint laws.

Crusader, you've been called--Dr. Seat Belt. Loving, patient father to Robert, and Priscilla, concerned physician who connected the health of the land with the people. It's sad, there are not many like you who leave the earth a better place for having been here. You, the most pure of heart person I've ever known. Did I tell you what I've learned from a poet I admired? On the night of 9-11, she said, "Everything's connected, everything changes, pay attention. You've lived like that--seriously alive. You would like this patch of woods, Bob. An old Sycamore gleams in the late sun, its interwoven roots riding the bank of Rummel Creek. Already the first Narcissi push up through dry leaves and Cedar Wax winds whisper their secrets.

Laddie Harton Neil

When Pat asked me to say a few words, about our early days in Tullahoma, I thought "Where would I begin? Start at the beginning." Bob was born on October 24, 1927, at 405 S. Jackson Street, and I was born the following August 15 at 300 Jackson Street, just one block away. So, you see, I guess I go back just about as far as anyone here today with Bobby. He was really my first sweetheart, and our friendship has been strong all these many, many years in this wonderful world.

Bobby and I reminisced about the school days we had in Mrs. Anderson's kindergarten where we thought Ring around the Roses was a pretty fun game. Then, we went to first grade at South Jackson Grammar School with Miss Carol Beam our teacher and many other special teachers like Miss Evelyn Daniel. Our grammar school had grades 1-8 and was directly across from the Sanders' home. Our neighborhood in Tullahoma was a good, safe neighborhood. We knew everyone on the street and maybe everyone in town. We walked to school, and we walked home for lunch. Of course, we just had to go across the street.

Playing night games in the early evening was one of our favorite things to do. We would play kick the can or three of our friends would stand on either side of the street and at the appointed time, we all pulled hard, and the cars that went by thought we were pulling a rope across the street. And, of course, the car would come to a screeching halt and we would *hide*. That was just about the most mischievous thing we did, I think.

Remember signing autograph books? Bobby always wrote a funny poem and ended with a silly cartoon at the end, and like Trudy said, he was a good artist, very creative and he had a wonderful sense of humor. He was fun to be with, and that's one of the reasons everyone loved Bobby. On the weekend we might go to the Strand Theatre for a movie and for a soda at the Tullahoma Drug Store. Some of us might venture out to watch the bombers land or maybe sit on the front porch and wave to the soldiers and convoys going to Camp Forest. Our crowd enjoyed learning to dance on the wonderful concrete floor of the Coca Cola plant. Good friends like Lester Freeman and Doyle Felts, Tommy Wiseman, and many others dancing to some of our favorite tunes like "String of Pearls" or "Chattanooga Choo Choo" on a fine Victrola. The Christmas Sub Deb dances were a real social event for teenagers, and I remember the excitement of receiving a gardenia from Bobby. I would pin it on in my hair. Pat, Bobby was really a little shy and a bit timid in those days.

Later, during the Christmas season, we would go to the cotillion dances in all of the surrounding towns like Lewisburg, Pulaski, and even Murfreesboro. We had a wonderful time then with long stag lines and even no breaks. Good times were had in the summer at Lake Tullahoma especially when Bob Couch and Bobby would entertain our crowd with their funny diving antics in their vintage bathing suits. They were a sight to behold. Tullahoma High School was such fun. Bobby played cornet in the band and MTSU band director Joe Smith played our drums. Betty Brown Tipps and I were two of the majorettes in our marching band of probably 20 or 30. Bobby was a wonderful athlete and a very fine student.

Several of our high school boys went to military school, and Bobby made quite a record for himself at Castle Heights Military Academy in Lebanon in the time that he was there. As a senior, Bobby was elected captain of the football team, and I was honored when he asked me to be his homecoming queen. I don't know if he was nervous about the game or more nervous about presenting me with those flowers before the game.

Even though Bobby didn't graduate from THS, he always kept up with his friends, and our class of 1946. Last October, we gathered in Tullahoma for our yearly reunion, and Bobby and Pat were there. Didn't we have a good time, Pat, and we have lots of pictures to prove it. Many of you can add much more, but Bobby, thanks for the memories and for being such a dear friend. Pat, Robert, and Priscilla, thanks for letting me share just a little of his love those wonderful years, and Pat, I will truly always treasure that smile he gave us a few weeks ago in the hospital.

Hello, everybody, my name is **Sylvia Sanders Kelly** and as you can imagine I am related to Bobby Sanders. He's my first cousin. I really wasn't prepared to say anything but I couldn't let the opportunity go by without saying thank you to Bobby Sanders, to Pat, Robert, and Priscilla on behalf of the Sanders family. I think he was the cousin who made us a family. He was so good, he was so kind to everybody that without . . . can you imagine what this family would have been like without Bobby Sanders? I can't. Just a quick vignette--just a--I think there are hundreds of stories that could be told about him but I went to my 50th reunion at Vanderbilt last year. Bobby and I fortunately ended up at Vanderbilt at the same time even though he's six years older than I am. And he took me under his wing. He wanted to be sure that I was happy, that I got adjusted, that I got all the advice that I needed, and that I had a good time. So I really didn't remember how much he had done for me until the trip from Atlanta to Vanderbilt and I wrote home everyday from Vanderbilt and I told what I had done that day and who I had done it with, so I had four years of memoirs. 1950 was the year with Bobby and I was reading it to my husband because he didn't believe that I had such a good time at Vanderbilt and I wanted to prove it and I read, Bobby Sanders took me over to the Sigma Chi house and wanted me to meet some people. Bobby Sanders called to see if I was getting along, if I had any questions that any professors needed--just about every line in 1950 mentions Bobby Sanders. I wanted to say thank you Bobby Sanders for the sendoff you gave me at Vanderbilt, for the self-confidence you gave me and all of us. Thank you Bobby Sanders for being such a wonderful cousin.

Rev. David M. Maynard

What a full life, what a long life you've heard reviewed and we've taken time to honor today. We'll take a few minutes now to hear something that you'd like to share with the rest of the group, that you will really regret if you don't share and this is a good time to do it, you're invited to do that and then we'll conclude with the playing of "My Sweet Daddy" by his daughter, Priscilla.

My name is **Dr. Mike Bachler**. I'm a retired teacher. My wife and I travelled up from Athens, Georgia to be with you all for this special event. We first encountered the Sanders family when son Robert joined Boy Scout Troop 364 at Hobgood School. Jim Jernigan was the Scout Master and my two sons were in the troop. We did a lot of camping in those days and of course we had to travel. Like father like son, son Robert was preaching the gospel of the seat belt and we didn't put a key in the ignition until young Robert was strapped in. And we tried to strap down as many of the others as we could but by the grace of God and Dr. Sanders, we all survived and it has been a pleasure to maintain a friendship with the Sanders family these many years. Bless you, thank you for being a friend.

I'm **Laurie Smith Ziegler**, and one of the most regrettable things I have had was not getting to spend as much time with Bob and Pat and Robert, and Priscilla these last few years. We've grown up together, Robert and I were in kindergarten together and our families got to know each other from then on, and Bob and Pat have both been such a strong influence in my life and my family. I could tell you many stories, as all of you have. Bob kind of lead me to the profession I'm in. He was there to help me through my 8th grade science fair project, was our physician who we'd call—not our main pediatrician, Dr. Lewis, if you're here, but if we needed somebody or had a question, Bob would stop by the house and check on us. He spent many hours heard his stories which have been very influential in my life. I pulled out the other night, Pat, pictures from when you and Bob stopped by and visited me in Charleston, South Carolina, after I moved there. I'm a pharmacist. Bob had some influence on me going into the medical profession. For years I thought I might be a pediatrician and then ended up deciding to go into pharmacy and started out as a pediatric pharmacist because of the influence that they've had and as all of you know, and I just had to take this opportunity since I didn't get to see Bob that much here recently that I love him, always have and Pat, you and Robert, and Priscilla, that you are such a very special part of our family. There are four of us. I'm the oldest of four but they are such wonderful special people and have been to our family and to everybody else in this community as you've heard all over the state and the nation, and we love you.

Hi, my name is **Veronica O'Grady**, and I'm a friend of Priscilla's. As everyone's been talking today, I just wanted to bring your attention to the stained glass windows that are in the middle of either side and all the stories about the sheep and I noticed that, I thought it was pretty interesting. And also that he has gone on, looking over here to the left.

As I've been listening to the stories, I wrote something very briefly and I'd like to share that with you. It's called "An Angel Walked Among Us."

We gather here to honor the passing of a soul whose life has touched millions of lives. We are blessed and continue to be blessed by the legacy of love he has given in so many ways to his family, friends, and all the children that he will never even know. Dr. Robert Sanders, Daddy Bob, as my daughter always called him, his voice sparkled with gentleness, his heart was pure, his eyes were clear and his laughter true. Everyone who had the honor of being embraced by his love was left with a place in their heart that was lighter and brighter and that light continues to grow. Yes, an angel walked among us and now he's gone home. May we continue to honor his special love by carrying that generous love and laughter into our lives every day.

Thank you

I'm **Bob Laughlin**. I was the lobbyist for the Tennessee Hospital Association for 22 years. And one of the opportunities I had to deal with the legislature was with Bob and Pat. Now you've heard a lot of things, but I don't know if you've heard the first year that they came down to the legislature was like two innocents into the Devil's den.

They had great things in store and wanted to really pass that legislation that first year, and they tried, but it just wasn't going to go that first year because you had to educate legislators to what the issues were. And they were so dumb it's unbelievable. And that's what Bob and Pat saw was how dumb we were.

Don't you understand what this legislature will do? Yes, but not this year. And so, it didn't pass that first year. Now John Bragg got hold of it. I think you all know John Bragg. And John really helped but we had to come back the second year. And of course what happened was we had time across the state to let them know what happened in Australia because I'm sure you all know that was where they passed the first seat belt law. We also had the information about how it had helped in Australia to save the lives of children. So the second year it passed. I have to tell you, I wanted to come and just say to Pat I know how much she wanted and I don't know if you all know, but she was there every day with Bob calling on every office she could get to and pushing that issue. The biggest problem we had, of course, was the fact that some legislators, not naming them, who were from the country kept saying two things. One, "Well, you know, people in the country have pickup trucks, and they just like to have children ride in the back." And the second thing was "Mothers with little babies like to hold them." Well, as you well know, mothers holding babies is one of the most dangerous things that you can have. Finally, as you well know, in 1981, the "Babes in Arms Amendment" was finally removed from the law.

Now the thing that made me come up here was if you think about how many children's lives have been saved in Tennessee since that time, that is the memorial to Bob and Pat. Thank you.

Bobby Sanders was my next door neighbor back in Tullahoma, my life-long friend and my hero. God speed, old friend.

I'm **Nan Keenan** and I always think of Bobby Sanders as a huge Oak tree and his extended arms having a Minor bird on them who have an extensive, magnificent vocabulary. And this is Pat and the two of them are synonymous and I've seen Pat in action. I've seen them both in action and they were most helpful to me when I was starting the County Beautification Committee and some other things that I worked on here— Recycle Rutherford--and it just was a joy to know them. They are a loving couple, and they love life and we love them.

Rev. David M. Maynard

Well, you wouldn't have been here if you didn't have a connection, if you didn't have memories. For all those that have been shared and those that remain in our minds and hearts, let us be grateful and let us bring this service of memory to conclusion with Priscilla's song, "My Sweet Daddy."

song: "My Sweet Daddy", by Priscilla Sanders

I still remember your morning whistle
On lazy weekend days
When I could get up late
We'd make pancakes on the griddle
Then sit and watch the birds eat with us
Thank you for holding me
After a nightmare
When I was scared
I felt so loved.
I didn't want Monday to come.

I know now that nothing lasts forever
At least not here on Earth
But I take comfort
That you will always be
Locked inside my memory.
My sweet Daddy, my sweet, sweet Daddy.

I'd sit on your lap when you drove the tractor
On top of the world
I was your little girl
Looking out on the wide green pasture

We'd talk to the cows that you had named
And we could get each other to laugh
With funny faces and joke making
We were such friends
I didn't want those moments to end.

I know now that nothing lasts forever
At least not here on Earth
But I take comfort
That you will always be
Locked inside my memory.
My sweet Daddy, my sweet, sweet Daddy.

When I was three
I would sit on your knee
And cry, "Daddy don't die — Please don't leave me"
You'd say "I'll be around a long, long time
Don't you worry now
It's gonna be all right."

I know now that no one lives forever
At least not here on Earth
But I take comfort
That you will always be
Locked inside my memory.
My sweet Daddy. My sweet, sweet Daddy.

Jim Howard

As a fellow member of the Unitarian Fellowship in Murfreesboro with Pat and Bob, it gives me a great deal of pleasure to read the benediction.

"Beauty is before me and beauty is behind me; above me and below me hovers the beautiful. I am surrounded by it. I am immersed in it. In my youth I am aware of it and in all days I shall wake in the beautiful trail. In beauty it's begun, in beauty it's ended."

Rev. David Garth

Please stand as the family makes its way into the common room where I hope you will join them and have refreshments.

APPENDIX: Child Passenger Protection Law, 2007

In the 30 years since 1977, the Child Passenger Protection Law has been improved and also strengthened. Below is the text of the 2007 version of the law on the books in the state of Tennessee.

55-9-602. Child passenger restraint systems - Violations - Penalties. –

(a) (1) Any person transporting any child, under one (1) year of age, or any child, weighing twenty pounds (20 lbs.) or less, in a motor vehicle upon a road, street or highway of Tennessee is responsible for the protection of the child and properly using a child passenger restraint system in a rear facing position, meeting federal motor vehicle safety standards in the rear **seat** if available or according to the child safety restraint system or vehicle manufacturer's instructions.

(2) Notwithstanding the provisions of § 55-9-603, any person transporting any child, one (1) through three (3) years of age weighing greater than twenty pounds (20 lbs.), in a motor vehicle upon a road, street or highway of Tennessee is responsible for the protection of the child and properly using a child passenger restraint system in a forward facing position, meeting federal motor vehicle safety standards in the rear **seat** if available or according to the child safety restraint system or vehicle manufacturer's instructions.

(3) Notwithstanding the provisions of § 55-9-603, any person transporting any child, four (4) through eight (8) years of age and measuring less than four feet, nine inches (4' 9") in height, in a passenger motor vehicle upon a road, street or highway of Tennessee is responsible for the protection of the child and properly using a **belt** positioning booster **seat** system, meeting federal motor vehicle safety standards in the rear **seat** if available or according to the child safety restraint system or vehicle manufacturer's instructions.

(4) (A) If a child is not capable of being safely transported in a conventional child passenger restraint system as provided for in this subsection (a), a specially modified, professionally manufactured restraint system meeting the intent of this subsection (a) shall be in use; provided, however, that the provisions of this subdivision (a)(4) shall not be satisfied by use of the vehicle's standard lap or shoulder safety **belts** independent of any other child passenger restraint system. A motor vehicle operator who is transporting a child in a specially modified, professionally manufactured child passenger restraint system shall possess a copy of the physician's signed prescription that authorizes the professional manufacture of the specially modified child passenger restraint system.

(B) A person shall not be charged with a violation of this subsection (a) if such person presents a copy of the physician's prescription in compliance with the provisions of this subdivision (a)(4) to the arresting officer at the time of the alleged violation.

(C) A person charged with a violation of this subsection (a) may, on or before the court date, submit a copy of the physician's prescription and evidence of possession of a specially modified, professionally manufactured child passenger restraint system to the court. If the court is satisfied that compliance was in effect at the time of the violation, the charge for violating the provisions of this subsection (a) may be dismissed.

(b) All passenger vehicle rental agencies doing business in the state of Tennessee shall make available at a reasonable rate to those renting such vehicles an approved restraint as described in subsection (a).

(c) (1) A violation of this section is a Class C misdemeanor.

(2) In addition to or in lieu of the penalty imposed under subdivision (c)(1), persons found guilty of a first offense of violating this section may be required to attend a court approved offenders' class designed to educate offenders on the hazards of not properly transporting children in motor vehicles. A fee may be charged for such classes sufficient to defray all costs of providing such classes.

(d) Any incorporated municipality may by ordinance adopt by reference any of the provisions of this section, it being the legislative intent to promote the protection of children wherever and whenever possible.

(e) Prior to the initial discharge of any newborn child from a health care institution offering obstetrical services, such institution shall inform the parent that use of a child passenger restraint system is required by law. Further, the health care institution shall distribute to the parent related information provided by the department of safety.

(f) (1) There is established within the general fund a revolving special account to be known as the child safety fund, hereinafter referred to as the "fund."

(2) All fines imposed by this section shall be sent by the clerk of the court to the state treasurer for deposit in the fund.

(3) Any unencumbered funds and any unexpended balance of this fund remaining at the end of any fiscal year shall not revert to the general fund, but

shall be carried forward until expended in accordance with the provisions of this section and § 55-9-610.

(4) Interest accruing on investments and deposits of the fund shall be returned to the fund and remain a part of the fund.

(5) Disbursements from, investments of and deposits to the fund shall be administered and invested pursuant to the provisions of title 9, chapter 4, part 5.

(6) The state treasurer may deduct reasonable service charges from the fund pursuant to procedures established by the state treasurer and the commissioner of finance and administration.

(7) The department of health is authorized, pursuant to duly promulgated rules and regulations, to determine equitable distribution of the moneys in the fund to those entities that are best suited for child passenger safety system distribution. Funds distributed pursuant to the provisions of this section shall only be used for the purchase of child passenger safety systems to be loaned or given to the parent or guardian.

(g) (1) (A) Notwithstanding the provisions of § 55-9-603, any person transporting any child, nine (9) through twelve (12) years of age, or any child through twelve (12) years of age, measuring four feet, nine inches (4' 9") or more in height, in a passenger motor vehicle upon a road, street or highway of Tennessee is responsible for the protection of the child and properly using a **seat belt** system meeting federal motor vehicle safety standards. It is recommended that any such child be placed in the rear **seat** if available.

(B) Notwithstanding the provisions of § 55-9-603, any person transporting any child, thirteen (13) through fifteen (15) years of age, in a passenger motor vehicle upon a road, street or highway of Tennessee is responsible for the protection of the child and properly using a passenger restraint system, including safety **belts**, meeting federal motor vehicle safety standards.

(2) A person charged with a violation of this subsection (g) may, in lieu of appearance in court, submit a fine of fifty dollars ($50.00) to the clerk of the court which has jurisdiction of such offense within the county in which the offense charged is alleged to have been committed.

(3) No litigation tax levied pursuant to the provisions of title 67, chapter 4, part 6, shall be imposed or assessed against anyone convicted of a violation of this subsection (g), nor shall any clerk's fee or court costs, including but not limited to

any statutory fees of officers, be imposed or assessed against anyone convicted of a violation of this subsection (g).

(4) (A) Notwithstanding any provision of subsection (f) to the contrary, the revenue generated by ten dollars ($10.00) of the fifty dollar ($50.00) fine under subdivision (g)(2) for a person's first conviction under this subsection (g), shall be deposited in the state general fund without being designated for any specific purpose. The remaining forty dollars ($40.00) of such fifty dollar ($50.00) fine for a person's first conviction under this subsection (g) shall be deposited to the child safety fund in accordance with subsection (f).

(B) The revenue generated from such person's second or subsequent conviction under this subsection (g) shall be deposited to the child safety fund in accordance with subsection (f).

(5) Notwithstanding any provision of law to the contrary, no more than one (1) citation may be issued for a violation of this subsection (g) per vehicle per occasion. If the driver is neither a parent nor legal guardian of the child and the child's parent or legal guardian is present in the vehicle, the parent or legal guardian is responsible for ensuring that the provisions of this subsection (g) are complied with. If no parent or legal guardian is present at the time of the violation, the driver is solely responsible for compliance with this subsection (g).

(h) As used in this section, unless specified otherwise, "passenger motor vehicle" means any motor vehicle with a manufacturer's gross vehicle weight rating of ten thousand pounds (10,000 lbs.) or less, that is not used as a public or livery conveyance for passengers. "Passenger motor vehicle" does not apply to motor vehicles which are not required by federal law to be equipped with safety **belts**.

(i) A person who has successfully met the minimum required training standards for installation of child restraint devices established by the national highway traffic safety administration of the United States department of transportation, who in good faith installs or inspects the installation of a child restraint device shall not be liable for any damages resulting from any act or omission related to such installation or inspection unless such act or omission was the result of the person's gross negligence or willful misconduct.

(j) Notwithstanding any provisions of this part to the contrary, for any child transported by child care agencies licensed by the department of human services pursuant to title 71, chapter 3, part 5 and transported pursuant to the rules and regulations of such department, such rules and regulations shall remain effective until the department amends such rules and regulations; provided, however, that the department shall either promulgate rules consistent with the provisions of this part or promulgate rules exceeding, based on applicable federal regulations or standards, the provisions of this part no later than January 1, 2007.

(k) (1) The failure to use a child restraint system shall not be admissible into evidence in a civil action; provided, however, that evidence of a failure to use a child restraint system, as required by this section, may be admitted in a civil action as to the causal relationship between noncompliance and the injuries alleged, if the following conditions have been satisfied:

(A) The plaintiff has filed a products liability claim;

(B) The defendant alleging noncompliance with this section shall raise this defense in its answer or timely amendment thereto in accordance with the rules of civil procedure; and

(C) Each defendant seeking to offer evidence alleging noncompliance with this section has the burden of proving noncompliance with this section, that compliance with this section would have reduced injuries and the extent of the reduction of such injuries.

(2) Upon request of any party, the trial judge shall hold a hearing out of the presence of the jury as to the admissibility of such evidence in accordance with the provisions of this subsection (k) and the Tennessee Rules of Evidence.

(3) Notwithstanding any provision of this subsection (k) to the contrary, if a party to the civil action is not the parent or legal guardian, then evidence of a failure to use a child restraint system, as required by this section, may be admitted in such action as to the causal relationship between noncompliance and the injuries alleged.

[Acts 1963, ch. 102, §§ 1, 2; 1977, ch. 114, §§ 1, 2; T.C.A., § 59-930; Acts 1981, ch. 86, §§ 1, 2; 1985, ch. 183, § 1; T.C.A., § 55-9-214; Acts 1986, ch. 866, §§ 2, 3; 1989, ch. 564, §§ 2-6, 9; 1989, ch. 591, § 113; 1995, ch. 112, §§ 1, 2; 2000, ch. 945, § 1; 2001, ch. 463, §§ 1, 2; 2003, ch. 299, §§ 1-9; 2004, ch. 809, § 1; 2005, ch. 55, §§ 1, 2.]

Magazine article:
Bless the Seats and the Children:
the Physician and the Legislative Process

written by: Robert S. Sanders, MD and Bruce B. Dan, MD
November 9, 1984, JAMA magazine, vol. 252:18; 2613-2614

"The care of human life and happiness, and not their destruction, is the first and only legitimate object of good government."
Thomas Jefferson

Motor vehicle accidents are the leading cause of death and injury for all children beyond infancy, and more than 90% of children ride unprotected in automobiles. Physicians have recognized that the current epidemic of highway casualties among our very young is essentially preventable and that state-by-state child restraint laws are the most practical approach to "immunizing" most of these children against their leading killer.

Since the nation's first child-restraint legislation, the Tennessee Child Protection Act, was implemented in January 1978, 49 states have enacted similar laws. In each state, pediatricians and other physicians have played a key role in lobbying for this effort. This heartening experience should stimulate physicians of all specialties to consider extending these laws to protect older children and adults from the carnage witnessed daily on our streets and highways.

The remarkable dividends resulting from the Tennessee law, as reported in this issue by Decker et al, document the merit of physician participation in safety legislation. Thus, we will review the Tennessee experience as a guide for future, inevitable legislative struggles.

The idea for legislation requiring the protection of small children while riding in automobiles evolved in 1974 as a recommendation from the Tennessee State Health Planning Council. Ironically, a legislative committee of this council in 1973 failed to approve this proposal, suggesting instead "educational" avenues. This detour in preventing unnecessary morbidity and mortality occurred despite evidence that during the three-year period from 1973-1975, almost 70 children younger than 5 years were killed in Tennessee automotive accidents and some 3,000 suffered serious injuries.

Thus the thrust for a means of protecting small children was a challenge accepted by the Tennessee Chapter of the American Academy of Pediatrics. Their arguments in favor of a *legislative* approach were that (1) educational efforts to convince adults to use seat belts had been notably unsuccessful, (2) restraint devices were known to reduce the chance of death by 90% and injury by 80%, (3) hospital and rehabilitation costs for accident victims are enormous, (4) young children, safely restrained, are better behaved during travel than unrestrained young riders, (5) unrestrained children are responsible for some accidents by disturbing the driver and, as flying missiles, injure other passengers during collision; and (6) most other industrialized nations mandate seat belt use. (The jurisdictions with seat belt laws, 1967 to 1984, are Australia, Austria, Belgium, Bulgaria, Canada (eight provinces), Czechoslovakia, Denmark, England, Finland, France, Hungary, Ireland, Israel, Japan, Luxembourg, Malaysia, the Netherlands, New Zealand, Norway, Portugal, Puerto Rico, South Africa, Spain, Sweden, Switzerland, USSR, and West Germany).

In Tennessee, the initial legislation in 1976 required all children younger than 4 years to be restrained in car seats while riding in any vehicle. The bill was killed in committee. The reasons stated for its premature death were reservations concerning individual liberties, difficulties in enforcement, and potential economic burden on low-income families.

However, during the next year, a major "grass roots" movement was started by a small but dedicated band of physicians and safety advocates. The law was rewritten to focus on the family unit, endorsements were obtained from the state's major medical and safety organizations, "fact sheets" were supplied to key pediatricians throughout the state for strategic distribution to legislators and the media, and presentations before legislative committees featured testimony from parents whose children had been severely injured in motor vehicle accidents (with a number of physicians present to "eyeball" committee members). Media coverage of the hearings and floor debates was also felt to exert favorable influence.

But the important factor in convincing elected officials that the legislation had merit was direct contact by constituent pediatricians and other physicians. That busy physicians would appeal to legislators in regard to a political issue that wasn't self-serving, except for the safety of little children, was considered refreshing by many Tennessee lawmakers.

The bill was passed in 1977. Unfortunately, an amendment (introduced by a legislator who recounted that his most joyous experience was seeing his newborn grandchild come home in his mother's arms) was attached, allowing adults to hold small children in their laps. Subsequent accident experiences demonstrated that these "Babes in Arms" were at an extraordinarily high risk, and the loophole was removed in 1981.

Dividends from the Tennessee law have been gratifying. Use of "kiddie car seats" has notably increased, deaths and injuries have been reduced, and enforcement innovations by state troopers have received commendation from the nation's safety community. Central in this national effort has been the American Academy of Pediatrics, which along with other medical and safety organizations holstered the thrust for widespread enactment and implementation.

Many physicians and safety advocates believe it is now timely and politically palatable to encourage state legislatures to assert themselves further in the protection of older children and adults. Two recent events support this premise.

174

The state of New York has enacted the nation's first mandatory seat belt law, and the Department of Transportation has issued a requirement for the gradual introduction of air bags or passive restraint devices into new automobiles, unless a significant number of states (accounting for two thirds of the U.S. population) approve mandatory seat belt laws by April 1989.

The Tennessee experience demonstrates that reduction in unnecessary morbidity and mortality may not respond to education efforts alone but may require protective legislation. Physicians are the ones who must annually attend to the 2.5 million broken bodies and witness the grief over the 50,000 dead. It would seem that active support for legislation requiring the universal use of seat belts, a simple yet responsible safety practice, would bear remarkable dividends.

Related reading:

Shelness A., Charles S: Children as passengers in automobiles: The neglected minority on the nation's highways. *Pediatrics*, 1975; 56: 271-284

Williams AF: Observed child restraint use in automobiles. *AJDC* 1976; 130:1311.

Decker MD, Dewey MJ, Hutcheson RH jr. et al: The use and efficacy of child restraint devices. The Tennessee Experience, 1982 and 1983. *JAMA* 1984; 252:2571-2757.

Sanders, RS, Casey EL: The Tennessee Child Passenger Protection Act: Origin, legislative success and national impact. Proceedings of the 23rd Conference of the American Association for Automotive Medicine, Louisville, Oct 4-6, 1979.

Tennessee Motor Vehicle Traffic Accident Facts: 1972-1975. Nashville, Tenn., Tennessee Department of Safety, 1972-1975.

Scherz RG; Restraint systems for the prevention of injury to children in automobile accidents. *Am J Public Health* 1976; 66:451.

Christopherson ER: Children's behavior during automobile rides: Do car seats make a difference? *Pediatrics* 1977; 60-69-74.

Hall WL, Council F. Warning. In cars children may be hazardous to their parent's health. Proceedings of the 24th Conference of the American Association for Automotive Medicine, Rochester, NY, Oct 7-9, 1980.

Children as Passengers in Automobiles:
The Neglected Minority on the Nation's Highways

written by: Annemarie Shelness and Seymour Charles, M.D., 1975
from *Pediatrics* magazine, August 1975; 56: 271-284

from Physicians for Automotive Safety, Irvington, New Jersey (A.S.), and Beth
Israel Medical Center and the New Jersey College of Medicine and Dentistry,
Newark, New Jersey (S.C.)

In its continuing efforts to reduce mortality and morbidity on the nation's
highways, the federal government is offering incentive grants to states passing
legislation that would require safety belts to be worn.

Infants and small children are specifically excluded from these Model Safety
Belts Usage Laws issued by the Department of Transportation (DOT) for states
to enact, although the use of special child restraints is "strongly" recommended.

It is ironic that a nation that ranks the welfare of children high on its list of
priorities is in the process of mandating the use of protective devices for parents
and older siblings, but denies the right to similar protection to the very young.
The reason for this policy is, however, understandable. Taking into account the
prevailing negative attitude to car restraints, the DOT anticipates strong
resistance to mandating their utilization. (belt laws were introduced in 26 states
but none were passed.) The legislation as proposed would simply require safety
belts already installed to be used; safety devices for infants and small children
would have to be specially purchased, such a requirement is expected to
jeopardize still further enactment of the legislation.

In the past, only about 20% of the motoring population were consistent belt
users. The ignition interlock system in 1974 model cars which prevents the
engine from starting unless front belts are buckled is claimed to have
substantially increased belt usage in vehicles so equipped. (The system was
outlawed by Congress in November 1974.) But the vast majority of children
continue to ride in cars either unprotected or restrained in devices that do not
afford effective crash protection. Failure to install devices correctly further
compounds the problem. (This statement, originally based on day-to-day
observations, has now been documented in a recently published study.)

Statistics or the year 1972 show that in the 0 through 4 age group alone,
1,000 vehicle occupants were killed and 77,000 were injured. (Contrary to
popular belief, more small children are killed and injured inside the vehicle than
outside.) Although the motor vehicle poses the greatest single threat to a child's
life once the neonatal period has passed, the protection of infants and small
children in automobiles has received minimal attention from government
agencies, industry safety organizations, and the medical profession.

Unlike crib deaths for which there is no known prevention, and trauma from poisoning, falls, drowning, and fires whose prevention is largely a matter of unrelenting parental vigilance, the prevention or attenuation of auto injuries requires only simply parental action at the start of each trip.

INFANTS AND CHILDREN NEED SPECIAL RESTRAINTS

Burdi et al. explain that, "A child's body dimensions, proportions, and biomechanical properties are so markedly different from those of an adult that a child can not for design purposes (of child restraints), be considered simply as a scaled-down adult: The following points are made:

In an adult, the prominent anterior superior iliac spines are used as anatomical anchor points for lap belts, but in children these spines are not well developed until about 10 years, and basically do not exist.

This fact, combined with the bulges of flesh in the pelvic region of a small child, makes correct positioning of a lap belt difficult; in an impact situation, the belt could ride up, possibly causing serious internal injuries.

In addition, the small child's higher center of gravity, resulting in greater body mass above the belt, may cause the child to whip forward more violently than an adult, placing relatively greater loads on the lap belt.

These and a number of other considerations have led to the conclusion that small children must be protected by distributing the force of the collision over a large body area. It is generally accepted that special restraints should be used until the child weighs at least 18.1 kg., preferably larger, but if no special restraints are available, use of standard belts is preferable to using no restraints at all. No special restraints accommodating a child weighing more than 22.6 kg are on the market at this time.

THE HISTORY OF CAR SAFETY DEVICES

Children's car seats were in use long before auto safety as we now understand it was even heard of. The Bunny Bear Company has been making such seats since 1933, but these devices were merely intended to provide support and confinement and raise the child up for better visibility thereby preventing interference with the driver. "Safety" was, indeed, a factor, but not *crash* safety.

Even in the second half of the 1960's when safety belts began to make their appearance and crash protection became a hotly debated issue, the special needs of children too small to wear belts continued to be ignored. The responsibility for design specifications was clearly the province of the DOT: The Twin Highway Acts passed by Congress in 1966 authorize the DOT to set safety standards for the design of motor vehicles and related equipment.

GOVERNMENT RULE-MAKING

More than four years were to pass before Motor Vehicle Safety Standard No. 213 for "Child Seating Systems" came into effect April 1, 1971. (Devices for infants not yet able to sit up without support were not covered).

Major innovations included: (1) means of anchoring the device to the seat of the vehicle with a standard lap belt; (2) provision of a harness to keep the child contained within the device, and (3) head support to minimize "whiplash" injury. It was further required that the device withstand a specified gradual pulling force, a "static" test requirement employing a wooden block to simulate the child occupant--a simple lab procedure. Manufacture of the popular bail-type models that hook over the back of the car seat was no longer permitted.

Although these were significant improvements, the new seats did not look much sturdier than their pre-standard counterparts, and it was soon confirmed that the test procedure required by DOT's National Highway Traffic Safety Administration (NHTSA) was, indeed, woefully inadequate. In October 1976, six months following the implementation of Standard 213, Dr. Verne Roberts, then head of the Biosciences Division of the University of Michigan Highway Safety Research Institute, the scientist in charge of the crash testing of child restraints under a government contract, felt compelled to expose the inadequacies before the final report on these tests was released by the DOT in September 1972.

Ten months later, in August 1972, the results of a series of simulated crash tests sponsored in the Consumers Union, also conducted at the Michigan research facility, drew national attention to the "shocking" shortcomings of the federal standard based on static load criteria. Of the 17 car restraints tested, all meeting government specifications, 12 were rated "not acceptable."

The Michigan research employed simulated crash tests, i.e.,"dynamic" tests, which reproduce the violent, split-second forces unleashed in real-life crashes. This consists of installing a device containing a properly restrained child dummy occupant on a standard car seat which, in turn, is mounted on an impact sled. The sled is propelled at predetermined speeds into a concrete crash barrier. The event is recorded with high-speed movie cameras and appropriate parameter technology of all strategic forces that come into play. The majority of devices tested at 30 miles per hour either collapsed, thereby adding to the injury potential, or pivoted forward, allowing the dummy's head to slam into the instrument panel. Furthermore, many permitted the vehicle lap belt to dig deeply into the dummy's abdomen despite indications that such loads may exceed the child's tolerance limits.

REVISION OF STANDARD 213

NHTSA's procrastination in revising test requirements as soon as it was shown that static tests were unrealistic in reproducing the violent stresses that occur in an actual crash situation is incomprehensible. An interim standard *could* and *should* have been issued to remove at least the worst seats from the market. At the same time efforts to formulate criteria for optimum crash protection should, of course, have continued.

It was not until March 1974 that a notice to revise Standard 213 was finally issued. The proposed effective date is September 1975, an interval sufficient to allow another 2,000,000 inadequate devices to be purchased by unsuspecting parents who put their trust in government regulations. At the time this goes to press, no final specifications for upgrading the standard have yet been issued; the effective date for new requirements, therefore, seems a long way off.

Under the proposed revisions *all* devices manufactured for the use of small children in motor vehicles will become subject to regulations, including car beds, and carriers for infants not previously covered. Dynamic tests would be substituted for the static tests required now. Proposed are frontal impacts at 30 miles per hour and lateral and rearward impacts at 20 miles per hour. Devices subjected to these forces would have to remain intact and retain the test dummy, limiting its head motion to 18 inches in front and 19 inches in lateral and rear crashes. The dummy would also have to be retained in a roll-over.

NHTSA has now seen fit to go from one extreme to the other. Test criteria required under the new proposals are so stringent a number of devices recently developed for crash protection are not capable of meeting them. Moreover, Melvin and Stalnaker question the advisability of restricting forward head movement to 18 inches.

In negotiating the usual compromise with manufacturers, it must be hoped that NHTSA will strive for a realistic balance between the optimum protection attainable, convenience of use, and child contentment. A parent who does not carry out all instructions for use because they are too cumbersome or time-consuming will greatly reduce or entirely defeat the protective properties of the device. A child who rebels at the restrictions the device imposes could succeed in exasperating the parent to the extent that the device may not be used at all.

AVAILABILITY OF EFFECTIVE DEVICES

Although a few effective devices developed by automobile companies have been available for a number of years, lack of public education and failure on the part of manufacturers to promote these products resulted in a deadlock: Companies blamed public apathy for their refusal to advertise, but at the same time parents anxious to obtain effective protection for their children did not know what to look for or where to look. As early as 1965 Ford introduced the Astro-Guard, but there was little demand for it and it was soon taken off the market. In 1967, Ford acquired the rights to a drastically innovative device, the Tot-Guard, which dispenses with a harness and, instead, surrounds the children

179

with a protective shield.

General Motors brought out a child safety seat in 1967; although superior to the flimsy seats available at that time, it failed to meet Standard 213 and was replaced by the Love Seat in June 1973. GM's Infant Carrier has been on the market since 1970.

In many instances Ford and General Motors dealerships, at that time the only sources of supply, had no knowledge of the existence of these devices, and some of those who did, refused to take orders! Orders that were accepted were followed by a long waiting period--often of several months. Senator Warren G. Magnuson, a dedicated safety advocate, accused Ford of "hiding the Tot-Guard away in its own dealers' parts departments, the place the consumer is least likely to look."

THE POSITION OF CAR SEAT MANUFACTURERS

Clearly in all matters of rule-making, NHTSA has industry opposition to contend with, in this case the Juvenile Products Manufacturers' Association (JPMA) whose member companies make a large range of equipment for children, e.g., playpens, cribs, strollers, bassinets, and so forth.

Originally, the pattern for JPMA opposition was the same as that of the motor vehicle manufacturers in their traditional resistance in all matters of rule-making proposed over the past eight years by the NHTSA. More recently the juvenile products industry appears to have recognized its responsibility to the public, and is now in support of upgrading design specifications of Standard 213.

While disclosures of the inadequacies of devices in general use clearly had little if any influence on speeding up government rule-making, the publicity created resulted in a number of articles in newspapers and family magazines as well as in television exposure. With awakening public concern, the demand for crashworthy products is increasing and manufacturers, skeptical in the past, are now finding that safety "sells."

At this time 12 devices are on the market, meeting safety criteria established by the staff of the Biosciences Division of the University of Michigan Highway Sagfety Research Institute. (These were developed voluntarily without waiting for government intervention, but several of these companies continue to market less expensive devices that conform to the deficient federal standards currently in force.) A comprehensive report on crash testing of these devices can be found in the March 1975 issue of *Consumer Reports*. The Consumers Union deserves much credit for the progress that has been and continues to be made.

FOCUS ON CHILD PROTECTION IN THE SCIENTIFIC LITERATURE

Safety advocates have long been aware that the protection of small children presented a problem. As early as 1960, Moore and Lillienfield expressed concern for the safety of child passengers, recommending that they occupy the rear seat. In 1962, Dye discussed "Securing the Package" to prevent ejection or contact with the vehicle interior.

In 1966, Aldman described the development of a rearward-facing seat in Sweden, explaining that the "proportions between the head and neck in small children are unfavorable for any restraint system that does not support the head. . ." (Rearward-facing devices which distribute crash forces evenly over the child's back are utilized in this country only for the infant. In Sweden the majority of older children also travel facing the rear.) In the same, 1966, Appoldt reported on crash tests which demonstrated the inadequacy of child restraints available at that time and the need for further research, concluding that all devices should be dynamically tested before they are marketed.

In March 1968 an article in *Physicians' Management* described devices then available for the protection of children, pointing out that pediatricians are in a "uniquely favorable position to advance parent and public understanding--and also that of the child--of this health problem that the National Academy of Science has termed the 'neglected disease of our society.'"

In October 1966, Siegel et al, reporting on a clinical study of occupants, left no doubt regarding the value of effective restraints to reducing the severity of injuries. The introductory remarks to the paper are as valid today as they were then: "The 'Battered Child Syndrome,' an injury pattern resulting from parental abuse, has been widely described in the medical literature and in the press. Yet automobile collisions are the most common cause of injuries in childhood and they have received little attention. . .The injury complex should be described as the 'neglected child syndrome,' since ample evidence indicates that a great many of these injuries could be readily prevented by simple parental action."

In the pediatric literature, Burg et al, made a strong case for involvement of the profession, presenting a helpful description and illustrations of devices then (1970) on the market. Alsever, (1971) and Glassauer and Cares (1972), reporting on two pediatric fatalities and two infants rendered paraplegic, respectively, made a plea for the use of restraints.

LITERATURE FOR PARENT EDUCATION

Among booklets covering accident prevention currently available to parents, *Congratulations to the New Mommy*, published by the Easter Seal Society in 1970, ignores auto safety entirely. Ironically, the Society's current Poster Child is the victim of a car crash. *The Cure and Safety of Children*, by Jav M. Arena, M.D., published by the Council on Family Health in 1972, deals with the hazards that confront the child in traffic but fails to mention the need for protection inside the car.

A 1971 edition of *Infant Care*, published by the Office of Child Development,

U.S. Department of Health, Education and Welfare, treats the subject all too briefly and also incorrectly. A diagram shows a child wearing a single diagonal strap combined with a lap belt positioned across the abdomen--the worst possible choice even from among the many unsatisfactory devices on the market. The illustration would more appropriately serve as an example of what to avoid. For safe protection, devices must (1) incorporate a crotch strap to prevent the lap belt riding up, (2) provide support for *both* shoulders and (3) provide for firm anchorage of the device to the seat of the car.

HEW's blunder is all the more surprising because as early as 1967 the same agency published a helpful folder entitled *Selecting Automobile Safety Restraints for Small Children* now out of print) which contained illustrations of the Tot-Guard and the original General Motors seat, infinitely happier choices than the one made in *Infant Care.*

NHTSA's own booklet, *What to Buy in Child Restraint Systems.* may have served a marginally constructive purpose when Standard 213 first came into force in 1974. But for patents seeking information now, the publication fails to throw any light on "what to buy" and only serves to add to the existing lack of understanding of the whole subject. Its withdrawal from circulation would in the authors' opinon render a public service.

The *Automobile Safety Belt Fact Book,"* published by the same safety agency, is packed with valuable information on the functions of belts, but parents are given little help on what to do to protect their little ones. Although the two devices illustrated are a type of infant carrier and the Ford Tot-Guard, respectively, no brand names or sources of supply are given. Until quite recently only car dealerships could provide devices resembling those shown (and presumably, therefore, also recommended) but the chances of parents finding them were remote.

It is, indeed, unfortunate that the policies of government agencies and so many other organizations, including professional associations, preclude identification of products by brand name, without permitting exceptions to be made even where no similar product exists. These policies have been partly responsible for valuable information failing to reach the public.

Among child care books currently in print, even recent publications are lacking in information: *Raising a Responsible Child* (1973) deals with youngsters' behavior in the car, warning that accidents can be caused by driver distraction, but no mention is made of the use of restraints. *Home and Family Medical Emergencies* (1973) covers auto safety at length and in considerable detail, demonstrating a concern for and understanding of the problem, but the authors' only source of information appears to have been the government safety agency, with the result that the deficient federal standard is endorsed. The only device illustrated is as poor an example of a "safety" seat as the one contained in HEW's *Infant Care* mentioned above.

182

Parents' Encyclopedia (1973) covers the subject correctly and in depth, but the listing of devices, true in 1971 when Standard 213 first came into effect, was long outdated by the time the book went to press. *A Parents' Guide to Child Safety* (1973) urges the use of restraints but contains incorrect information, some effective devices are, however, mentioned by name. *Today's Child* (1972) includes a discussion on children's car seats but provides confusing information and leaves parents in the dark about the names of effective devices.

But progress is being made: *Let's Stop Destroying Our Children* (1974) deals with the subject all too briefly but the information given is correct and effective devices are named. Two books giving auto crash protection the attention it merits are due to appear shortly: *The Child Health Encyclopedia,* edited by Richard Feinbloom, M.D., of the Boston Children's Medical Center, is due to come out in the fall of this year. The *Parents' Almanac,* edited by Glenn Austin, M.D., is scheduled for publication in January of next year.

Among books on child care currently in print covering accident prevention, 19 either do not deal with auto safety at all or do so inadequately and/or incorrectly(Appendix). This includes Dr. Benjamin Spock's all-time classic *Baby and Child Care* whose latest edition (1974) mentions cars only in connection with "automobile polish poisoning."

Exceptions worth noting are Jean Carper's *Stay Alive,* (now out of print), which discusses the protection of children in cars with a great sense of urgency, advocating the use of what limited means of protection were available at that time (1965). *How to Protect Your Child* which covers the subject adequately within the scope of knowledge available in 1968, and *Belts On, Buttons Down,* sponsored by Boston Children's Medical Center, which is a helpful publication dealing exclusively with children traveling in cars. Published in 1971, much of the information it contains is now, unfortunately, outdated.

Parents turn to books on child care for guidance on child-rearing. The protection of children in cars is a vital aspect of child health, and we urge that information on the subject be added and/or updated before a publication is reprinted.

Naming the effective devices and referring readers to sources of authoritative up-to-date information are essential at this time and will remain so not only until the revised government standard comes into effect, but until it can be safely assumed that stock piles of inadequate devices have been taken off the market (Implementation of safety standards applies to the date of manufacture--not sale.)

CHANGES IN RECOMMENDATIONS MUST BE ANTICIPATED

The subject of child restraints is involved and far from resolved. The sate-of-the-art is of recent vintage, and what was true at one time may quickly be superceded by more recent research findings. It is therefore essential to keep in close touch with developments in the field.

For example, recommendations for positioning an infant car bed have been changed. It was formerly suggested that the bed be placed in the fore-aft position, i.e., parallel with the long axis of the vehicle. More recent findings have shown that it is preferable to place the bed, which should be of strong construction and well-padded, on the seat of the car, cover it with a net, and anchor it with two vehicle lap belts. The bed should be positioned with the child's head in the center of the vehicle. But there are no strong, well-padded beds on the market, and securement also presents quite a problem. It is probably much safer and certainly far more convenient to transport an infant in one of the four effective carriers now on the market, at least until car beds meeting safety specifications are developed.

Another case in point is the safety harness. Use of a harness is frequently advocated on the grounds that it offers the child greater freedom of movement. Crash testing has, however, shown the "freedom" to be potentially hazardous. A harness should keep the child firmly in place.

As research continues, it is quite possible even now that further changes in recommendations will be made. It would be helpful, therefore, if publications on child care indicated sources of up-to-date information on the subject. Such a source is Physicians for Automotive Safety, an organization which has made child auto safety one of its major areas of concern over the past seven years. *Don't Risk Your Child's Life!*, a pamphlet developed in consultation with the staff of the Biosciences Division, University of Michigan Highway Safety Research Institute, provides the public with continually updated information. First published in April 1971, the folder is now in its 12th printing, totaling 250,000 copies, of which seven contained major revisions and most contained minor changes. (A sample copy and price list are available on request.)

A primary source of information for research purposes is, of course, the Michigan Safety Research Institute, Action for Child Transportation Safety, a citizens' group affiliated with Physicians for Automotive Safety, can also be relied upon to furnish authoritative information.

THE IMPORTANCE OF USING SAFETY DEVICES CORRECTLY

Too many parents continue to look upon children's car seats as "positioning" rather than crash safety devices, and the intended function of these restraints must, therefore, be brought to their attention. All too often one of the expensive effective devices can be seen merely resting on the seat of the car. Sometimes the seat itself is anchored, but the child sitting in it is not strapped into the harness.

At present, Standard 213 requires only weight and height limitations and a declaration of compliance with government specifications to be affixed to the device itself. Instructions for installation and use are usually supplied loose inside the carton where they are easily overlooked. A brief explanation of the function the device is intended to perform and of the critical importance of correct installation and use must be prominently posted on the device itself. This is far more important than the information now displayed on the seats, and should be required under the revision of Standard 213.

A number of seats must be anchored at the top (Table) to prevent them from breaking and/or pivoting forward in a crash. This requires joining a strap leading from the top of the device to the lap belt in the seat behind or to an anchorage assembly bolted to the rear window ledge. The former method renders a set of belts inoperable, as well as creating an obstacle for rear seat passengers, while the latter necessitates permanent installation of an anchorage assembly--an added inconvenience and expense.

The authors' ongoing scrutiny of restraining devices in use shows that the majority are *not* anchored at the top. Similar findings are being reported by other users including Melvin and Stalnaker.

PERFORMANCE RATINGS OF CHILD RESTRAINTS

The consumers union rates products in order of merit based on efficiency of performance in relationship to price--including any other criteria applicable to a particular product--to enable the consumers to obtain the best possible value for their money. In the testing of child restraints cost was not a factor. The first two test series rated safety performance alone, but the report on the most recent tests stresses the importance of correct installation and use, and convenience was taken into consideration in the determination of ratings.

A similar rating was adopted in recent editions of the Physicians for Automotive Safety pamphlet on child protection (Table) but its value to the public is being questioned and the practice may be discontinued. Too much emphasis is being given to differences in performance, differences that are in many instances only minor. *All* restraints meeting established dynamic test criteria offer infinitely better crash protection than those merely meeting current government requirements. They are also more effective than standard safety belts which give virtually *no* protection in side impacts.

Parents naturally wish to purchase a device with a high safety rating. But those with the highest safety performance ratings are also the most difficult to use: if not used correctly, devices top rated for safety performance will give less protection than those awarded a lower rating. The Ford Tot-Guard, for example, which is by far the most convenient (and versatile) device to use, is being turned down by parents because of poor side protection. (Table). Yet use of the lap belt alone ensures effective crash protection. Convenience is a key factor in proper utilization.

IN-HOSPITAL EDUCATION OF NEW PARENTS

Of the 3,000,000 infants born in the United States each year, most go home in a car. Traditionally the infant is held in its mother's arms. This is inconsistent with accepted principles of crash protection.

Credit for the spreading practice of educating expectant and new parents on the need for appropriate restraints for the infant goes to Dr. Arnold Constad of Union, New Jersey, who recognized that the most appropriate time to begin instruction is at the time parents prepare for the care of a new baby. At Overlook Hospital, Summit, New Jersey, he initiated an educational program involving physicians, nurses, and volunteer staff. Instruction begins in the course of antenatal visits and is reinforced post-partum in the hospital and during subsequent visits to the pediatrician.

Through the efforts of Dr. and Mrs. Constad on behalf of Physicians for Automotive Safety, the program, funded by grants from the New Jersey State Department of Health and the New Jersey Chapter, American Academy of Pediatrics, is now functional in most of New Jersey's maternity centers. A number of hospitals throughout the United States and Canada are also using the teaching manual, film, and handout literature developed for the program.

In the states of Washington and Wisconsin progress is being made through the initiative of Dr. Robert Scherz of Tacoma, Washington, chairman of the American Academy of Pediatrics Committee on Accident Prevention, and Mr. Ernest Cooney, a health educator of Madison, Wisconsin.

Dr. Scherz has gathered significant evidence of the effectiveness of the program he initiated more than three years ago at the Madigan General Army Hospital in Tacoma, Washington. Mr. Cooney reports similar findings from his work in Wisconsin, where a state-wide "Child Safe" program is currently being launched.

While the most immediate objective of the program is to ensure that the infant leaves the hospital safely "packaged," in an appropriate carrier--an essential first step towards continued protection--the value of repeated reminders as part of the child's regular check-ups has been demonstrated. Dr. Constad believes the understanding that brings about acceptance of restraints for the newest member of the family can motivate parents to protect their older children and indeed the safety belts themselves.

Key to "System Used" and Explanations of
Approaches to Crash Protection
1. For the infant:
   A device facing rearward or sideways is recommended; the infant rides in a semi-upright position, restrained with a harness. The carrier is secured with a lap belt.
   2. For the child able to sit up without support
   a. The shield: In a collision, the child would be thrown into an impact-

186

absorbing shield which distributes crash forces evenly over a large body area. The device is secured with a vehicle lap belt. No harness is necessary (except for the Bobby-Mac which requires a harness in conjunction with the shield); the child is adequately protected by the shield alone.

b. The "conventional" car seat: A five-point harness restrains the child; the seat is secured with a vehicle lap belt. A number of seats require top anchorage as well.

c. The safety harness: Effective protection is provided at low cost. Anchorage assembly must be bolted to the floor of the vehicle or the rear window ledge. The child may sit on a booster cushion.

Several devices combine the design features of 1 and 2, a & b.

There are effective devices currently available (1975). Among them are the: Astroseat, Bobby-Mac, Guardwell, Infantseat Harness, Infant Carrier, Kantwet Car Seat #885, General Motors, Motor Toter, Safety Shell #74 & #75, Sweetheart II, Tot-Guard, and the Wee Care #597.

Related Reading:

Collins, Robert D., M.D., *Ernest William Goodpasture: Scientist, Scholar, Gentleman*, Hillsboro Press, Franklin, Tennessee, 2002

Grayson, Robert, M.D., *Robert S. Sanders, M.D. Oral History Project*, American Academy of Pediatrics, Pediatric History Center, April 20, 2004

Hemby, Lisa, Immunizing Against the Highway Epidemic, *The Tennessean Magazine*, supplement of the *Sunday Tennessean* newspaper, February 1978, pp: 22-24

Meador, Clifton K., M.D., *Med School: A Collection of Stories About Medical School, 1951-1955*, Hillsboro Press, Franklin, Tennessee, 2003

Merrill, Robert E., M.D., *Amos Christie, MD, The Legacy of a Lineman*, Hillsboro Press, Franklin, Tennessee, 2006

Price, Susan Crites, Robert Sanders: Lifelong Advocate for Children, *Childhood Injury Prevention Quarterly*, summer 1992, 4:1

Rowland, Betty, *Bob and Pat Sanders oral history project*, Gore Research Center, Middle Tennessee Oral History Collection, MTSU, December 15, 2000.

Scherz RG; Restraint systems for the prevention of injury to children in automobile accidents. *Am J Public Health* 1976; 66:451.

Honors Received Related to Child Passenger Safety

1977

1. Distinguished Alumnus, Castle Heights Military Academy, Lebanon, Tennessee, May 1977.
2. Certificate of Appreciation from the State of Tennessee, signed by Governor Ray Blanton, Nashville, Tennessee, October 20, 1977.
3. Special Certificate of Appreciation from the Committee of Accident and Poison Prevention, American Academy of Pediatrics, New York, NY, November 8, 1977.
4. Tennessee Public Health Association Health Worker of the Year, Nashville, Tennessee, November 17, 1977.

1978

5. Special Certificate of Appreciation from the Tennessee Child Passenger Safety Program, Nashville, Tennessee, May 10, 1978.
6. Ross Award for Distinguished Service in Maternal and Child Health Care, Southern Branch, American Public Health Association, Nashville, Tennessee, May 16, 1978.

1979

7. Distinguished Public Service Award from the Tennessee Academy of Health Education, Inc., May 1979.
8. Certificate of Special Recognition from the American Association for Automotive Medicine, Annual Meeting, Louisville, Kentucky, October 5, 1979.

1980

9. Distinguished Service Award from the Tennessee Medical Association, Nashville, Tennessee, April 9, 1980.
10. Service to Mankind Award from the Murfreesboro Sertoma Club, December 16, 1980.

1984

11. Distinguished Service Award from the National Transportation Safety Board during the Lifesavers III National Conference on Alcohol Countermeasures and Occupant Protection, Orlando, Florida, May 8, 1984.

1986

12. Tennessee Highway Safety Award from the Tennessee Safety Belt Use Coalition, Knoxville, Tennessee, May 23, 1986. (Presented to Bob and Pat Sanders)

1988

13. Murfreesboro Education Association Community Award for Distinguished Service to Murfreesboro City Schools, March 1988. (Presented to Dr. and Mrs. Robert S. Sanders)

14. Advocated for Children, Certificate of Merit, presented by Contemporary Pediatrics, New York, NY, May 9, 1988.

1991

15. Tennessee "Pediatrician of the Year" (Tennessee Pediatric Society, Chattanooga, Tennessee, September 1991).

1992

16. Lifetime Achievement Award, (National Safe Kids Campaign-Washington, DC, May 1992).

1994

17. Paul Harris Fellowship Award, (Murfreesboro Rotary Club, Murfreesboro, Tennessee, June 1994).

1995

18. Rutherford County Health Department Clinic Building named "The Robert Smith Sanders Public Health Clinic." (Murfreesboro, Tennessee - June 1995).

1996

19. Public Service Award: National Highway Traffic Safety Administration -NHTSA- (national convention: Women's Highway Safety Leaders- Nashville, Tennessee, September 1996).

1997

20. Amos Christie Memorial Award for Continued Commitment to Public Service, from Vanderbilt Center for Health Services, Fall of 1997.

1998

21. the Annemarie Shelness Award for lifetime achievement in child passenger safety, at the Lifesavers Conference, Cleveland, Ohio, March 27, 1998.

22. the 1998 World Traffic Safety Award, "In recognition of commitment as an advocate for the safety of children and dedication to influencing legislation that increased vehicle occupant protection throughout the nation." World Traffic Safety Symposium, New York, NY, April 16, 1998.

2003

23. Distinguished Career Award presented to Robert S. Sanders, MD, "In recognition of outstanding dedication and leadership in injury control and emergency health services with contributions and achievements that have a significant and long term impact on the problem of injury." Injury Control

and Emergency Health Services Section, American Public Health Association, November 2003.

24. Award for Superior Achievement presented to Robert S. Sanders, MD, FAAP,

"In appreciation for your lifelong leadership and outstanding contributions to child   passenger safety. The agency is forever grateful for your exceptional accomplishments, and your selfless dedication to saving and preserving the lives of American children." U.S. Department of Transportation, National Highway Traffic Safety Administration, November 2003.

2004

Robert S. Sanders, M.D., FAAP, MD, '55, HS'55, '59, FE'62-'63, CF, '80-'89, of Murfreesboro, Tennessee, received the 2004 American Academy of Pediatrics Fellow Achievement Award, given to an AAP Fellow who has made an exceptional contribution to the area of injury and poison prevention. He was given the award for his work with the AAP Tennessee Chapter's Committee on Accident Prevention, leading efforts to require the use of infant safety restraints. The Tennessee Child Protection Act, the first such law in the country, was passed in 1977. Since then, Sanders worked to create a mandatory seat belt requirement for older children and adults, which became Tennessee law in 1986. Sanders, who is recovering from multiple strokes at home, and his wife, Pat, are very proud of their children - Robert, Jr., who has written an autobiography book, "Overcoming Asperger's: Personal Experience & Insight," and daughter, Priscilla, a singer/songwriter in Nashville, who has just released a CD, "Ride a Wave with Me."

2006

The Dr. Robert S. Sanders Award for Outstanding Public Policy Achievement in Child Passenger Safety, presented by Safe Kids Worldwide, Washington, DC, awarded to Safe Kids Kansas, October 19, 2006.

2008

Vanderbilt Distinguished Medical Alumni Achievement Award, presented to Bob's wife Patricia Pelot Sanders, October 24, 2008.

HEALTH DEPARTMENT SHOULD HOLD NAME OF
DR. ROBERT S. (BOB) SANDERS
the *Daily News Journal*, February 19, 2006, Murfreesboro, Tennessee

Louis Armstrong's "What a Wonderful World" was played at the memorial service for Dr. Bob Sanders when he was eulogized Feb. 4, 2006 at the First Presbyterian Church. It was a fitting song for a man who spent his life trying to make this a better world, especially for children.

When Bob and Pat Sanders moved to his family's historic farm on Armstrong Valley Road in 1963, he opened a pediatric practice, but he couldn't bring himself to charge much and his patients' parents couldn't afford to pay much. Not long afterward, he entered the public health field, commuting some days to places like Carthage, Smithville and Lebanon to treat children.

In 1969, Sanders was afforded the opportunity to stay a little closer to home when he became the director of Rutherford County Health Department and chief physician at the historic building on 303 N Church Street near downtown Murfreesboro.

Always known for his calm demeanor, Sanders was adept at working with little children. One of his subtleties was drawing a small animal on tongue depressors to get the attention of his young patients and encourage them to hold still and open their mouths long enough for him to check the back of their throats.

In the mid-'70s, Bob and Pat started their odyssey toward passage of child restraint laws, an attempt to protect small bodies from becoming projectiles in bad car crashes.

The Sanders ran into a firestorm of protest when they went to the state Legislature, where members felt their freedoms would be stripped away by such a new law. Consequently, when the law requiring kids to ride properly strapped in child-restraint seats passed in 1977, it contained an amendment allowing older persons to hold children in their arms while riding.

We know now, of course, that the "Babes in Arms" loophole was a foolhardy measure that, in fact, endangered children more than it protected them, because children who ride in the laps of their parents are likely to be crushed immediately against the steering wheel or thrown through the windshield in crashes.

The Sanders persevered, nevertheless, and in 1981, the "Babes in Arms" provision was removed. Now, state law requires everyone riding in a vehicle to wear a seat belt, and it all started with the Sanders' efforts some 30 years ago.

Their concern for children and refusal to give in to political pressure led to protections that saved the lives of countless children over the years, and now our seat belt laws are protecting the lives of all Tennesseans.

Subsequently, Bob Sanders earned the nickname, "Dr. Seat Belt," but the humble Sanders was never one for bragging. So let us do it for him.

For his years of dedication to public health, his bedside demeanor, and his heroic efforts in seat belt legislation, along with those of his wife Pat, the new health department at the corner of Maple and Burton Streets should be named the Dr. Robert Sanders Health Department.

Public health would not be what it is today across America without his efforts.

U.S. Congressional Record
HON. ALBERT GORE, JR. OF TENNESSEE
IN THE U.S. HOUSE OF REPRESENTATIVES
Monday, January 30, 1984

Mr. GORE. Mr. Speaker. I am delighted to join with Congressman GLENN ANDERSON to introduce H.R. 4616 a bill to improve child passenger safety.

Over the last three decades we have seen the death rate for preschool children decline by 53 percent. Virtually all of this decline resulted from a 62 percent reduction in death rates from medical illness. In contrast, the rate of child passenger deaths remained unchanged. Highway death is the only major cause of death for these children that has not declined. In fact today it is the single leading cause of death of children. For this reason I believe we must immediately recognize that highway deaths and injuries are the number one public health threat that all our children face.

The bill we are introducing provides a program to meet this challenge. It encourages each State to combine their wisdom and expertise in ad-ministering programs within their State to put forth a child passenger safety program that will work best in that individual State.

Last session I introduced the bill H.R. 3483, the Child Highway Safety Act. While I continue to believe the concepts embodied in that legislation are those that we must ultimately strive for, H.R. 4616 represents an important first step on that road.

The Federal Government's interest in protecting the Nation's children has a long and successful history. Federal dollars have been well spent for State programs in maternal and child health, nutrition, primary care, and immunizations. The combined Federal/State programs in these areas have resulted in the significant decline of deaths due to medical illness I cited earlier. We must now turn our attention to motor vehicle safety and put an end to the senseless and easily preventable tragedy of so many of our children needlessly dying on our highways.

I have a special interest in this legislation for two reasons: First, as a father of four young children I have a special empathy for families who have had to suffer the death or crippling injury to a child involved in a motor vehicle accident; and second, this bill builds upon the hard work of many of my fellow Tennesseans, as Tennessee was the first State to enact a law requiring the use of child safety restraints 7 years ago. I particularly would like to note the efforts of Dr. Robert Sanders, Dr. Sam Carney. Dr. Ed Caldwell, and Mr. Edward Casey. Mr. Casey of Nashville, Tenn., first had the idea for a child passenger safety law back in 1975. Dr. Robert Sanders of Murfreesboro, Tenn., with the help of his wife Pat and Doctors Carney and Caldwell, worked tirelessly to see that vision realised.

Through an act that has truly demonstrated unique dedication, they have taken Mr. Casey's idea and today deserve the thanks of all of us for the great strides that have been made. Because of the overwhelming success of Tennessee's child highway safety law, 40 other States plus the District of Columbia have passed similar laws mandating the use of child restraints by preschool children.

Hearings on this legislation will be held before the Subcommittee on Surface Transportation following the February district work period. I am hopeful and optimistic that with the broad, bipartisan support this legislation enjoys, it can become law before the end of year.

U.S. Congressional Record
U.S. House of Representatives
Tuesday, January 31, 2006
U.S. Representative Bart Gordon
Honoring the Life of Dr. Robert Sanders

MR. GORDON. Mr. Speaker, I rise today to honor the life of Dr. Robert Sanders, a generous man who dedicated his life to keeping our children safe. Dr. Sanders passed away earlier this month.

Dr. Sanders wore many hats in my hometown of Murfreesboro, where he resided. He was a husband, father, farmer and pediatrician. He served as Director of the Rutherford County Health Department from 1969 to 1991 and served as the county's medical examiner from 1983 to 1999.

As a pediatrician, Dr. Sanders cared for thousands of Murfreesboro's children. As an advocate for child safety restraints in vehicles, he saved the lives of countless more. Because of Dr. Sanders' tireless efforts, Tennessee became the first state in the nation to pass a law requiring children in vehicles to be restrained in safety seats. Every other state in the country eventually followed Tennessee's lead.

Even after the passage of that law in 1977, Dr. Sanders kept working to keep children safe while riding in vehicles. His efforts led to a state seat belt law and loaner programs to help low-income families acquire child restraint seats.

The Tennessee Medical Association, Tennessee Public Health Association and Tennessee Pediatric Society all have honored Dr. Sanders for his great service.

Although Dr. Sanders' dedication to a noble cause will benefit children for generations to come, I know he will be deeply missed by his family, his friends and countless Middle Tennesseans like me.

The following books are available directly from Robert S. Sanders, Jr. They may also be ordered at retail price directly from Ingram Book Company of LaVergne, Tennessee, or from www.Amazon.com and www.Amazon.co.uk .

ORDER FORM

Please send me:		quantity	amount
Dr. Seat Belt: the Life of Robert S. Sanders, MD	@$22.95 _____		$_____
Mission of the Galactic Salesman *special reduced price*	@$12.00 _____		$_____
Mission Beyond the Ice Cave: Atlantis-Mexico-Zotola	@$15.95 _____		$_____
Heritage Findings from Atlantis	@$15.95 _____		$_____
Galactic Salesman Trilogy Synopsis	@$ 9.95 _____		$_____
Walking Between Worlds:			
a novel of an American in Mexico	@$19.95 _____		$_____
Overcoming Asperger's: Personal Experience & Insight	@$17.95 _____		$_____
On My Own Terms: My Journey with Asperger's	@$19.95 _____		$_____
En Mis Propios Términos: Mi Jornada con Asperger's	@$19.95 _____		$_____
My Hikes in California's Sierra Nevada Mountains	@$ 9.95 _____		$_____
EXODUS: the Dolph/in Saga (by Martin Enticknap)	@$16.50 _____		$_____
Arc of the Ancients and other Poetry (by Martin Enticknap)	@$14.95 _____		$_____
Tennessee residents add 9.25% sales tax to subtotal			$_____
– Out of state orders, NO sales tax –			$ 0000
Plus shipping and handling for one book			
(surface rates: $3.50 within USA, $7.00 foreign)			$_____
Plus shipping and handling for each additional book			
(surface rates: $3.00 within USA, $5.00 foreign)		_____	$_____

Please remit funds in US dollars.　　　　　　　Total enclosed　$_____

Make checks or money orders payable to: **Robert S. Sanders, Jr.**

Discounts:
10 to 99 books:　　10% off
100 or more books: 20% off

Books make great gifts and/or Christmas presents for your friends and relatives.

Send order to:
　　　　Name_____
　　　　Address_____
　　　　City_____State_____Postal Code_____
Phone number _____

Send orders and checks payable to:
Robert S. Sanders, Jr.
P.O. Box 1275
Murfreesboro, TN 37133 USA FAX: 615-893-2688

Westview Press

5500 Central Avenue • Boulder, Colorado 80301
Frederick A. Praeger, Publisher • (303) 444-3541

Available in paperback

A PRACTICAL GUIDE TO THE CONDUCT OF FIELD RESEARCH IN THE SOCIAL SCIENCES

Elliot J. Feldman

This book guides social science students in defining problems for research and in organizing and conducting a research program. Confronting philosophical as well as practical problems, it will serve both graduate students and under-graduates well, providing the former with assistance in preparing their theses and informing the latter on how to develop research papers. Dr. Feldman addresses basic questions about topic selection, interviewing, surveys, documentation, and other research methods. While his emphasis is on comparative research, any student pursuing field research will

"Solid in concept and highly practical in execution. The approach and techniques which it presents are ones I would like . . . students in social research to command."
—Gilbert F. White

A Practical Guide to the
Conduct of Field Research
in the Social Sciences

Other Titles of Interest

The Modern Middle East: A Guide to Research Tools in the Social Sciences, Reeva S. Simon

International Terrorism: An Annotated Bibliography and Research Guide, Augustus R. Norton and Martin H. Greenberg

Bibliography on World Conflict and Peace: Second Edition, Elise Boulding, J. Robert Passmore, and Robert Scott Gassler

Aging and the Aged: An Annotated Bibliography and Library Research Guide, Linna Funk Place, Linda Parker, and Forrest J. Berghorn

African International Relations: An Annotated Bibliography, Mark W. DeLancey

A Select Bibliography on Economic Development: With Annotations, John P. Powelson

National Planning in the United States: An Annotated Bibliography, David E. Wilson

About the Book and Author

A Practical Guide to the Conduct of
Field Research in the Social Sciences

Elliot J. Feldman

This book offers students in the social sciences simply stated, direct guidance in defining problems for research and in organizing and conducting a research program. Confronting philosophical and practical problems, it will serve both graduate and undergraduate students well, providing the former with assistance in preparing their theses and informing the latter on how to develop research papers. Dr. Feldman addresses basic questions about topic selection, interviewing, surveys, documentation, and other research methods. While his emphasis is on comparative research, any student pursuing field research in political science, sociology, anthropology, geography, social psychology, and other branches of the social sciences will find the book helpful. The concentration on data collection, rather than analysis, will make it particularly useful for those undertaking a research project for the first time.

Elliot J. Feldman, director of the University Consortium for Research on North America, is assistant professor of politics at Brandeis University and research associate at the Harvard University Center for International Affairs. Dr. Feldman was formerly visiting assistant professor of policy analysis at the University of British Columbia and was assistant professor of European politics and political science at the Johns Hopkins University School of Advanced International Studies. A former Woodrow Wilson Fellow, Dr. Feldman has also received fellowships from The Fund for Peace, the German Marshall Fund of the United States, and the United States Arms Control and Disarmament Agency.

A Practical Guide to the Conduct of Field Research in the Social Sciences

Elliot J. Feldman

Westview Press / Boulder, Colorado

Copyright © 1981 by Westview Press, Inc.

Published in 1981 in the United States of America by
  Westview Press, Inc.
  5500 Central Avenue
  Boulder, Colorado 80301
  Frederick A. Praeger, Publisher

Library of Congress Cataloging in Publication Data
Feldman, Elliot J.
  A practical guide to the conduct of field research in the social sciences.
  Bibliography: p.
  1. Social sciences—Field work. I. Title.
H61.F37   300'.723   80-15796
ISBN 0-89158-980-5
ISBN 0-89158-981-3 (pbk.)

Printed and bound in the United States of America

For Gilbert F. White and Theodore J. Lowi,
scholars who have been my teachers and friends

Contents

4. Organizing and Managing Field Research

Foreword

Many research workers in social science will be skeptical about the need for a guide to the conduct of field studies. Some may argue that the apprentice investigator can learn best at the elbow of the seasoned scientist or by trial and error. And it will be asserted that an abundant number of disciplinary treatises and handbooks on study methods are already available.

A few years ago I would have been inclined to place less emphasis upon the utility of writing down rudimentary suggestions. There is a kind of mystical belief among certain field workers that they have learned the art and can communicate it to others through association on the job. They consider that little else is required.

As I look over the results of a goodly number of recent studies I conclude that this skepticism is unwarranted in most instances. The record shows that some field investigations have gone astray and that Murphy's law has been at work on the very points enumerated by Elliot Feldman. More than a few young social scientists are going into unfamiliar field situations without adequate preparation. Much of the literature on methodology in anthropology, geography, political science, psychology, and sociology appraises the issues involved in approaches to interviewing and observation. However, these treatises more often deal with such questions as the validity of interview responses and the danger of impressing an external view on a local culture than with the more earthy problems of planning and carrying out the study. In addition to dealing with these problems, Feldman looks at the extremely sensitive and complex ethical issues of inquiring into individual and community lives.

I strongly recommend that any young investigator contemplating going into the field take a look at the Feldman guide. The book also makes a convenient checklist for the old hand, and it is likely to suggest points that may otherwise be overlooked. Even if it illuminates no new techniques for the experienced researcher, it will underline the basic importance of high-quality data and the way in which field technique determines the validity of the data. All too often broad generalizations and sophisticated analysis are based on data drawn from casual and inaccurate information obtained through inquiry on the ground.

The guide draws heavily upon two lines of investigation that have been expanding and in which Feldman and his colleagues have been most active. One is the growing emphasis upon policy-oriented research, which typically is interdisciplinary. The other is the interest in comparative studies across cultural and political boundaries. Such studies tend to involve collaboration with local residents. Both types of research may call upon field workers with different experience and training. For them, a few common ground rules may be helpful, and a simplified and direct review of lessons may be especially important in assuring valid and precise information.

The questions raised by Feldman inevitably arise in the course of field study. Better they do so sooner than too late.

Gilbert F. White
Institute of Behavioral Science
University of Colorado at Boulder

Preface

Social science research has long been regarded as mysterious. There always has been an apparent need or desire to give to social science research the scientific legitimacy normally attributed to laboratory work. To this end, social scientists frequently have been vague about exactly what they do and exactly how they get their information. When not vague, explanations are so frequently laden with jargon that even other social scientists cannot figure out what is being done.

The objective of this book is to demystify one area of social science research—field research—by describing in simple terms what it is and some of the ways in which it can be pursued effectively. Three areas of social science field research have received substantial treatment in the past: the work of anthropologists, the work of sociologists, and the work of behavioral scientists refining surveys. My own orientation is toward policy research, and I have given this volume a modest bias accordingly. Furthermore, since the value of comparative research is becoming more fully recognized, I have decided to discuss field research problems often in terms of comparative efforts. The difficulties and advantages of comparative research are poorly understood, the special features of comparative research nowhere articulated. Despite these two biases, however, the discussion here ought to serve all social science field research.[1]

This volume is a "handbook," a volume of "how to." Social science graduate students frequently complain of two principal deficiencies in their education: (1) they receive role models but little or no guidance in how to teach; and (2) they receive countless examples of research but little or no guidance in how to conduct research themselves. They are asked to find out things, but they are rarely told where to look or how to find out. When they set out on master's and doctoral theses, they all too frequently find themselves in the field uncertain of what to do. Many social scientists have suggested to me that up to three months of settling down and getting acquainted should always be allowed before serious research can begin. In the days when grant money was more abundant and few felt rushed to complete their degrees, such an assertion was especially convenient for foreign vacations. My own experience in the field tells me that the disorientation is more the consequence of ignorance than of natural causes, that it is not always a necessary feature of research, and that, to a large extent, it can be avoided.

It is certainly true that every research project is different, that every individual who conducts research will have peculiar personal qualities that affect procedures, and that every locus of research dictates particular needs. It is also true that some places take more getting used to and that some kinds of projects require a slower pace than others. My own research has taken me to five foreign countries and six different regions of the United States. I have found that, despite the peculiarities, certain general factors emerge that can be applied to almost all settings and situations. From this experience, and from discussion with colleagues also engaged in field research, I have concluded that this "practical guide," at least for the advanced industrial world, has a universal application.

Some of the suggestions will raise complex and serious moral questions. Because this book is intended as a practical guide and not as a philosophical treatise, I will point out where I think moral issues are involved but will not discuss these issues. They are surely appropriate subjects for concerned discussion and debate, and they are not ignored here as if to suggest that they should be avoided. Rather, it is up to each researcher to evaluate moral implications in a given case. A practical guide, unfortunately, can do no more than point out where what is practical may not necessarily be ethical. I think I would be remiss if, because in some instances ethical judgment would discard apparently practical solutions to problems, I therefore failed to suggest, for all cases, practical solutions. This choice, too, of course, may be criticized, but it is a choice I make in an effort to be honest and consistent in the fulfillment of the objectives of this guide.

This book emphasizes data collection, not analysis. The behavioral literature is concerned more with analysis, but as we shall see, serious doubts are raised over the quality of data. Hence, behavioralists, whose basic inclinations may differ from my own, may at least pause here to reconsider the source of the numbers on which they so heavily rely.

In the field, numerous problems arise that seem peculiar. This guide should reduce the number of apparently peculiar problems by indicating that many such problems arise elsewhere, have been experienced by others, and tend toward a general solution. Not all suggestions here should necessarily be followed. The researcher's own intuition may in the end be the best guide. Nevertheless, the weight of experience has proven the worth of many solutions proposed here.

Although this volume makes particular reference to field research, I want to emphasize that it should be useful to all social scientists who leave their libraries (and more recently their laboratories) to collect data. The examples used are all drawn from my personal research experience and occasionally the experience of colleagues, which means they are real, not abstract, examples. Furthermore, I have attempted to put things in simple—even inelegant—terms, for I do not attempt here to justify or to defend field research, but rather to provide some guidance for it. The novice then may accelerate in becoming expert by using this guide. Those uncomfortable, and often unprofitable, first months of quiet desperation may be better managed in light of another's experience. And I hope the experience of new research will bring from some reader a new guide with better tips and more helpful information. The ultimate objective is to expand the number and improve the quality of people conducting field research in social science, so that we may know more, sooner, about our social, political, and economic world.

Elliot J. Feldman

Notes

1. Eugene Bardach has argued that the requirements of policy research differ from those of other social sciences. In some respects (due especially to short deadlines and political volatility) policy research does impose different requirements, as in lining up expert defenders and timing carefully the release of results. Nevertheless, the similarities far outweigh the differences, and experiences are applicable across the social science disciplines. See Eugene Bardach, "Gathering Data for Policy Research," *Urban Analysis* 2 (1974): 117–144.

Acknowledgments

I have been fortunate to have had the opportunity to test the effectiveness of these ideas on students of four different levels in three different institutions of higher education. Originally developed as a series of lectures in 1974, the manuscript underwent changes based on what students found difficult to understand and put into practice. At the Johns Hopkins School of Advanced International Studies, master's candidates used the presentation as an introduction before conducting intensive field research on airport development and citizen participation in Milan and Paris; at the University of British Columbia, fifth-year commerce students followed these guidelines for a series of team field projects in Vancouver; at Brandeis University, a team of undergraduates, ranging from sophomores to seniors, put the suggestions here into practice on the common problem of solid waste disposal in Greater Boston, and their efforts were followed by a similar team of doctoral candidates. In each instance I was able to profit from their experience and further refine and improve the presentation.

Liz Shultis and Alice Levine of Westview Press have contributed unerring professional advice for achieving order and clarity without ever losing the spirit or style of a teaching book. A number of scholars, in addition, have provided thoughtful and useful ideas for the manuscript. Gilbert F. White of the University of Colorado first taught me the joy of field research and was the first to give the manuscript a sympathetic and useful reading. Others who contributed significantly to a final version include Theodore J. Lowi of Cornell University, Jerome Milch of the University of Pittsburgh, Stephen Weinberger of Dickinson College, Bill Zumeta of UCLA, Peter Sheras of the

University of Virginia, and Clark Gilmour of the University of British Columbia. This list includes scholars in political science, geography, history, psychology, business, and policy analysis. But the most valuable observations came inevitably from my wife, Lily Gardner Feldman, whose own sensitivity to students and their needs helped me to seek out the clearest phrases and the most intelligible examples. Whatever remains unclear or incorrect is my own fault.

E.J.F.

A Practical Guide to the Conduct of Field Research in the Social Sciences

1
Choosing Subjects and Objects of Research

What is research? What does it mean to do research? Let us agree that a directed inquiry involving evidence that must be gathered—not just intuited—is research. Research involves the collection of information for some specific purpose associated with answering questions, solving problems, or generating understandings. We undertake research in order to know, to understand, to explain, or to predict—or all of these things or some of them. The key, however, is that research is a purposeful task.

The wonders and the ills of the world present us with more than enough questions to occupy us superficially for many lifetimes. If we choose to inquire—that is, if we are inclined to research—how do we decide what to do research on? For our purposes, there are three pertinent responses to this question. The first is that we are engaged in research within the disciplines of social science. We each have our own peculiar explanations for why we engage in social science research instead of, say, the study of the atom. I will not try to answer here why we do this kind of research; let it suffice that we have made this particular disciplinary choice our first premise. But, given that premise, what do we mean by it? That is, what is social science research?

Let us agree that by social science research we mean the inquiry into problems involving human and institutional interaction. More particularly, I am referring to research concerned with the way men and women interact, as individuals and as groups, and with the way they structure their governments for the purpose of managing, guiding, and directing their public affairs. Social scientists are concerned with individual, group, and institutional goals and processes and with what men and women seek and how their aims are pursued individually and through institutions. Research into social activity—whether political or economic—is social science research.

Given that we are engaged in social science research, two responses remain to the question "How do we decide what to do research on?" One response concerns the questions we ask, the *subject* for our inquiry: What do we want to know about? The other response concerns the vehicle for the subject, which is the *object* of research: How will we find out about it?

Choosing a Topic

The choice of a research topic is intensely personal. Choices are made consciously, half-consciously, subconsciously, and unconsciously, and the quality of the research, in the long run, may well correspond to the kinds of choices we have made. You can best choose a topic by asking: What is most important to me? What question would I most like answered? Obviously, there are some boundaries within which such questions must be posed. If you declare that what interests you most is the meaning of life, you will be hard-pressed to pursue an effective program of research. However, there is an order of inquiry that will guide you to discover just how narrow your question must be. Once you have asked your question—that is, once you have defined your subject—you must then ask, "What will I do to find the answer?"

Effective research is systematic. Traveling as far as possible for as long as possible may be a popular method for investigating the meaning of life, but it will not qualify as a program of research. What questions, exactly, will we ask? Where? Of whom? On our travels, to whom will we speak? Our mortality obliges us to appreciate that our time is limited. We cannot speak to everyone. We must choose among the multitudes. What will be the basis of our choices? Shall we speak only to the rich? Only to the poor? Only to the powerful? Only to the weak? To some of each? Shall we sample opinion? How many views in each category shall we solicit? As soon as we begin asking these kinds of questions, we cannot help but discover that (1) we must be selective, and (2) we must be systematic. These two discoveries must guide the rest of our inquiry.

The subject of research should be something of personal importance or consequence. It is true that what is important to us may not be important to others, but because it is important to us, we can hope to be committed and to persevere when the answers seem few and the questions seem to multiply. Pursuing personal interests does, however, carry with it a problem involving the values we bring to bear in the very choices we make. We must consider carefully why something seems important to us and whether its importance is generated by selfish interests, by intellectual curiosity—or by both. There is no harm in pursuing research generated out of selfish interest, but there *is* harm in not being aware of our own motivations. We must separate our selfish interests from the systematic task and make every effort to suspend our judgments while selecting evidence. We might set out to prove something, but only the evidence—and not our own interests—can ultimately prove it. If we delude ourselves into accepting certain conclusions before the evidence is gathered, the research is destined to fail.

The distinction here is a very important one. Our research is committed because we choose both subject and object, but we cannot predetermine or prejudge the outcome of our inquiry. Our research is ideological because we choose what questions to ask, and our choice of questions cannot help but be a profoundly ideological proposition. Thus, there is no suggestion here that research is value-free. Rather, I am suggesting that in reaching conclusions we must suspend judgment, collecting and weighing evidence with open minds, conscious of the reasons underlying the choices of subject and object that we have already made.

What's First: Subject or Object?

Whether we choose the subject or the object first, the subject must be *matched* with the object. That is, we may not have a burning question we want to answer, such as (a burning question for me, at least) "Why was Weston, Illinois, chosen as the site for an atomic accelerator?" but we might be interested in knowing everything possible about atomic accelerators.[1] The object of our research, then, will be atomic accelerators, and the research will involve collecting all the information we can about these machines. In beginning to assemble this information, we will be obliged to ask a subjective question, for, whereas the object provides the vehicle for data collection, the subjective question is the instrument for putting the information into some kind of order. We will be confronted by what I call the "So what?" of our inquiry. The object may come first, but we must inevitably attach the subject to it if the results are to be reported systematically.

It is not certain, either, whether it is preferable to choose the subject or the object first. But let us consider for a moment what we must do after we have chosen a subject. For research purposes, we probably cannot ask, "What is the meaning of life?" There is nothing wrong with the question, but the method we must adopt to answer it cannot bear up to such breadth or vagueness. Given the constraints on our time, we must select a systematic method for examining the question. That method must involve something or someone. If we ask, "Why was Weston, Illinois, chosen as the site for an atomic accelerator?" we can identify within the question at least four objects for inquiry: the village of Weston, the state of Illinois, atomic accelerators, and choosers of the site. And if we focus our systematic inquiry on these four objects, we are likely to formulate at least some hypothetical answers to our subjective questions. Furthermore, if we ask a broader question, such as "How do sites for science projects get chosen?" it is probable that our case study will lead the way to a tentative answer. For, no matter how broad the question (defining the subject), the answer needs examples. Cases and examples are derived from objects.

Choosing the subject, then, tends to identify the objects for study. We could pose any number of subjective questions in this vein. A question such as "Why do experts exclude ordinary citizens from important technical decisions?" would lead us to examine experts, ordinary citizens, technicians, and technical decisions.[2] "Is conscription necessary to raise an army?" leads us to conscription as a program, necessity as a concept, and armies.[3] In every instance, our first task after posing the subjective question is to ask, "What must we look at in trying to answer this question?"

Choosing the object first is sometimes easier (especially if we do not have any burning conceptual questions of our own), but it is often harder to do effective analysis by proceeding this way. We may sense, for example, that cities are decreasingly habitable, but our vague feelings on the matter may lead simply to a desire to know all about urban planning. If urban planning is to be the object of our inquiry, we must then ask more specifically, "What *about* urban planning?" Ultimately we will have to pose a subjective question. It might be, "Are cities less habitable because of poor urban planning?" or "Could urban planning improve the plight of our cities?" Again, we should seek to identify the object of inquiry by carefully examining the question we pose. If we ask whether cities are less habitable, we will need to examine cities, urban planning, and the concept of habitability. That is, the terms used in asking the question will always determine the first stage of our inquiry. Even if we have started with an object, we must ultimately pose a question about it. The great "So what?" should hang over all research, and it should oblige us to think hard about the "what."

The problem here is not one of merely defining the terms. Rather, it is a problem of grasping concepts. Let us pursue the urban planning example to see how we acquire a focus in our research. What does it mean for a city to be less habitable? For that matter, what kinds of communities shall we include under the name "city?" Shall we choose communities on the basis of geographic size, population size, population density, local law? By determining what it means to be habitable (and, therein, more or less habitable), and by deciding what to include in the category of "city," we are setting down criteria. Those criteria will guide our choice of objects into narrower areas. For example, we may suggest that crime and cleanliness are principal measures of habitability. For the first of these we can seek a variety of statistical measures. We can see whether there are trends in various categories of crime, though we may find ourselves obliged at some point to judge whether the incidence of one crime is preferable (i.e., makes the city more habitable) to the incidence of another. If there are more rapes but fewer armed robberies, for example, is the city becoming more or less habitable? All criteria we choose—and all measures we take— will at some point force us to make judgments of this kind. But we will have other measures—or other criteria—to help us as well. On the matter of cleanliness, we might look at how often a city cleans its streets. We might also ask how good its equip- ment is and what kind of cleaning it does. Are the streets merely swept, or are they also washed? Is the labor manual or mechanized? Where is garbage dumped, and how often? We will necessarily have to judge whether the city is clean and whether it is getting cleaner or dirtier on the basis of these and other such questions. But we will also be able to use this judg- ment about cleanliness along with the judgment about crime as we push toward an answer to our original question.

We will seek other measures of habitability, but we will also narrow our scope of object in terms of city. However we choose to define "city," we will need to examine *examples* of cities rather than *all* cities. Furthermore, if we examine more than one city for *relative* habitability, we introduce comparative research. But for just a moment we are getting ahead of ourselves.

I have said that the subject of research must be tied to an ob- ject and that if we begin subjectively, the first questions we ask must come directly from our subjective question. In posing the subjective question, we have—whether secretly or openly— created a hypothetical answer. In the question "Could urban planning improve the plight of our cities?" we have already im- plied that our cities are suffering in some relative way and that urban planning is a possible remedy. Thus, there is an unstated hypothesis that urban planning can or cannot improve cities. Our hypothesis raises innumerable other questions, such as "Who does the planning?" but it is the recognition of the hypothesis that is most important. With that recognition our in- quiry becomes all the more purposeful. We seek to prove whether urban planning has a consequence, and, if so, in what way. Our evidence may support or refute the hypothesis, but what is more important is that we are able to formulate the hypothesis in order to guide our inquiry.

The hypothesis—which, if we think about it, inevitably asks whether something is true or is false, is one way or the other—leads implicitly to a model. If urban planning does improve cities, then we can suggest that urban planning is a cause whose effect is better cities. And if we propose the contrary—that urban planning does not improve cities—then we suggest that either (1) cities cannot be improved or (2) forces other than planning will bring improvement. Again, there is an implied causal model. The question ultimately reduces itself to the classic hypothesis: if A then B. If we persist in formulating and reformulating our questions until we recognize the hypotheses and the models implicit in them, we will always find a path along which to pursue our inquiries.

Testing the Hypothesis

Since this book emphasizes comparative research, the comparative method is therefore central to how we will test our hypotheses. Many methods are available, of course,[4] but in every test we need a standard—something against which to measure. Cities are either more or less habitable according to some ad hoc or abstract criteria, or they are more or less habitable relative to each other. In both cases, we judge according to some norm or standard. Comparative research tends to prefer the latter standard—in this case that one city is more or less habitable than another—without precluding the possibility of abstract criteria for judgment. All noncomparative research ultimately depends on abstract or ad hoc criteria. Comparative research seems superior to me because it provides concrete grounds for judgment while improving our awareness of a wider range of choices and possibilities.

No matter what method we choose to use, we must define our terms with some care. To understand what the comparative method is, we must first establish what a method is. In the broadest sense, a method is a way of going about something—usually a problem. It is a way of asking a question, conducting a discussion, observing a phenomenon. A method can also be an instrument or device for testing hypotheses or evaluating information. The identification of a method involves at least two choices. First, the way we go about investigating a problem depends above all on the problem we choose. Second, the method we then choose must in some intelligible way correspond to the problem. This point is not to be taken lightly. Many are the research designs that fail because methods are poorly related to problems.

I would like to emphasize here the notion of choice itself. We must remember that when we choose a problem, we choose one problem among many, and that when we choose a method to solve that problem, we choose one among many possible ways of solving the problem. These choices are value-laden; they carry with them biases and constraints, screening out some possibilities while maximizing others. If, for example, we want to know the impact of a new airport on a community, we may choose to interview community and citizen-group leaders. That is a methodological choice, but we might also choose to examine medical records statistically over time to establish whether health is affected by pollution from the airport. Spokesmen may guess, and doctors may know for their own groups of patients, but only through a thorough examination of all medical records can we verify this information. Even then, not all ill people see doctors, and not all doctors keep good records. Changes in health might be coincidental and not caused by the airport. This information, moreover, only pertains to one aspect of a multifaceted problem. For this aspect we have chosen a method—the inspection of medical records—but there are other aspects that may call for other methods. At some point we must decide—or *choose*—how many aspects are sufficient to determine "impact" and which aspects are the most useful to know. For each of these concerns we must also seek evidence in support of our choices.

Each time we make a choice, then, we involve a method, and each time we involve a method, we make a choice. These methods are instruments—ways of asking and explaining—but they are not value-free. A survey, for example, implies that we trust in some way what people tell us. If we survey prior to an election, we assume people will tell us something useful for predicting how they will behave—that is, how they will vote.

They may in fact vote as we predict, but it is only our *inter-pretation* of their answers that permits us to claim they voted a certain way for any particular reason. Can we know for sure why people vote as they do? We do not stand in the voting booth and can never know why they make a particular choice when they actually pull the lever. What they tell us may be anything from conjecture to rationalization. When we choose to use a survey, or any other method that relies on unsworn testimony, we must recognize this problem.

Ideally, methods are designed to resolve hypotheses that form predictive models: if A then B. If A is present or occurs, then B also will be present or occur. The ultimate problem lies in the *then*, for even if we are able to predict as the result of ex-perimentation, we cannot explain *why* except through the inter-pretation of our hypothesis. Had we a paradigm—that is, had we an embracing, testable, and apparently reliable theory with quintessential examples, such as Newton's gravity to explain falling apples—our problem, superficially at least, would be solved. In social science, however, there are competing paradigms; disagreement abounds over valid interpretation and adequate and appropriate evidence. Choices of methods, there-fore, are debatable. For all of them there is, at heart, a simple problem: All we have to go on is what is written down, what we ourselves can see and hear, and what people tell us. In the first case we can never know if we have found everything that has been written down. In the second case we can never be sure that our own eyes and ears have provided a full account. And in the third case we can never be absolutely certain that we have been told the truth or that we have compensated for every possible inaccuracy and fallacy. Together these difficulties leave us on uncertain ground. The best research designs, however, seek to minimize these weaknesses by reducing their probability. Minimizing their influence is ultimately the key to good social science.

If a method, then, involves the way a question is asked and the techniques employed to answer it, what does the com-parative method involve? If we multiply the difficulties of methods and methodology to however many things we want to compare, we can begin to appreciate the difficulties of the comparative method. In effect, there is no single comparative method. Scholars disagree about appropriate methodology in general, and the comparative method is one of many competitors. In the case of the comparative method, however, there is further disagreement because there are many possible ways to compare. Hence, we have two tasks. We must understand the comparative method as one of many methodologies, and we must establish separately what the—or a—comparative method is itself.

What does it mean to compare? What can be compared? In grammar school we learned not to add apples and oranges except in quantity—yet we were taught to compare them. One was smooth, the other rough; one orange, the other multicolored, and so forth. If we had ten oranges and ten apples, we could generalize only by consolidating categories, reporting that we had twenty pieces of fruit. Ten pears added in would give us thirty pieces of fruit. Now we add ten rocks—that gives us forty what? We compare the ten rocks to the ten apples. We have the same number so we describe their different and relative qualities. In so doing, we choose criteria, and we introduce standards, or norms. We might say, for example, that one is softer than the other; the standard for soft is then the consequence of a norm between the two. Now let us imagine these rather flexible norms in a more political context. If we say that Belgium is more developed than Italy (ignoring the problem of defining "developed"—a problem little different, really, from defining "softness"), we might also note that France is more developed than Belgium, that Germany is more developed than France, and that the United States is more developed than Germany. If the apple is soft, which country is developed?

This problem is inescapable. Social science obliges us to offer definitions and to construct categories. Comparative social science obliges us to distinguish not only among these categories, but also among sets of categories. And so, in the definitions we choose and in the methods we apply, we introduce evidence and interpretation. We make judgments, we display preferences, we make moral commitments. But the comparative method also provides us with standards—at least to the extent that we ensure comparability between and among categories.

We will test our hypotheses, then, by defining criteria that may be applied from one category to another. Given the question "Is airport service in Milan superior to service in other cities in Italy?" we can identify as objects of inquiry airports, airport service, Milan, other Italian cities, the deliverers of services, and criteria for "superiority." We must also recognize that our question is not "Is airport service good in Milan?" This question would require some standard of "good." Our question, in fact, provides a standard, but to answer it we must compare Milan's services to services elsewhere. Thus, we must see to it that (1) by "airport" we mean more or less the same thing in more than one place; and (2) by "service" we refer to phenomena more or less the same from place to place. For these objects, at the very least, we must derive consistent definitions that assume what we measure in Rome is more or less the same as what we measure in Milan. For each item we seek to make comparisons; we also tally within the categories and among the categories from place to place. Given comparable things to measure, we will eventually develop a composite whereby we can seek to answer, finally, the question of whether Milan's airport services are, indeed, superior.[5]

There are really two levels at work here—one related to the subject and the other to the object. Our subjective question, for the purposes of comparative analysis, must have meaning wherever we ask it. This problem is a serious one. When Gabriel Almond and Sidney Verba set out to ask Mexican peasants and German businessmen the same questions, their assumptions about comparability—that the questions would have a common meaning in different cultures, occupations, socioeconomic classes, and languages—necessarily undermined the quality of their study. *The Civic Culture*, although generally regarded as a landmark in comparative research, would serve as well as an example of doubtful methodological assumptions.[6]

Almond and Verba discovered, as we shall discuss later on, that people answer most questions they are asked. However, comparing the answers assumes common questions. Although the questions, to an American scholar, may appear to be the same, once posed through linguistic, cultural, social, economic, and political filters, the questions in one place may bear no resemblance to the questions in another. Even "yes" and "no" can take on different meanings. The question (that is, the subject) must be pertinent in as many places, in as many languages, and in as many cultures and socioeconomic classes as it might be asked. It must be asked by equally skilled interviewers making similar impressions on respondents. If the question is not comparably pertinent, we can only learn which questions are pertinent in different places; our comparison can go no deeper.

Comparability must be assumed at the objective level as well. We might inquire about cities, but we should be aware that Milan and Bologna are not wholly comparable, even though they both are called cities and they both have airports. To establish this comparability we need to enumerate characteristics within a reasonable range. "Reasonableness" is, of course, a judgment we make, but we can offer a strong defense to the extent that we have been systematic in reaching that judgment—that is, to the extent that we can enumerate demonstrably important criteria. (For example, Milan's airports are international and intercontinental and serve a population in the millions; Bologna's airport is principally domestic and serves a much smaller public.)

Comparability, at both the subjective and objective levels, is not fixed. In theory anything can be compared, but like rocks and pears, the broader the category, the more abstract the comparison. And the more abstract the comparison, the more superficial the insight is likely to be. Different data lead to different questions, and these differences may multiply within categories in such a way as to render the comparison across categories senseless. Although we must not make data "fit" our hypothesis or our commitment to compare, we must nevertheless be prepared to pursue, item for item, problems of comparability. To this end we will now consider some of the practical problems associated with the pursuit of comparative research.

Maintaining Comparability

There are several prerequisites to maintaining comparability in research. First, the subject must define a universe that has a corresponding and measurable object. Thus, from "Can urban planning improve the plight of our cities?" must flow the choice of particular cities and particular urban plans or possible plans. Second, the objects being compared ought to have both geographic and intellectual proximity. Let us consider the notion of intellectual proximity first.

All cities have something in common, and the ills of all cities may be subject to similar cures. But the research necessary to demonstrate the crucial common features of all cities—those located in all countries and cultures—has not yet been done. Hence, although cities may all be somewhat alike, the proposition is as yet hypothetical. Moreover, the greater the intellectual distance—as would be found, say, by comparing Paris with Lagos—the greater the number of variables that may intervene to disrupt the appreciation of possible causal relations. Cities may be set in environments so different as to render them, in fact, incomparable. Water, for example, may be a problem for all people in all human communities. Yet David Bradley and Gilbert and Anne White show vividly in their remarkable study *Drawers of Water* that the problem in East Africa is of so much greater a scale than in the advanced industrial world that the very concept of water as understood in New York is utterly different from the concept in Kenya.[7]

Of the old notion of "compare and contrast," we should remember that we are trying, first, to compare. The contrast may bring the concept into bold relief, but the comparison is more likely to deepen any insight. Thus, it is probably preferable to choose objects that fall within plainly similar universes. It may be that the results of the research that follows will yield greater possibility for comparing previously thought noncomparables, but it is probably best to start in the center of some circle and move concentrically outward. Put simply, the research task will probably be more fruitful if the researcher compares cities within the advanced industrial world or within the Third World, rather than comparing between the two.[8] Eventually, sensible comparabilities may be found between the two, but if experience in comparative social science research so far is any guide, that "eventually" is not yet with us.

Intellectual distance involves intellectual problems— problems concerned with the identification of criteria and the purpose of study. Geographical distance involves more practical problems. Comparing manpower policy in the United States and China might prove fascinating, but what chance is there that we will be able to shuttle like Henry Kissinger between Washington and Peking? I use the word "shuttle" because, as we will see in a moment, comparative research does not work best by examining single cases one after another.

There are only two possible solutions for comparing objects separated by significant geographic distances. One solution involves finding a reliable colleague with like interests who will run the same tests, seek the same data, stay in constant communication, and perform the research at approximately the same time. These conditions will be explained in a moment. The other solution requires money and time. The old maxim "If you want something done, do it yourself" is as true for research as for other things in life. Team research is exhilarating but difficult and often aggravating. On the other hand, the scale and scope of much comparative research requires it. When undertaking ambitious projects alone, especially over great physical distances, there is no substitute for money and time. Perseverance, dedication, commitment—none is enough.

It is fundamental to research that all paths of inquiry are not predictable. The scholar needs to be prepared to travel down whatever path beckons with the most promise. But what happens when in, say, Boston, we discover while pursuing an urban planning problem that, as Jane Jacobs suggests,[9] government—not planning—is central to improving the plight of our cities? Suppose we are comparing Boston with Montreal. In Montreal we might find that wherever planning was comprehensive, the outcome—on our scale of habitability—was preferable to outcomes where planning was less apparent. Then, in Boston, we find that the questions asked in Montreal are no longer the most pertinent. Do we conclude that planning makes a difference in Montreal but not in Boston and leave it at that? Or should we pursue the new line of inquiry in Boston and then return to Montreal to test it? In other words, do we maximize the original advantage of comparative research? Comparative research, you will recall, has the particular advantage of providing standards for testing hypotheses. When we tested the Montreal findings in Boston, some of them were denied and another hypothesis was suggested. Must we not return to Montreal to test the Boston findings?

This line of questioning opens up another central problem of comparative research. Do we look particularly for what is similar or for what is different? What is it we are really trying to learn? The answers to these questions must, again, be highly personal. Much of comparative research has been dedicated to demonstrating the "family of man"—demonstrating that we are "all in the same boat" with similar problems subject to similar solutions. But anthropologists, especially, have shown that the incredible variety of human culture distinguishes problems and solutions. In areas of East Africa, demands might be satisfied by the simple availability of clean water. In New York, however, such demands would also require that the clean water be no further away than the kitchen or bathroom tap. A pool of clean and available water in Central Park simply would not be an adequate solution for New Yorkers. Differences are great enough to warrant hope for the discovery of the range of possible preferences rather than a single answer. The range of human experience and preference informs us of possibility, whereas commonality suggests a certain inevitability. To the extent that we study social science in the belief that human choices matter, we must necessarily be inclined to explore differences before similarities.

Here there is a persistent tension that stalks all comparative social science research. The problem is that the objects of analysis must be similar enough to remain within the same universe of discourse, yet different enough to warrant thorough investigation. Furthermore, as we explore for differences we must constantly be sure that everything remains reasonably similar. There is the potential for a dilemma here, but really the matter is more a tension than a dilemma.

There can be little doubt that if we are to benefit from the comparative method in our study of Boston and Montreal, we will have to return to Montreal. Furthermore, we must be prepared to shuttle between the two places and test changing hypotheses. This shuttling proposition can sometimes be resolved through team research, but the range of cooperation must be very great. Whether shuttling or working as a team, researchers must recognize that the need to retest may result not only from changes in the overall hypotheses, but also from less dramatic differences in evidence in one or the other place that support or deny the hypothesis. When the smaller pieces of evidence vary, the maintenance of comparability becomes the most difficult of all.

Suppose we hypothesize that perception is crucial to the habitability of a city and that, therefore, people's responses to the survey question "Do you like living in this city?" will suggest whether the city is more or less habitable. Suppose, further, that in Montreal, across all manner of people on a first run of the survey, we receive positive responses. Then, in Boston, rich people seem to respond positively and poor people seem to respond negatively. In Montreal we did not sample systematically between rich and poor, nor did we in Boston. It was only after a quantity of negative responses in Boston that we detected a relationship between these responses and other characteristics. Now we are obliged to test systematically—in both cities—whether the correlation holds. The consequence is another trip—more money and more time. The alternative is a faulted hypothesis. Yet this matter of perception may be one of many indicators we are testing. In that case, we may save up a number of discrepancies and return to Montreal with all of them at the same time. Nevertheless, discrepancies—variations on the hypotheses between objects—may not always appear in different categories— or with respect to different variables—at the same time. We cannot count on one return trip to check out everything. As a line of inquiry develops we must check it out at our other site for guidance as to which direction might be pursued.

This need crosses all the research materials. If we seek, for example, to know about expropriation and changes in land value, we may consult transfers of land titles and deeds in a U.S. county office. When we ask for the same documents in provincial offices in Italy, we may learn that there are no comparable documents, but that through other materials we can collect other information about the land. We must then return to the county offices—or ask our research partner to return to the counties—to see if the kind of material in Italy can be matched in the United States. Documents will vary. What people say will vary. Furthermore, events in one place may influence events in another, which means that the *time* when questions are asked may be pertinent to when they are asked in another place.

Consider, for example, an inquiry of airport officials in Rome that reveals no concern at all for problems of noise. As we complete our inquiry, a special report is released by an investigating committee of the International Civil Aviation Organization (ICAO) concluding that noise is the most urgent problem on the airport agenda. We arrive in Milan to ask airport officials the same questions we asked in Rome. In Milan we find strong expressions of concern for problems of noise. Are these expressions of concern a consequence of greater awareness and sensitivity among officials in Milan or a consequence of the ICAO report? We will probably never know for sure. Had we been able to be in both Milan and Rome at the same time asking the same questions of comparable officials, the problem would have been less likely to occur. Being in two places at once means being two people—a feat that can be accomplished only by a research team. If the cases must be examined in series, the chances of variables intervening necessarily increase. The Rome-Milan problem might not have proved insoluble for the independent researcher, who may have turned to other sources in the historical record to establish whether there had been concern in Milan prior to the ICAO report. Our independent researcher may or may not have found other suitable documents, however. Even if he had, he still had to work harder to achieve like results.

Such a shuttle assumes that we, as comparative researchers, have a high tolerance for unstable existences. For the duration of a research project we must be prepared to move with some regularity between or among the objects we are analyzing. Our tolerance for such instability must therefore affect our choice of objects and, perhaps, our choice of subject as well.

In addition to being able to cope with this inescapable instability, we must be equipped with certain skills. Above all, if our objects are separated geographically, we must be equipped with appropriate language skills. Where the language is the same but the dialect or accent is different, we must also be sufficiently aware of cultural biases to overcome antagonisms we might unconsciously generate. If we speak Italian with a southern Italian accent, Milanese are not likely to take well to our inquiries about migrant labor, any more than a cultivated northern accent in Mississippi provokes sympathetic or helpful answers to questions about integration. Language can be a total barrier to the successful conduct of any research, but especially to the conduct of comparative research, where frequently more than one accent, dialect, or language is needed. The language problem can often be assuaged by deliberate cultural integration into the environment where the object of analysis is set, however. This approach requires personal skills of adaptability and sociability that must be sensed more than consciously taught or learned. No one can educate us to be natives if we are not born natives. Still, if we want Romans to give us honest answers, we might try following the oldest of maxims as much as possible: "When in Rome, do as the Romans do." Reduce the visibility of obviously conspicuous tasks, and try not to call inordinate attention to the inquiry.

Summing Up

Let us review briefly the key points we have considered thus far. The definition of a subject involves the recognition and choice of object(s). Whether the choice of a research topic begins conceptually with a subjective question or pragmatically with an object, every subject must be given an organizing framework, and every organizing framework must have examples. It is probably more efficient to choose the subject of research first, since this choice dictates the direction the inquiry will follow. In any event, subject and object must be seen together. Furthermore, the best place to begin the choice of object lies within the terms of our subjective question.

Subjects and objects imply hypotheses and models that, in turn, require testing. "If A then B" must be considered in light of all possible explanations: Although B might follow from A, it might also follow from C. Or it might follow from A in only some cases or under certain conditions. To find out whether B alone follows from A and whether it follows only from A, we must compare "If A then B" with, for example, "if C then B." And if we want to know whether A is "better" than B, we must compare them by applying identical criteria for each.

We test our hypotheses, therefore, through the establishment of norms and through comparison. The central dispute among people who do comparative social science research is whether comparison should be between highly similar or highly dissimilar objects. The preference depends on the purpose of research. Most comparative researchers now seem to seek the demonstration of similarity, whereas we are suggesting here that similar objects need to be chosen but ought to be employed for arraying choice and variety. Thus, the intellectual distance between objects must be sufficiently similar to impart like meaning to like questions, but the inquiry should seek to array the variety and scope within those common terms. Geography may also be a great impediment to our choices for comparison, for access to the objects of research is fundamental.

Finally, we have noted that comparative research requires certain skills, especially linguistic skills, and we must be sure that we are equipped sufficiently before we set out. Other skills, such as sociability, also matter but are less subject to modification or immediate development. Perhaps we should let our choices of subject and object be guided by our personal estimates of what methods we can execute best, accounting for whether we like interviewing or observing (e.g., going to meetings), or whether we tend to get along better with some kinds of people than with others. This personal assessment needs to be taken quite seriously; it concerns a fixed factor that unlike other skills is not readily subject to alteration or improvement.

All analysis depends upon good description. Thus, the quality of our observations determines the potential quality of all research. Once questions are framed and skills assessed, we must pursue the methods that will assure accurate, thorough, and impartial description. Much criticism has been leveled at description in social science; nevertheless, there can be no useful analysis without it.

Notes

1. The answers to the Weston questions may be found in Theodore J. Lowi, Benjamin Ginsberg, Elliot J. Feldman, et al., *Poliscide* (New York: Macmillan, 1976).

2. Discussion of this question is in Elliot J. Feldman and Jerome Milch, *Technocracy vs. Democracy: The Politics of International Airports* (forthcoming from Auburn House).

3. See Elliot J. Feldman, "An Illusion of Power: Military Conscription as a Dilemma of Liberal Democracy in Great Britain, the United States and France" (Ph.D. diss., Massachusetts Institute of Technology, 1972).

4. See, in particular, Robert K. Merton, "The Bearing of Sociological Theory on Empirical Research," *Social Theory and Social Structure*, rev. ed. (Glencoe, Ill.: Free Press, 1957), pp. 95–99.

5. Results of the relevant study may be found in Elliot J. Feldman, *Airport Siting as a Problem of Policy and Participation in Technological Societies: The Case of Milano-Malpensa* (Cambridge, Mass., and Torino: Harvard University Center for International Affairs and Fondazione Luigi Einaudi, 1978).

6. Gabriel A. Almond and Sidney Verba, *The Civic Culture: Political Attitudes and Democracy in Five Nations* (Princeton, N.J.: Princeton University Press, 1963). See especially the survey provided in the appendix.

7. Gilbert F. White, David I. Bradley, and Anne V. White, *Drawers of Water: Domestic Water Use in East Africa* (Chicago: University of Chicago Press, 1972).

8. See discussion in Elliot J. Feldman, "Comparative Public Policy: Field or Method?" *Comparative Politics* (January 1978):289–293.

9. Jane Jacobs, *The Death and Life of Great American Cities* (New York: Random House, 1961).

2

Field Research Methods

There are *not* many ways to collect information for social science analysis. The laboratory where controlled experiments may be undertaken is, among social scientists, almost uniquely the domain of some psychologists. Most social scientists are denied a variety of experimental techniques. The attitudes, cognitions, perceptions, values, choices, and actions of people that concern us are not easily distilled or replicated and are certainly not likely agents for test-tube reactions. Moreover, since this book focuses on research that is neither psychological nor psychiatric, much observational data lie outside what we can use. We are not psychoanalyzing respondents. However sophisticated the techniques for data analysis may be, by and large, all social science techniques for data collection reduce themselves to what we see, what we hear, and what we read.[1]

Each of these means of collecting data suffers from a variety of important limitations. What we see, for example, is, in fact, only what we think or believe we see. Certainty depends on verification. We can increase certainty by collecting the testimony of witnesses, but we know from the eyewitness accounts of an accident, for example, how short of verification we can fall. If a book descends from my desk to the floor, I may say it fell; someone else may swear that I dropped it; another observer may say it was pushed over by accident. Moreover, not only does such testimony rely on what we and others think we see; it also depends on the honesty of the witnesses. How can we be certain witnesses have not conspired to deceive us? (Indeed, famous cognitive dissonance tests conducted by Muzafer Sherif at Columbia University revealed that the conspiracy of witnesses can be very effective in deceiving someone collecting testimony for verification.[2]) Thus, in trying to verify what we think or believe we see, hear, or read, we confront the problem of sufficiency. How much testimony, whether visual or aural, is enough? Is the legal guideline of one or two corroborative witnesses sufficient in social science? In any event, we must accept at the outset that we deal strictly in probabilities and that we are, in effect, never certain of anything. We can be no more certain than we are confident in the consistent reliability of our personal faculties. As imperfect beings, we are inevitably imperfect data gatherers.

Armed with the certainty that our data collection is inevitably imperfect, we must choose techniques that will (1) correspond in the tightest possible fit to the information we seek to gather; (2) maximize reliability; and (3) reduce error as much as humanly possible. All social science techniques for collecting data constitute sophisticated forms of seeing, hearing, and reading. These forms vary a great deal from one another, however. Perhaps the most important factor to consider in choosing among them is economy, in terms of both time and money (even when the two are not necessarily equivalent). Since we cannot read everything or talk to everyone, we must keep our study confined as much as possible to our chosen objects and we must try as scrupulously as possible to collect only information pertinent to our subject. Everything else is extraneous—a burden to collect, catalogue, and maintain. Being selective in what we collect and what we ask is one of the hardest of all research tasks. We should therefore be vigilant and remind ourselves constantly of just what our subject is as we examine the object. We must always remember why we are studying a particular object beyond any intrinsic interest suggested by the object itself. It is very easy—and very unfortunate—to waste time and energy.

Surveys

The survey[3] is perhaps, next to reading, the most popular yet least economical of social science field methods. Its popularity stems from several factors. (1) It appeals to our egalitarian instincts by permitting us to include many objects of potentially countless backgrounds and interests, while creating jobs when done on a mass basis. (Some social scientists may consider this last point insulting or irrelevant, but surveys have provided considerable employment for graduate students, and the function of surveys in this respect has not always been purely incidental.) (2) The survey permits us to gather quantities of similar data within fixed time periods. (3) The survey, if conducted in a sufficiently random way, can normally be replicated and therefore seems to simulate best the laboratory experiment. (4) The survey holds many variables constant simultaneously, which increases reliability. (5) Surveys can be at the same time fancy and fun. All these factors have contributed to the survey's unparalleled prominence in the methodology literature of sociology and political science. It also has been by far the most favored tool of comparative political scientists. But let us consider some disadvantages.

Surveys are expensive. It is necessary either to expend enormous amounts of personal time and energy or to employ others to ask the questions. For every person questioned, a separate form must be prepared. There must be a code to keep the data from different respondents classified in a common way. Without a code it is extremely difficult to compile the data. There must be mathematical computation, and if there are more than twenty people in the survey, a computer may be necessary to analyze the data. Computers and computer time are expensive.

Surveys are also not as reliable as they may at first seem. Although sufficiently large samples may compensate for error or deceit, every answer depends upon the respondent's interpretation of the question. The range of possible interpretations—and hence misunderstandings—is infinite. Not only might the language lead to misunderstanding, but an abundance of literature now reports that the questioner's unconscious biases often betray themselves in subtle ways to respondents. Respondents may answer with these biases in mind.[4]

Surveys can also be unreliable because they account for those who answer but say little or nothing about those who do not. Catching people on a street corner and asking, "Hey, could you answer a couple of questions?" might seem reasonably random, but it is impossible to know whether those who never have the minute to stop constitute a more important or coherent sample. Those who do stop may represent a population only of the "stoppers." But before going further in this general statement about surveys, let us systematically categorize the kinds of surveys and make more precise suggestions about each of them.

Demography Versus Attitudes

Broadly speaking there are two kinds of surveys—or, at least, there are two kinds of information that can be gathered in a survey. We can ask people for certain facts about themselves—demographic questions—such as how old they are, where they live, or how much they earn. We can also ask people what they think, how they feel about something, or how they have behaved or might behave (as in voting); these are attitudinal questions. Some surveys are demographic, others are attitudinal, and, inevitably, some are both.

We should be aware that when we ask people for facts about themselves, the "facts" are not always clear. For one thing, people are not always ready to give away certain information. Conventional women may not reveal their correct age, and conventional men might not reveal their correct income. How often would a casual acquaintance answer your inquiry about their parents' income? Deception may be deliberate, or it may be completely accidental. And some simple facts may not be discernible. For example, a tenant farmer may be perfectly cooperative but nonetheless unable to cite a cash figure for his income. Although he may receive some meager wage and live in a rundown shack, probing may reveal that he uses the shack free of charge, including the utilities, and that the owner's truck is at his disposal. He may also be able to hunt and fish on the land and, consequently, has an excellent diet without ever spending anything but his spare time to feed himself and his family. The rent, utilities, transportation, and food all come as fringe benefits, but surely must be regarded as income. A cash figure for his income, therefore, is elusive, even though he is sincere in his effort to satisfy our factual request.

If demographic data sometimes prove elusive, attitudinal data are normally available in abundance. Generally in surveys, if we ask a question we get an answer. Unfortunately, not every answer is meaningful. People have opinions on most subjects. We can try to test the reliability of attitudinal answers by asking the same question in different ways at different points in the survey, but the respondent may or may not prove consistent.

The difference between probing for demographic data and probing for attitudinal data involves a difference in purpose. In asking demographic questions, we have already defined some group and now want to describe it. That group may live in a certain geographic area, attend a certain school, church, function, or meeting, or share some other factor we identify. We begin by identifying something in common and then inquire whether that particular factor is related to others that are shared: Are the neighbors all middle class? Are they all approximately the same age? Are their families the same size? We might also ask more attitudinal questions: Do they have similar aspirations? Do they envision the world the same way? Are they concerned about the same issues? All these questions, whether demographic or attitudinal, arise after we have already identified some respondent group *as a group* that we then want to describe. In such instances we begin with a demographic inquiry.

When we begin with an attitudinal inquiry we tend to ask whether an apparently heterogeneous sample of people shares certain patterns of behavior or belief. Are there linkages or "bundles" of beliefs, and can we locate any variables that will predict others? For example, will people who profess a fervent belief in organized religion also profess a preference for the Republican party? Attitudinal and demographic information *may* prove highly related. Whatever the commitment to organized religion, for instance, rich people may prove more likely than poor people to support Republicanism. The point is, however, that our sample tends to be random and from it we seek to identify groups or clusters on the basis of attitudes or ideology. To identify such groups, we must have hypotheses, for they determine what questions we will ask.

Few surveys are either completely demographic or completely attitudinal—most combine the two kinds of information and, indeed, attempt to correlate between them. Nevertheless, we should note that the departure point for each type is different because of a basic difference in purpose.

Survey Methods

There may be only two basic kinds of information to be gathered in a survey, but there are several different approaches to collecting this information. Let us consider some of them.

There are four main ways in which a survey can be administered: (1) the survey can be mailed or left on the doorstep for people to fill in, and it can be returned by mail or picked up by the investigator; (2) it can be delivered to people to fill in while the researcher waits and perhaps helps; (3) the questions and format can be kept by the questioner who personally asks each question of the respondent; or (4) the survey can be conducted over the telephone. The relative advantages and disadvantages of these four methods depend largely on cost. Delivering the survey, leaving it for completion, and returning to collect it is certainly the cheapest method. It also eliminates variation in presentation. However, this method has certain unfortunate aspects. For one thing, it normally means that the survey results are not reliable for individuals but must be regarded more in terms of households. Husbands and wives— however much they may be asked not to—often will collaborate if they are at home together facing the same questions on separate forms. For another thing, there is usually a high level of unreturned forms, and there is simply no way of knowing— short of subsequent personal follow-up visits—who does not respond and why.

Remaining present while the respondents complete the survey involves a considerable sacrifice of time. It also can seriously inhibit the respondent, who may feel embarrassed or pressured and, hence, hurry to complete the form, hesitate to ask questions, or both. The personal administration of a survey is probably the best method, but it is not free of important disadvantages. Many people will refuse to talk with a stranger in their homes. Not only is interviewing in people's homes clearly the most expensive method, but it also places an enormous burden on the questioner, who must instill confidence in the respondent and pose each question in a clear and unambiguous manner.

The way in which the questioner dresses and talks can have a serious impact on the results. Jeans and T-shirts may provoke honest and useful responses in a university dormitory, but only hostility can be expected in response to such attire at a meeting of the board of trustees. If the sample is to be random on the sidewalk (or over the telephone or door-to-door through various neighborhoods), it may be extremely difficult to anticipate how to dress or how to talk. But, unfortunately, appearances and impressions count.

The telephone is used most frequently by national polling organizations and political candidates. When located within the community being sampled, the caller operates at the lowest telephone rates and eliminates all other travel costs. The telephone also enjoys the advantage of an impersonal interview, reducing the influence of appearances on results. But the time of day may define the sample: Working people will not be home most of the time, and evening calls frequently conflict with dinner hours. Many people will not want to spend time answering questions over the telephone, and it can be difficult to generate a reliable random sample. Overall, the telephone can be a cheap and desirable instrument for testing acquaintance with a product, but it is less reliable for lengthy inquiries or for defining a respondent group.

Open-ended and Closed Surveys

In addition to these four methods for conducting surveys, a survey may be open-ended or closed. That is, it may be loosely structured so that the researcher can ask different series of questions depending on the responses given, or it may have a fixed set of items allowing for a specified range of answers. It is possible to alternate between these two types if the survey is administered personally, but basically, open-ended surveys are administered personally, and closed surveys do not require such personal attention.

A closed survey assumes not only that the questions to be asked are the same for everyone but also that all questions will be asked and understood in the same way. The phrasing of a question can alter its meaning or can alter the understanding conveyed to different respondents. Avoidance of errors attributable to this kind of misunderstanding depends upon consistent phrasing. As we will mention in Chapter 3, it is often necessary to "probe" for answers, even on closed surveys. Nevertheless, the principal feature and value of the closed format is its relative assurance of consistency in the phrasing and presentation of questions.

Scaling and Coding

Whether the survey is open or closed also affects how it is scaled or coded. Scaling and coding are necessary for the storage and retrieval of information. If we merely write down whatever we are told, we will face a wealth of disorganized prose defying later analysis. Unfortunately, the precise way in which people say things is often much more accurate and honest than the categories into which we might force their answers to suit our purposes. For example, suppose we ask a woman if she buys eggs at the supermarket. We have coded her possible responses as $1 = yes$, $2 = no$, and $3 = sometimes$. She might answer that she used to, doesn't at present, but will again as soon as the supermarket fulfills its promise to improve the quality of its eggs. Her answer is not "yes," because she does not at present purchase her eggs at the supermarket; her answer is not really "no," because she used to make such purchases and will again soon—only at this moment is "no" accurate; nor does "sometimes" correspond to what we have been told, since at present the answer is "no." For the purpose of computer analysis, we are asking all our questions on the basis of three possible answers: 1, 2, and 3. (The computer analysis will match the 1's, 2's, and 3's and thereby indicate clusters.) But all answers do not always suit our coding, and we have therefore thrown out numerous answers unwittingly.

Similarly, we might scale answers. For example, we might ask, "On a scale of 1 to 10—1 being terrible and 10 being wonderful—how do you rate this course?" On this particular item the respondent might say, "This course is fragmented: the readings rate a 10, but the lectures rate only a 1." Perhaps the survey offers separate items for the readings and the lectures, but if it does not, shall we conclude that the course is rated "5" or "10" or "1"? Consider whether you have ever seen a course evaluation form that did justice to what you wanted to convey about the subject and the professor. Both coding and scaling normally require us to increase the number of discrete items to heighten detail. However, shades of difference in items may not always be apparent to respondents. Furthermore, the amount of time a respondent is prepared to devote to a survey is limited, and a point can be reached rather quickly after which there are either no answers or the answers are capricious. The respondent may be pleased to have as many discrete items as possible when trying to find a love-match by computer but may be somewhat less disposed to answer a like number of items concerning his shopping habits.

Hence, there are advantages and disadvantages to various kinds of scaling and coding that depend, above all, on the purpose of the survey. Some scaling or coding is inescapable. But we should take this particular problem one step further: When preparing a survey, we should ask ourselves repeatedly not only about the purpose of the whole survey but about the purpose of each item as well. We should ask ourselves, "If we have an answer to this question, what will we then know or be able to deduce?" If we are unable to specify the value of any given question, it should be excluded from the survey. Surveys often begin with questions (or observations) about age, sex, profession, and income; yet, this (and other "standard") information frequently proves unrelated to the survey's objective. For each such piece of information it is essential to have a hypothesis (e.g., if any group supports a military draft, it will be the people over draft-eligible age). Coding then should be adjusted to the hypothesis. If the hypothesis involves bracketing respondents into two main age groups—those within and those above draft-eligible age—then specific ages need not be recorded and can only add time and expense to later analysis.

Every survey, if at all possible, should be pretested for the value of each item: the phrasing, and order of questions; and the overall format and length. Pretesting—practicing with the survey on a small number of people—should guide us to eliminate some items and to include others, to alter scaling or coding to allow for answers in fact given, to alter the order of questions, to restate items that apparently are not clear, and to lengthen or shorten the entire survey.

Choosing Populations

In preparing a survey, then, we must specify our purpose and check each item for its phrasing, for the specific information it can provide, and for its contribution to the overall purpose. We must establish a format that is easy to follow, clear, and precise. We must set down questions in a logical order, especially where some questions depend upon prior answers. We must try to be both brief and complete. And, finally, we must decide who will answer these questions—that is, we must choose a population.

The choice of population depends, of course, on our purpose. If we want to know whether airport neighbors are economically and socially homogeneous, we have to ask people who live near airports about their economic and social situations. If we want to know whether Italians are likely to vote more for the Communist party in the next general election, we need to draw a sample from all of Italy. What we are trying to find out determines whom we ask, but there is also a quantitative problem: How many members of the relevant population do we question? Do we examine all of the population? Some fixed percentage? If we cannot reach an entire population, then we need a random sample. There is disagreement as to how many people constitute a sufficient statistical sample, with the minimum number in steady decline despite the "law of large numbers," which promises greater statistical validity with bigger samples. Some social scientists have even suggested that samples of less than one hundred are reliable.[5]

Although it may be true that it is quite enough to survey fewer than one hundred people of a given population, we must be very careful about how we draw our sample. If, for example, our target group is airport neighbors, it may be important to know that several different legal districts border the airport. These districts may have different zoning ordinances that in turn govern whether rich or poor people are likely to be found in a given district. Suppose, moreover, that these districts tend to be ethnically exclusive and that the last names of people in these ethnic groups cluster around different letters in the alphabet. We randomly open a telephone book (which is consolidated for all these districts) and choose every tenth name to draw a sample of, say, twenty-five people. We subsequently may discover, much to our dismay, that we are interviewing twenty-five people from the same ethnic group and from the same neighborhood—hardly a representative sample of airport neighbors.

This set of unusual conditions may seem somewhat contrived. Nonetheless, it should warn us that randomizing may require being aware of numerous conditions first. In this instance, we may have to avoid the telephone book and randomize by street addresses. Once we overcome the peculiar conditions of a given case, we may then draw a random sample.

Drawing the random (or stratified random) sample does not complete the task. Suppose we generate responses from only ten of our set of twenty-five? (Fifteen may not return the survey forms, may hang up the telephone or not answer, may not be home, or may slam the door in our faces.) Ten people do not a survey make. We will have to try again. For this reason another rule of thumb is that an initial sample should be at least one-third to one-half larger than necessary. Experience shows that in a normal survey one-third to one-half of the drawn sample will not provide responses for whatever reason. This percentage, furthermore, may vary depending on the manner in which the survey is administered. Percentages are better for personally administered questionnaires, worse for forms put in the mail. Financial inducements, follow-up, and high-status sponsorship all may increase the return, but each adds to the time and expense involved. It is best not to sample at all, but rather to aim for the whole population. Obviously, a 100 percent response reduces sampling error. Unfortunately, such an aim is rarely practical.

Administering the Questions

Besides drawing the sample, there is the problem of who will administer the questions. It is normally best to do it ourselves. We know better than anyone what we are trying to find out, what we are really asking, and what we really mean by a given question. If we seek a large number of people (whether aiming for 100 percent of the village expropriated for an atomic accelerator or surveying Italians on their voting preferences), we must find others to ask some questions on our behalf. In this case it is important that we find people who (1) speak the language of the respondents; (2) know enough about the respondent population to know how to dress and present themselves inoffensively (miniskirted women should not administer questionnaires in Palermo); (3) are familiar with the survey, its purpose, and its content; and (4) have practiced—either with this survey or with others—asking questions and recording answers. This last item of training is especially important if those who conduct the survey are expected to code or scale while administering the questionnaire.

Summary

We have now treated—however briefly—most of the ways in which surveys are administered and questions are posed. We should remember, however, that for all the survey's attractions it is expensive and time-consuming. Its purpose must be very clearly defined, or its payoff will not be at all commensurate with its costs. It is important in all social science research to ask a fair number of people basically the same questions, but the systematic survey is not always the best way to accomplish the objective. Let us remember finally that in comparative research, all of the different populations under investigation must be asked the same questions, and requirements of randomization, sampling, and method of administration must apply equally to each population as if it were an entirely separate undertaking.

Let us turn now to some of the other ways in which we can collect information—in particular, to elite interviewing and documentary collection and analysis, both of which will be discussed again in Chapter 3.

Elite Interviews

By elite or "in-depth" interviewing, we do not mean asking questions only of heads of state, corporation executives, or the like. We mean any elite within a given culture or subculture.

Thus, we might be talking to heads of state, but we might also be talking to tribal leaders or the directors of the local Boys Club or YMCA. The elite is comprised of the leaders or decision makers, whatever they are leading and whatever they are making decisions about. But we must make our distinctions finer to appreciate fully that mass surveys are not the same as elite interviews.

The central difference between the survey and the elite interview is the purpose of each interview and the technique employed. Although many of the same questions must be put to different people in a designated elite, *no two interviews are exactly alike.* This is so because each person has been deliberately, not randomly, chosen. We do not seek a sample of a population. We seek sworn testimony from as much of a particular population as we can reach.

In the early 1960s Daniel Lerner and Morton Gordon ran a mass survey of European elites.[6] They asked leaders, decision makers, civil servants, and businessmen—so-called opinion makers—the same set of questions in closed interviews. Their population was chosen on the basis of reputation and apparent social, political, and economic importance. They surveyed attitudes and opinions on a wide variety of subjects related to the development of Europe. In terms of our definitions, Lerner and Gordon conducted a mass survey, not elite interviews.

Every member of an elite plays (or has played) a unique role in the set of events or decisions we are studying. We choose the people we see to learn as much as possible about that role—in order to understand as much as possible about the entire process of decision making or about the entire set of events. Thus, elite interviewing is always conducted in part for information that we cannot find written down somewhere—information that only members of an elite seem to know.

There is also a second, often more important, purpose in elite interviewing. Elites have certain perspectives, sometimes shared, sometimes in conflict. Decisions are sometimes consensual and sometimes strife-torn. People we might have assumed were important may have played no role, while others we had discounted may have been crucial. We need to see enough people to establish who was involved and who was not, what roles were played, and what positions were taken. But above all, perhaps, we want to know something about the perceptions of the decision makers or leaders. That is, we want to find out what each of them thought they were or are doing, what motives each defines, what general views are shared or in conflict. In this area—the perceptual area of our inquiry—elites should be subjected to the same questions, in contrast to the informational part of our inquiry, which focused on the uniqueness of each role player. However, even in this stage, there are still important differences between this method and the survey.

Elite interviews must be open-ended, and the structure must be flexible. Although we may plan to ask our questions according to a certain priority, we must be prepared to pursue them in the order the respondents perceive pertinent. The respondents may be prepared to answer all our questions, but they might think the tenth item on our list second in importance. As they speak, without ever seeing our list, they may skip to that item. On the one hand, we must be flexible enough to follow. On the other, we must be firm enough to cover the ground we deem most important before the respondent meanders into other subject areas and then terminates the interview.

Elite interviews also afford an opportunity to hear more than one version of the same story. The technique of storytelling is common to psychological interviewing; the difference here is that we know much of the story must correspond to some event generally perceived as having happened. The psychological interviewer is likely to amass a good deal more fiction than fact from a respondent. Each elite version of a given set of events or decisions will yield peculiar and important perspectives and perceptions.

For the sake of nomenclature, I should explain here that in-depth, open-ended interviewing with a precisely chosen set of people (for example, all the people who participated directly in the decision to invade the Suez Canal) will involve most of the same methods as elite interviewing. We might have to go about arranging interviews differently—a subject we will take up in Chapter 3—but the actual conduct of the interview and the range of things we might want to find out are probably similar.

A unique population group—which we identify as unique and as a group *before* we conduct interviews—will, for the sake of our terminology here, constitute an elite.

Summing Up and
Reflecting on Elite Interviews

Elite interviews, then, involve a specific group of people, require open-ended and flexible inquiry, and are likely to involve both informational and perceptual components. Furthermore, elite interviewing does not normally allow for sampling. Rather, the object is to reach as many people as possible who are identified as part of the group. Constraints of time, money, or language may prevent our conducting all elite interviews ourselves (or, for that matter, conducting any of them personally in a question-answer session). But let us be candid: In studying an elite—especially one with a story to tell—there is no substitute for face-to-face meetings.

Elite interviews have a number of obvious advantages over other research methods. Besides offering an "inside" story and an "inside" perspective, they often provide vital information. These apparent advantages should not be overstated, however. Elite interviews are expensive. They may not require the manpower of a survey, and they may not involve the computer or complex statistical compilation, but they do involve quantities of time. We will discuss in Chapter 4 some of the more specific constraints and time demands. Let it suffice here to note that at least two hours must be allowed for an elite interview, including travel and waiting time. As the research advances, interviews will last longer, even when the value of the extra information begins to diminish. Since we might be able to read anywhere from fifty to one hundred pages of documents, books, or articles during two hours, we should be sure to ask ourselves before conducting an elite interview whether the chosen respondent is apt to contribute enough to merit time that might be better spent reading. It is often true that matters become clearer to us when we learn them in conversation or discussion, but if particular information is already written down and we have not taken the trouble to find or read it, we may be wasting our own time and the respondent's.

We should be aware, furthermore, that the more we know about a given problem the more marginal the return on elite interviews is likely to be. Finally, we should be conscious that elites may be scattered geographically. If we propose to see them, we may have to travel great distances. While it is usually easier to arrange to see people whose roles were played in the past, those currently active are likely to dwell in one geographic area. People out of power or responsibility or who are no longer unique, though more receptive, are also more likely to be dispersed. The trade-off on our time and resources in this choice should not be taken lightly. During World War II every American citizen was urged to ask when driving—in the name of resource conservation—"Is this trip necessary?" We should ask ourselves a similar question in preparing and conducting elite interviews.

Documentary Research

Interviewing, whether as survey or as open-ended elite inquiry, is almost always the most enjoyable part of social science research. It has a certain sense of adventure and challenge that is not common to other research methods. However, there is an almost inescapable pleasure/pain principle in social science research, meaning that we often have to endure a considerable amount of pain before we ever get to the pleasure of interviewing. It is not so much that other research tasks are painful. Rather, it is that their productivity is not always apparent to us. They can also be isolating, even alienating, and they can be tedious. But for all that, they cannot be avoided.

The "they" to which I am referring involves the collection and examination of written materials. These materials may be found in library books, government releases, public statements, personal papers, official documents, archives, and newspapers. There is no substitute in this task for a good and complete library, but it is highly unlikely that any single library will contain all the materials pertinent to a study. We must go out and look for materials—from both private individuals and from institutions—and we must keep in mind some of the problems that frequently haunt a researcher.

Common Research Fears

A researcher can probably never know when everything pertinent, such as papers, reports, and other studies, has been found. There is always the worry that somewhere someone is doing the very same thing—writing the very same story—and better. Whereas this worry cannot be discounted, it ought not to be inflated either. When two people are engaged in the same research, the probability of their crossing paths is extremely great. Furthermore, it may be attributable simply to the wonders of man, but when we have a problem or a question that we have a burning incentive to explore, the probability that someone else has precisely the same problem or question— framed precisely the same way—is almost negligible. Even the most obvious and apparently vital subjects often constitute virgin research ground. Some aspect of what we are doing might suddenly appear elsewhere, but it is not likely to overtake our whole project.

A similar fear is that what we are doing has already been done. This worry haunts the historian far more than the student in comparative social science. Indeed, the student of contemporary problems may hope fervently that all the background to the present subject already has been assembled. However, before embarking full throttle on a piece of research, we must do substantial preliminary inquiry. We should begin with the recognized scholars and experts in the field. If we do not know who they are, we should go to a library and find out who has written on our subject and on related subjects. We should examine the books in the field. We should examine the bibliographies. The University of Michigan maintains an almost complete collection of doctoral dissertations and can report on research in given fields and subject areas. Government agencies, such as the National Academy of Science, maintain lists of work in progress, and there are several services that publish abstracts of major journal articles. We can also ask scholars and experts (including journalists) whether they know of any work that preempts our plans.

These preliminary studies and inquiries narrow considerably the likelihood that we will fall midway into our research onto our whole study already done by someone else. It is not impossible that we will discover ourselves replicating other work, therein making no new contribution, but the probability of doing so is very small.

A researcher is also haunted by the possibility that all of his other research may depend completely on one unavailable document, record, report, or testimony. Good research opens enough avenues, asks enough challenging questions, and relies on a sufficient diversity of sources to escape such a problem entirely. Every piece of research does not answer every question raised, and this or that unavailable piece of information may hold the answer to a particular question. Nevertheless, good research raises more than one question, and there is always more than one way to get at least an approximate answer. We might not be able to state what Neville Chamberlain's intentions were without Neville Chamberlain's papers, but does it matter? The testimony of others interpreting Chamberlain's motives surely reveals the important historical data, for the explanation of the behavior of actors in the international arena lies in what the actors perceived in each other. Chamberlain may have been misunderstood. What is more important is how he was understood by others and how, consequently, they behaved. His papers may help us apologize for him, but they probably will not help us much in our social science understandings. They may be nice to have, but they should never be crucial or decisive. We began, after all, by suggesting that the greatest certainty in our inquiries is uncertainty. No single piece of information or set of materials can provide us with certainty. We must have other materials in order to make a case.

Another, and even more compelling, research fear is that one will find not too little, but rather too much. As in the task of interviewing, we must constantly try to stay focused on what we are asking and on what we are trying to find out. It is unnerving that apparently extraneous materials often prove pertinent long after we had been inclined to discard them. This tendency leads us to collect a great deal that does, indeed, prove extraneous. There is no convenient rule to follow in this matter, but there is something we can try always to remember: whatever we collect we will have to analyze. Data may be nice to have, but we need only consider the quantities of data collected, stored, and ignored by government bureaucracies everywhere to appreciate that data are important only when they are analyzed. We should attempt, therefore, to confine our collection to what we have some reason—however vague—to believe we can and indeed eventually will use. Our research involves becoming expert in something. Hence, we may try to read everything on the subject. In some instances, so little will have been said or written or analyzed as to make this objective perfectly feasible. However, more often this objective will be impossible. Consequently, we need to emphasize again the importance of selectivity. We must husband our time as our most valuable resource.

Sources of Information

An important thing to remember about documentary research is that valuable data may be in unlikely places. Political scientists, for example, rarely begin where they should: by reading statutes. Laws define the tasks of agencies, the values of societies, the rules of behavior. They constitute the norm against which performance in a given sphere can be measured. One of the first tasks of a political scientist, therefore, should be a visit to a law library to read exactly what rules govern the phenomena under investigation.

Students of political science should also read the debates of the law makers. What a congressman has done in voting for a law and what he *thinks* he is doing when he casts his vote often offer a fascinating study in contrasts. Reading debates affords us the opportunity to consider what objectives and goals are on the agenda or what the society or the government is at least trying to accomplish. Similarly, since many of the laws have been refined or redefined by the courts, court decisions are an important resource for understanding competing views of law and the prevailing view of interpretation at any given point in time. Court decisions are an invaluable resource for learning about social conflict and social and political rules.

Other information sources include statements and reports from government agencies. The army, for example, might sponsor a law to appropriate money for a new weapon. What has the army said on the matter? What studies did it conduct? What evidence or information did the army submit to the law makers? Answers to these questions will be found in the official record. The army's press officer or public relations officer may provide them; the newspapers may report them; and the records of the law makers may display them. They constitute documents.

Governments and private agencies also frequently hire consultants. Consultants write reports that often can be made available and often include raw data, analysis, and recommendations. Whether in a study for building a dam (of value to geographers) or a weapon (of interest to economists and political scientists), the consultants' efforts can be of great value in research. Remember, however, that agencies we might not expect to deal with certain subjects sometimes do. The Bureau of the Census in the United States, for example, maintains excellent documents on housing. We need to investigate the less than obvious offices.

Scholars are often unjustifiably critical of newspapers. Newspapers constitute a daily record, however, and while the stories may be superficial or incomplete, much basic information will be found there. Moreover, newspapers over time can prove surprisingly thorough. Little news emerged, for example, from the publication of the Pentagon papers. Albeit piecemeal, the newspapers had already carried most of the stories. Inadvertently, journalists constitute a worldwide research team whose data collection may serve social science analysis. The scholar who rejects this source may affect superiority but is ultimately foolish. Sometimes a story may not be carried, but a journalist may be willing to share copy. The newspapers of record—like the *New York Times, Toronto Globe and Mail, Le Monde*, the *London Times*—and journalists' notes are fundamental documents.

Institutes and libraries may provide special services that make available materials otherwise difficult to use. Not only do some libraries and archives maintain special collections and private papers, but the Royal Institute for International Affairs in London, for example, maintains a press library of cut, catalogued, and cross-referenced newspaper stories from all over the world. The collection, though suffering from certain biases and gaps, is peerless in its breadth, depth, range of time treated (since World

War I), and efficiency. The Council on Foreign Relations in New York and the International Institute for Strategic Studies in London also offer press services (though not nearly as comprehensive and for subjects sometimes more narrowly defined). Newspapers themselves, furthermore, often keep their stories organized, as in the *Times'* yearly index. Newspaper compilation of this kind can save considerable time over reading the daily paper for periods of several months or years. Shortcuts such as organized press collections are not always available, especially in some fields. Nevertheless, it is useful always to explore for them before embarking on some endeavors ourselves.

In every instance where institutions are involved there are institutional records. They may not always be immediately accessible, but more often than not perseverance will produce them. If we are interested in the socioeconomic composition of airport users, it may pay to ask the airport authorities if they have collected such data before rushing off to run a survey. That step would be normal in data collection. But we might also discover an institute specializing in air transportation or in market research that has also undertaken this area of concern. Political parties often maintain files on a host of nonpolitical issues and also have official positions available from the party headquarters. Furthermore, consumer organizations collect data on all sorts of products and services.

In short, the directly responsible agencies and parties may not be the sole sources of data. Field research should be empirical, which means it results not only from collecting new data but also from exploiting data collected by others. Such data often may be found in organization offices, special institutes and libraries. Established scholars and journalists will frequently know of these sources, and they should be asked.

We should remember that many officials have private papers or personal libraries which, on request, they may share with us. These constitute an invaluable documentary resource. Sometimes it will be necessary to request access in writing; it is preferable to ask personally at an interview. Either way, we should not forget the possibility that such papers may exist and that we may be allowed to use them. When documents are offered, especially during an interview, we should never fail to accept them, even if at first we doubt their value. Later on, they may surprise us in their usefulness. And when respondents have mailing lists for the release of documents, we should sign up.

There are other kinds of documentary information readily available. The mass public registers its general tendencies on issues in only one way—voting. We must be very wary of voting data, for, as we have said before, we never know *why* people vote as they do. But voting data can tell us whether change is occurring. Voting data can serve admirably both as a barometer and as a thermometer of society. The more people vote, the higher the passions, and whether voting is stable or changing is an important storm gauge.

Much social science methodology concerns statistical measures. Statistics are not the product solely of government studies or reports, however, nor must a researcher conduct a survey or rely on someone else's. There are many ways other than surveys to gather statistics, and the most imaginative tend to be the most successful. Anything that can be counted can also be calculated, graphed, compared.

The Risks of Using Events Data

Many social scientists rely on what they call "events data." Such data are used in quantitative analyses for measuring indicators and testing hypotheses. Events data usually are derived from newspapers, magazines, and journals. They record an event. For example, one might scour the *New York Times* for reports on strikes and then add up the number of occasions when a strike has occurred. Newspapers might also be the source of counting incidents of violence, whether in individual crime or in riots or mob behavior.

Using these data is risky. We are obliged to depend on the observations of others, particularly journalists, who may have a particular point of view or a need to report something a particular way. A sensational press might report a peaceful demonstration as violent, or a crowd of angry people as a riot. A pro-government newspaper might estimate a crowd of 100,000 demonstrators as nearer to 25,000, which seemed to happen often during the early days of anti–Vietnam War protest. We compound such misleading reporting when we aggregate the inaccuracies. We might also misinterpret across different national experiences. A strike in Italy may last only a few hours and be motivated politically, whereas a strike in the United States may last months but be concerned only with the size of a paycheck. The intent and character of each is different, but both are called "strikes" and to the untrained or ethnocentric observer they may appear similar.

We must remember, then, that the analysis of data can be only as good as the data themselves. The value of the data, in turn, depends on the quality of observation. Events data represent the compilation of observations, usually from the perspective of others; they must be treated accordingly.

Visual Techniques of Data Collection

We listen to answers in interviews, and we read the documentary record. We can also see. If we want to know how often the municipal government cleans streets in different neighborhoods, there are three possible ways to find out: (1) we can ask municipal officials; (2) we can ask residents of the neighborhoods; and (3) we can visit the neighborhoods and see for ourselves. Does a neighborhood still change rapidly under ethnic pressure? Perhaps the best and easiest way to answer the question is to cruise the streets counting "For Sale" signs.

There is a great deal we can observe outside the laboratory without asking questions or reading documents. The meaning we impart to what we observe visually is no less valid than what we observe aurally, and it is much less obtrusive. However, we often have to be imaginative in developing useful indicators. For example, one indicator of the wealth of a neighborhood or community may be the percentage of new automobiles in front of homes. Or perhaps we can count the number of garages built for more than one car. The number of different doorbells on a building may tell us how many families reside inside, and we can see for ourselves the size of the building.

Visual techniques are especially valuable in community or neighborhood research. They are obviously less valuable in studying, for example, bureaucratic decision making, but observing the books and documents on desks and shelves in offices where we may be interviewing can give us useful clues to relevant data. We should always remember that what we see can be as important as what we hear. As we are systematic in seeking information we will hear, we ought to be systematic in seeking information that we see. Our basic human faculties in social science field research are limited, so we should use them all to their fullest.[7]

Research Priorities

Research that can be completed at home before going into the field should have priority. All data that can be collected without asking for anyone else's time, which means without interviewing, should be undertaken with priority in the field. And all activities—reading and collecting documents, interviewing, and surveying—should take place simultaneously, as much as possible, once the order described here has been respected the first time through.

It should be clear, then, that considerable research precedes going into the field, that documentary research must continue in the field, and that in the field we are confined basically to reading, to listening, and to seeing. The problem lies in what we get to read, what we take the trouble to see, and to whom we get to listen. These concerns depend on how we present ourselves and how well we define exactly what we are doing. These most practical of matters will be our next principal concern.

Notes

1. A fourth means—employed by geographers, anthropologists, criminologists, and others—is taste. I have no experience with this method in social science and will not discuss it further.

2. See research beginning as early as 1945, as, for example, Muzafer Sherif and Hadley Cantril, "Psychology of Attitudes," *Psychological Review* 52 (November 1945):295–319 and 53 (January 1946):1–24.

3. I am using the term "survey" in preference to "questionnaire" because it is more embracing. "Questionnaire" implies a set of fixed questions eliciting coded or scaled responses. "Survey" suggests a variety of ways in which different problems, questions, or issues may be presented to a large number of people.

4. See especially Herbert H. Hyman et al., *Interviewing in Social Research* (Chicago: University of Chicago Press, 1954) pp. 83–137.

5. See the discussion in Hubert M. Blalock, Jr., *Social Statistics* (New York: McGraw-Hill Book Co., 1960) pp. 165–167.

6. Daniel Lerner and Morton Gordon, *Euratlantica: Changing Perspectives of the European Elites* (Cambridge, Mass.: MIT Studies in Comparative Politics, 1969). Robert Putnam did similar and more effective surveying later, reported in Robert D. Putnam, *Comparative Study of Political Elites* (Englewood Cliffs, N.J.: Prentice-Hall, 1976).

7. A useful source of ideas is Eugene J. Webb, Donald T. Campbell, Richard R. Schwartz, and Lee Sechrist, *Unobtrusive Measures* (Chicago: Rand McNally & Co., 1966).

3
The Conduct of Research

Once we have defined a subject of inquiry and have identified an object of study, certain problems present themselves in sequence. First, we must consider the precise methods for examining the object. If we have decided to use a survey, for example, we must prepare the instrument, pretest it, and prepare the requisite number of forms before going into the field. Appropriate and available literature should be read; accessible scholars and journalists familiar with the subject or the object should be visited.

All of these activities involve exploring the resources available where we are before we make the investment of going into the field. Field research must be thoroughly prepared so that the time in the field is spent profitably. Profitability, however, implies money, which is necessary if we are to go into the field. Unless we are independently wealthy, or unless we conduct the study near home, we need to raise funds for getting to the object of study, living there for a time, communicating with people, transporting ourselves to interviews, preparing forms, purchasing materials and documents, and so forth. The best-planned research can never see the light of day without an adequate supply of funds for such things.

Grantsmanship

Getting money often has very little to do with the quality of research, although few established social scientists would ever admit it. This fact should raise moral problems for those who give as well as for those who receive, but it does not change the practical issues of locating support for serious researchers. Until those who give show greater concern for the quality of the product of research, and until those who do research are uniformly more serious and honest in their undertakings, the necessity of playing the game known as "grantsmanship" will be difficult, if not impossible, to avoid.

It is hardest to get money the first time. That is, when you are unknown (and perhaps unpublished), it is especially difficult to interest someone in paying for the work you propose to undertake. The first necessity, therefore, is to find a patron. A patron can be anyone with an established reputation who inspires confidence on the part of those who have money to allocate. Entrusting funds for research does require some measure of confidence in the recipient. If you are unknown, the next best thing is to find someone who *is* known who will vouch for your project and the individual(s) planning to conduct it. It is up to you to find a patron.

With the support of the patron, you must then inventory those foundations, agencies, and individuals who support academic research in general and your area of research (subject *or* object) in particular. It is usually best to begin with governments. Federal and state agencies allocate substantial sums to research, and they are often looking for someone to carry out projects of interest.

Government agencies tend to pay for research in one of two ways: through contracts (which is the most popular way) or through outright grants. In general, contractual research is the product of—again—two possible methods. In the first, the agency issues a "request for proposal" (RFP). (This is especially true in the United States.) The RFP is normally sent to established scholars, consulting companies, research laboratories, and university departments. Often the RFP is "guided," which means very few people ever see it, and the agency hints strongly that a response to the RFP is likely to generate funds. Sometimes the RFP will even specify the sum available for support. An unknown researcher can get in on an RFP in basically one of two ways. He or she can either persuade the recipient to file the proposal and grant him or her supervision of the project, or the researcher can work on the project under the supervision of the RFP recipient. Obviously, the former is preferable; it is also more difficult to achieve because established scholars are understandably reluctant to risk their reputations on an unknown.

Apart from responding to an RFP, you might secure a contract from a government agency by submitting an unsolicited proposal in hopes that the agency will be interested in your specific area of concern. It is much more difficult to secure a contract this way. If you choose to pursue this route, however, you should consider how you might improve your chances of catching a bureaucrat's eye. At the least, you should try to know the name of the official likely to be responsible for receiving your proposal, and you should apply directly to that individual instead of to the whole agency. At the most, you should make contact with the most highly placed person in the agency whom you either know or can contact through someone else's acquaintance. You should enter into preliminary discussions to test for agency interest, and in this way, you may find someone in the hierarchy who will agree to guide your request personally. When someone in the agency takes a personal interest in your project, you stand a much better chance of securing funds than if you enter blindly hoping to catch someone's eye.

If a contract is issued, there are a number of concerns of which you should be aware. For one thing, a contract involves a specific agreement. The agency expects you to produce some specific thing. If, in the course of your research, you discover interesting questions that any good and responsible scholar might be inclined to pursue, the contract may not allow it. You might be obliged to defer, or even to cast aside completely, the study of this interesting path. The money has been given to find or study a particular problem, and the contract obliges you to stick to the specific task.

Because of the nature of contracts, scholars tend to seek vague terms and ambiguous promises. The scholar's independence and freedom is inversely related to the specificity of the contract. Moreover, the contract may put restrictions on the ownership of the materials, and the recipient may find it difficult, if not impossible, to publish results. Therefore, contracts need to be read carefully and negotiated.

The above restrictions—and many others—make contract research much less desirable than research done on outright grants. Contract research leans toward problem solving; grant research poses broader questions. Contract research is almost unscholarly by definition, for it involves research deliberately in service.[1] It is possible that the research interests will coincide precisely, but every deviation of interest between the contractor and the recipient is a challenge to intellectual independence.

As already indicated, there are two basic ways to secure money from governments: one is by contract, and the other is through outright grant. Sometimes grants are made through a general research agency, such as the national science foundations in the United States and West Germany. More often, however, grants are made through specific agencies concerned with specific problems. The greatest single source of funds for research in the United States, for example, is the Department of Defense, but it is erroneous to assume that the department itself controls strictly all research conducted with its money. On the contrary, much of the research paid for by the Pentagon yields results that are outside the apparently established interests of the agency. The key here lies more in the difference between contract and grant than between one agency and another. The terms of a grant should include the freedom of the researcher, with which no agency should—or normally will—interfere. For this reason, scholars should always prefer grants to contracts, and, indeed, some scholars will not work on contract under any circumstances.

There are also two ways to pursue a grant from a government agency. One, as described, involves a general inquiry. The second way can be more fruitful. The agency may sponsor a grant program whose terms provide for undertakings consistent with our research intentions. For example, the U.S. National Science Foundation may sponsor a program that provides research funds for doctoral dissertations. Whenever there is some specific program under which you can apply, it is preferable to file an application directly with the agency sponsoring that program. When an agency has established a granting program, it prefers to allocate research funds through such established procedures.

In all cases, whether we seek a contract or a grant, we need to make preliminary inquiries concerning agency interest and agency allocations. These inquiries are best made through personal contacts; they are admissible when writing to appropriate officials. If the agency has a particular format or wants particular supporting information, it is necessary to have complete details before filing. There are deadlines, usually early autumn, and it is important to meet them. Inquiries must begin, therefore, in spring or summer—some twelve months before support is needed. Finally, it is important to know whether more than one agency can receive the same application at the same time. In the Federal Republic of Germany, for example, only one government agency can consider a research proposal at a time. Application to more than one can damage severely the chances of securing support. When such restrictions on applications pertain, it is especially important to establish with which agency an application is likely to fare best.

While governments provide the greatest amount of research funds, they do not have a monopoly. Foundations and independent organizations have established research programs or are often willing to pay for certain kinds of research. The best place to begin an inquiry about such funding sources is among senior scholars. University bulletin boards also display information about grant programs, and most universities have development offices responsible for monitoring sources of potential funding. In addition, there are several volumes found in the reference section of most libraries that list foundations, their resources, their addresses, and the objectives of their support programs. It may be necessary to adjust the terms of a proposal somewhat in order to enhance the chances of eliciting interest in a given program or foundation, but the programs and foundations chosen should truly correspond to your interests. Nonetheless, if the terms of different programs are not precisely identical, it should be possible to adjust the scope of your project for the purpose of multiple applications.

The Research Proposal

Research proposals are essential for fund raising, but they also have a more general use. When formulating a project, we should always set to paper a detailed plan. First, we should write a one-page summary of the question we seek to answer and how we will try to answer it. This summary, sometimes called an "abstract" or a "précis," will guide all our subsequent preparation. Many students and scholars wait to prepare such a summary until after they have completed the research proposal or even, in some extreme cases, until after they have embarked on their research. The abstract loses much of its value if not prepared early, for it helps us to answer the questions we will most frequently hear from others: "What are you working on?" and "How are you doing it?" A succinct written statement of the subject and objects, with an indication of appropriate method, will be our most valued single document.

The research proposal itself should be short. Its purpose is to state the importance of the research, the status of the literature and the discipline in the given subject area, the questions to be raised, the method we will use, and the reasons we are especially worthy of support for this particular research. In other words, the proposal should be a clear description of our subject, our object, our method, our reasons, and our worthiness, and each of these areas should be blocked out separately.

The importance of the research refers to its significance, both for a general public and for our particular discipline. What proposal to fund cancer or heart research would not begin with dramatic statistics concerning fatalities from these and related diseases? If we want to study an ethnic group, we need to say at the outset how many people are members of this group and why learning about them will be useful for other peoples. Research on Canada surely must note the vast territory the country covers, the critical alliance that Canada shares with the United States, the valuable natural and human resources that help give it one of the world's highest standards of living.

If the research concerns a specific case, we must explain what it is a case *of*. Research may be intrinsically interesting, but it will only find an audience—or a sponsor—if it has potential for general lessons or can teach something new that will suggest understandings beyond the case itself. We must convince our readers—and ourselves—that this research is particularly worthy of support and attention and that it should be given preference over other efforts when scarce resources of time and money require selection among projects. Often this statement need only involve an articulation of how and why we chose the subject of research, since what made it important to us often will have a more general importance. Too often, students lose sight of the large questions posed by their research; this statement of importance becomes all the more useful for such cases.

In addition to explaining the importance of our research, we must also show that it has not been done before and that it will profit from previous work conducted in our own, or in a related, discipline. Hence, we need to demonstrate some familiarity, however modest, with relevant literature so that a reader can see where our project fits in the grand schemes of social science.

Having stipulated the questions we will ask, how we will ask them, why they are important, and the relevant accomplishments of our colleagues (and ourselves) to date, we must articulate an appropriate methodology so a reader will understand what exactly we intend to do with our time (and perhaps their money) in order to answer the questions or solve the problems we have chosen. This statement should include where the research will be conducted, whether we have secured cooperation from scholars or facilities there (or whether there is any cause to anticipate difficulty in doing so), and whether we have the requisite skills (language, statistics, interviewing, etc.). It is in this statement that we must demonstrate our own particular worthiness, convincing our readers—by citing prior accomplishment and preparation—that we are the right people to conduct this research.

Finally, our research proposal must include a budget. Many programs specify budget support, but more often we can expect to be asked, "How much money will you need?" It is always best to estimate on the high side, since if our estimates turn out low, it is almost always difficult to raise additional money (unless we indulge in the famous "cost overrun" of contractual research and development). Furthermore, proposals will rarely, if ever, be selected on the basis of sums involved. If a proposal generates interest but appears too expensive, we may be asked to propose another budget or another method to execute the research at less cost. But interest in the proposal is not likely to fall through because we ask for too much cash. In fact, the opposite often seems to be the case. If we ask for a sum of money that seems too little for the effective execution of the research, the proposal runs a risk of not being taken seriously. Agencies tend to think research ought to cost even more than it normally might. We should not forget to include, therefore, any overhead expenses we may be charged for working in a research center or institute. Finally, a research proposal will be considered in the same bureaucratic way whether much or little money is involved. First comes an examination of the merits of the idea and the interest or apparent value or importance of the research; then comes consideration of whether it can be afforded. (All this depends, of course, on whether the research proposal falls within the province of what the foundation or agency generally sponsors within its own charter.) Logically, a small sum of money ought to be more forthcoming than a large sum. This logic, however, does not normally apply in "grantsmanship."

Researchers are often asked when making a proposal, "What is the thesis?" or "What do you expect to show or find out?" These questions ask us to have some sense of the research results before we have actually done the research. Needless to say, it is almost impossible to know the results beforehand. We may entertain a number of theories or hypotheses, but it is generally contrary to our assumptions about free inquiry to have the answers before we begin. Nevertheless, there is an apparent reluctance on the part of granters of funds to accept this ignorance.

Let me suggest here one possible solution to this problem that may seem facetious but should be considered seriously. As I said earlier, the first grant is always the hardest. There is something of a cumulative effect after the first grant. When an agency recognizes that others have thought us worthy of support before, it is easier to instill confidence than when our slates are blank. For this reason, we are hard-pressed the first time around. Since it is much easier to explain what a particular research project can discover after it has been done than before (and also easier to know what it will cost after it has been done and money has been spent), it is easier to seek funds for research already completed. The funds allocated can then go into a new project or a more advanced phase of the present one. If we are prepared to withhold our results until the next project or final completion of the present work (thus staying one project ahead in the use of funds), we will be able to budget precisely and propose subject, object, hypothesis, and thesis with little difficulty.

Let's call this idea the "one-project-ahead" or "one-grant-ahead" method. If the new funds pay for the last project—that is, if the monies we use for a new project are based on an old one—we are more likely to please those who pay and our own results may be of better quality. Since precise proposals are better than vague ones, we should not discount the potential value of such an approach to grantsmanship. This approach raises moral issues, but the practice is much more common than might be supposed, and its practitioners do not consider themselves immoral. We should always remember, however, that poor-quality research may make it difficult to secure subsequent support.

Setting Up Shop

Once we have the money and can go into the field there are a number of immediate problems that must be solved. The greatest of these is almost always finding living accommodations. An official affiliation with the use of an office is invaluable, for it may provide an official address, the use of telephone, and possibly other services. In many cities there are institutes that provide space for visiting researchers, and every attempt should be made to use that space. Access can often be gained directly by writing in advance or even by arriving at the door. However, chances of securing space to work and use facilities improve substantially when (1) the foundation or agency providing financial support either provides space itself or makes a request at an institute in our behalf, and (2) some personal contact within the institute in question can provide help. However it is secured, office space reduces enormously the burden of living accommodations.

If there is no office space, then the housing problem takes on special dimensions. Single researchers might be able to take a

room in someone's home; for couples or families such an arrangement is more difficult. If we intend to do any interviewing,
a telephone becomes a necessity. In Europe, a telephone may
not be in a given apartment, and the cost and wait for installation is forbidding. Since one room is likely to become a constant
work space, at least two rooms will be needed. In an urban setting an automobile may be hard to operate or afford; if research
is to be concentrated at certain libraries, institutions, or agencies
or in certain neighborhoods, it will be important to live near
these places or at least near good public transportation. These
prerequisites can drive up the cost of housing as well as increase
the difficulty in finding something. Time spent looking for accommodations is time lost from research. On the other hand,
long daily travel or inadequate work space can present a constant drain on resources as well.

To meet these needs we should be prepared, yet again, to exploit contacts. Do we know anyone living in the place where we
are going? Might they know of a suitable or sufficient accommodation? Is there a university with a housing office that might
help? It is hard to accept housing before arrival, though something temporary is always needed.

The search for housing can vary widely from city to city and
country to country. In London, for example, the *Evening Standard* newspaper, which appears in the early afternoon, has many
pages of advertisements for housing. Unfortunately, many of the
listings lead back to a few agencies that seek fees, and the many
telephone calls necessary to learn this advertising device can
prove frustrating and expensive. The *London Times*, whose listings are far more brief (and whose daily edition costs twice as
much), often proves more reliable and useful. In addition there
are numerous agencies, both within the immediate areas where
we might want accommodation and in the Center for the
Greater London area, but since they all work (except the "estate
agents") on commission from those who seek a place to live,
they seek to convince clients to take more expensive accommodations.

Often embassies and consulates provide housing lists. In
Florence, for example, the British consulate maintains an informal list on which Americans (who find no like service in the

bigger American consulate down the road) frequently rely. It also can help to place an advertisement in the local newspaper, stating who you are (e.g., "American research student . . .") and what kind of accommodation you seek. Many people reluctant to advertise their housing may respond to the reversed roles. I can attest personally to the efficacy of this method—much to my own surprise—in Italy.

Living arrangements, though they may seem trivial, constitute one of the most serious problems of field research. They cause considerable anxiety and lost time. As much as possible should be done before arriving in a new place, but you should also be resigned to the likelihood of difficulty once you do arrive.

The Researcher's Affiliation

Once housing is found it is possible to set out on the task of research itself. But there remains yet another preliminary problem. We must decide how we will present ourselves—that is, what or whom we represent and with whom or what we are associated. There is no simple answer. Suppose we come from a university, have a grant from a foundation, and have office space in an institute. Here we have at least three different affiliations. And what are we doing? "Research" is rarely a satisfactory identification for people being questioned. In general, we had better be writing a dissertation or a book. The questions "Why are you doing this?" and "Whom are you doing this for?" will be asked repeatedly. We had better be armed with good answers.

This problem of identity can be extremely complicated. Suppose, for instance, we have a grant to study political conflicts over airports from the airport authority. The grant is without qualifications, and we are pursuing independent and free research under the auspices of a university. But we need to ask questions of local people in conflict with the airport authority. If we answer one of the above questions with, "The research is paid for by the airport authority," we can rest assured we will receive no worthwhile answers from hostile and suspicious local citizens. For the local citizens, then, we are doing university research. But we also need to raise questions with the airport authority's bureaucracy, which is suspicious of universities. There we must give the answer we could never have contemplated giving to the local citizens. We are obliged to divide our multiple identity.

In another example, suppose we do research sponsored by the Department of Labor concerning local manpower programs. To local groups, people who work for the government are not to be trusted; to local government agencies, independent researchers are not worthy of precious time to answer questions. So we are independent for the locals and we work for the government as far as the agencies are concerned. Our entire identity, if revealed, could destroy our research, not because we do necessarily work for anyone or out of anyone's interest, but because people answering questions normally doubt the concept of independent or free inquiry and because the research sponsor may indeed seek to influence our research. If we study German-Israeli relations with a German grant, the Israelis are inevitably suspicious. If we study automobile workers with a grant from FIAT, the workers must certainly be suspicious. So we must identify with some independent institution.

Multiple identities often can be exploited valuably, even though the use of them may raise moral questions. Are we less than honest if we are less than candid for the sake of data collection? How much must we tell, given that we expect others to tell us everything? And if we tell less than everything, what happens if we are found out?

Above all, we must be consistent. That is, even if we don't tell all, we must never tell something other than the truth. We must never claim to work for the government if we do not; we must never claim to be enrolled in a university if we are not. The sources of money can complicate enormously our research tasks, no matter how honestly we pursue our research. Consequently, we must be especially careful. If we work for a newspaper, it is foolish and immoral to pretend we do not. Once found out, we can never proceed again. It is normally best to be independent and to be affiliated with a nonaligned or impartial institute or university. Unfortunately, this ideal is rarely achieved when money is needed. Not only must we resist any attempts to be influenced by those who pay us; we must resist permitting the sources of money from interfering in any way with the pursuit of honest research.

We should note that it is almost always necessary to carry some form of identification. This identification should be fancy enough to impress and simple enough not to confuse. In general, the solution is the personal calling card. Before setting out to see people, you should have cards printed with your name, address, and phone number (if you know them in advance), and your most neutral official affiliation. Prestigious affiliations always have a certain value, but we should be constantly aware that prestige in the field relates more to neutrality than to power; better to identify—on a card that may be circulated—with a university than with a government or agency.

Furthermore, whatever titles you have should be displayed. Asking people to cooperate with research involves a demand on their time for which you offer meager compensation at best. Unless people just like to be helpful or just like to talk—which happens less often than might be desirable—you are obliged to convince them that you deserve their help. The best, and most honest, way to convince people to help is by convincing them of a serious purpose. Serious purposes are associated with serious people and serious institutions. If you appear important—because you have degrees or titles or come from a notable institution—you are more likely to elicit cooperation than if you appear to be just another student, bent on interfering with people's time and lives. We may doubt the justice in a world of such bias, but we would be foolhardy to doubt the truth of it or to fail to draw appropriate conclusions in order to conduct ourselves.

The calling card should not necessarily tell all, but it should tell that which can be told to everyone. A fair supply should always be at hand, and we should not hesitate to use them. In general, however, one hundred cards are a lot of cards. They will last at least a year in most research.

In addition to carrying calling cards to identify us, it is also helpful to carry letters of reference or introduction. If we know someone who knows someone else that we want to see, we should carry a letter of introduction. The institutions with which we are affiliated should provide general letters asking for cooperation on our behalf from other institutions, libraries, individuals, etc. We should head into the field armed with these letters, and if someone can write ahead personally on our behalf, that opportunity should be seized.

Launching the Inquiry

Research should begin always by identifying the local resources: Where are the archives? Where are documents kept? What is kept in which libraries? We should make ourselves known to curators and librarians and arrange visiting and (if possible) borrowing privileges.

If there is a local newspaper, we should read it. We will learn, at the very least, the local issues of the day, which will make our contact with people easier because we will be familiar with what is important to them. At the most, we will find stories about the subject of our study. We also will learn the names and roles of key actors.

We should then contact the local nonpartisan experts on our subject. University people and journalists tend to be the two principal resources. Then we can hope to frame issues better by acquiring a better understanding and feel for local perceptions and a sense of who is perceived as knowledgeable and important. In this way we can begin to compile a systematic list of the people we want to see and what, more precisely, we should ask them.

In setting out to visit archives, libraries, and local specialists, it is often best to announce ourselves in writing first. The pattern (which should be repeated when seeking interviews in the field) should involve writing a short letter identifying ourselves and our project, asking for an appointment, and explaining precisely what we intend to do at a meeting if it is granted. We should propose a time and date, invite a reply, and promise to telephone for confirmation within some specified time if no written reply has been received.

A follow-up telephone call, if necessary, should not descend into an interview. To this end, it is often best to ask on the phone for a secretary or someone who keeps a person's calendar. If the party we want to see gets on the other end of the phone, he or she is likely to launch a series of questions obliging us, in effect, to present our own questions then and there. Telephone exchanges have many disadvantages, the greatest of which is the most obvious: We cannot establish eye contact, so we cannot judge effectively when a question might lead somewhere else and when something is, at least for the moment, better left alone. Whenever possible, telephone interviews are to be avoided. The best way to avoid them, again, is never to get on the phone with the party in the first place. If it is unavoidable, we should state our business as succinctly as possible with an eye to arranging a convenient meeting.

The practice of writing letters is especially valuable because it assures that the party we intend to see will have something in front of them with which to associate our voice on the phone or, later, our presence in the room. It sets a formal, businesslike, and serious tone to the task. If the letter can be sent on some kind of official letterhead, so much the better. In any event, formality suggests respect for the other parties. When people feel respected, they cooperate and help. We should always make every effort, therefore, to generate a feeling of respect.

For many research projects, we can begin almost immediately to contact some sources of information; other cases may require a slower approach. If the research concentrates on a bureaucratic or government elite, we can move ahead formally and officially without a major concern for ingratiating ourselves. If, on the other hand, we are studying local activists, workers, trade unions, or political parties—or for that matter any group of people out of power and struggling for it—the approach must be different. There is a certain, often justified, paranoia among such groups. They often have been infiltrated or subverted. Their self-conscious challenge to established authority makes them especially suspicious of our purpose and method. They may have a clear but unspoken hierarchy that we are expected to observe and respect. We walk into such settings largely ignorant, and a few early mistakes—which offend people or cast doubt on our seriousness or honesty or generate a lack of trust and confidence—can destroy our entire research effort.

In settings where we are studying local groups out of power, we must present ourselves discreetly and somewhat less formally. We must inquire quietly how things are arranged and organized and who is recognized as the local leadership. We might have to visit the bars or cafés, the local church on Sunday, and so forth. The accounts of such research are numerous, ranging from *Street Corner Society*[2] and *Tally's Corner*[3] to Edgar Morin's *The Red and the White*.[4] We should familiarize ourselves with this literature and with the experiences of others in pursuing this kind of delicate research before we set out ourselves.

Since we must establish trust, we usually need to allow a great deal more time for local community research than for elite study. The need for more time has been demonstrated amply by Laurence Wylie in *Village in the Vaucluse* and *Chanzeaux*.[5] We need to find a place to live, and we also need to build trust and a network of contacts. A general rule of thumb is that setting up shop for good community field research can be expected to take three or four months. Only then will we have established ourselves in the community such that people will be open, lead us to other people, and so forth. Since we are normally obliged to indicate how long a research project will take before we launch it, these factors must be taken into consideration.

As I have emphasized before, the choice of research object is closely tied to the choice of subject. Similarly, we should be conscious of the choice of site. Whether we work in a big city, a small neighborhood, or a small town depends, of course, on the questions we want answered. But we should remain conscious here that the choice of site affects in major ways the conduct of research and the time needed. Moreover, it affects when we begin our research or move to a particular site. It may be necessary to arrive before the end of a term of parliament when all the legislators return to their constituencies or before the end of the university term when students and faculty scatter to their homes; or it may be important to know when landlords and landladies tend to holiday, lest we arrive without hope of finding a place to live for a while. Elite research in Europe during the Christmas holidays is a futile undertaking, just as it would be in Washington in August. These local conditions are also part of the information we need to launch research, to structure our time, and to calculate our timing.

Getting Interviews

As in contacting resource people shortly after our arrival, we should also arrange interviews more directly related to data collection through formal approaches. The formal and official request for the allocation of time is universally flattering. Flattery can, in research, get us everywhere, so we should write a letter and follow it with a telephone call. Often, of course, this procedure is not possible, and in some communities it is not necessary. In Washington, D.C., for example, much can be arranged directly by telephone because the American capital prides itself on a daytime, efficient informality. Such informal approaches in Paris would be—in far too many cases—disastrous. We can never go wrong being formal. Informality involves risk. In general, especially at the beginning, it is best to follow these formal procedures.

Getting interviews can often be facilitated through third parties, which is one reason why we should begin with those people we think most likely to be sympathetic to our enterprise. Whenever a third party offers to arrange an interview, it is usually worthwhile to accept the offer. Accepting the help makes the helper feel as though he or she is contributing, and it helps make the person to be interviewed feel somewhat responsible both to the interviewer and to the intervening third party. Such dual obligation can and often should be exploited.

Some networks may seem impenetrable. Potential respondents communicate with each other and seem to conspire not to see us. Alternatively, each time we arrive at an office we are greeted with a reference to the person we just left. There is no solution to the inconvenience of communications among respondents, but there are ways in which we can penetrate a network. One particularly valuable approach is to exploit the "young boys' network." Somewhere within the orbit of the parties concerned we may have an acquaintance or two. They may have been classmates in high school or college or graduate school. They may be former students, teachers, cousins, or even friends of friends. If we can locate them anywhere in an appropriate bureaucracy, we may discover they can reach into the network of respondents for us.

We may be inclined to neglect these contacts because they are not situated in the upper echelons of the bureaucracy. They are not, themselves, the elites we seek. However, it is important to remember that the directors of agencies, like the generals of armies, usually are not familiar with day-to-day operations. Agencies are run by the colonels, not the generals, and the colonels often can prove to be the most valuable sources of information. The "old boys' network" may be beyond our reach, but it may also be populated by generals. The young boys' network, closer to our own generation, may contain the lieutenants and colonels.

Some people may not want to give an interview but would prefer to be credited with being too busy rather than unwilling. We must decide in such cases how important such a person really is for us. If important enough, there are time-honored journalistic methods for getting to see someone. We can wait religiously at the office or at the home. We can offer to ride along *en route* somewhere, carry a suitcase, or open a door. We can have others write letters or place telephone calls on our behalf. We can simply telephone every day. Whatever we do, we must be fair. Hence, before applying pressure tactics we must have offered to meet at any time, in any reasonably accessible place. If we have been this accommodating, we can then more vigorously seek an audience.

Businessmen, lawyers, and doctors will occasionally inform us of the unique cash value of their time. They will be happy to see us, they may say, if we are prepared to pay the one hundred dollars per hour (or whatever the sum) to which they are accustomed. Each researcher must decide whether an audience with a particular individual is worth such an investment, for it may prove, on very rare occasion, worth taking up such a challenge. In general, however, it should be remembered that no single person, like no single document, is likely to be worth the expense.

Another point to consider is that we may be granted an appointment for only a very brief interval. Rarely do such interviews terminate when scheduled, however, so we should accept such appointments rather than think the time allowed to be too short and consequently not go at all.

It is also possible that we will be asked to submit our questions in writing before the interview. We should never hesitate to comply, remembering that if we are given an audience we will probably have the opportunity to probe. By "probing" (which will be discussed later) I mean the exploration of certain answers to gain clarification or further information. Probing is always necessary in open-ended interviews and is frequently necessary in closed interviews.

We may resent the suggestion that respondents are vulnerable to attractive members of the opposite sex. On the other hand, female interviewers often do have difficulty getting respondents to take them seriously, and men may be subject to the problem of sex bias as well. In instances where a man or woman has difficulty getting an appointment and senses a sex bias, he or she should find someone of the opposite sex to telephone or accompany him or her to the interview. This person should be identified as a research partner. For interviewing executives, there is nothing better than the presence of an attractive person of the opposite sex. For interviewing government officials and others in male-dominated circles, attractive young women may do better if accompanied by serious-looking young men. The researcher can conduct the inquiry and can indeed do all the talking. It is the presence of the other person that makes the difference.

Finally, we should recognize that many people will answer written requests despite a refusal to meet with us. Although the face-to-face interview is preferable, the value of written answers should not be discounted. If we are able to put precisely both our informational and attitudinal requests, we have every reason to expect useful replies. When someone has refused to see us due to time constraints, we should write asking if written questions would be acceptable. Upon the granting of our request, the questions should then be sent as quickly as possible.

The Place of the Interview

It is sometimes possible to choose where the interview will be held. Usually this choice will be between a respondent's home or office. There are advantages and disadvantages to both, but in general, if it is possible to see someone at home, the likelihood of a more forthright exchange is improved. Away from the office a respondent is inclined to feel removed from others who might overhear. Even though documents and reference materials may all be at the office (which may create a handicap), a person interviewed at home may prove willing to assemble pertinent documents in the office later on. For these reasons, despite the risk of being deprived access to some documents, the home should normally be preferred whenever choice is available.

Many interviews will probably be conducted over meals, especially lunch and occasionally dinner. When we are invited, we should try to accept, but we should remember at least two points. (1) It is very difficult to take notes and out of the question to operate a tape recorder during a meal. Although food and drink may lead a respondent to be especially lucid, it is best, whenever possible, to arrange for the meeting to continue after eating. This way, important ground can be repeated, and notes can be taken. If the interview cannot be continued after the meal, however, the interviewer is faced with being wholly dependent on memory, which is likely to be impaired by food and drink. (2) If the interview takes place at a restaurant, the respondent—who has usually extended the invitation—will normally propose to pay the bill. Purists will feel that to permit such payment may create a measure of indebtedness; the respondent may expect us to tell our story casting him or her in a favorable light. We must each make our own judgment on this question. I think that when respondents perceive us in their debt, they often are even more forthcoming; it is up to us to overcome the bourgeois response that associates financial outlay with moral indebtedness. A single meal is not a vicuna coat; if we distort the story, we are more culpable as poor social scientists than as takers of bribes. One caveat, however: If we are working on contract, these matters are more delicate than if we are wholly independent. And if we are on expense accounts, we should be prepared both to extend the invitations and to pick up the bill.

The Interview Itself

Once the interview is arranged, several rules should be followed: (1) be on time; (2) do not be early; (3) dress as if you are going to be interviewed for a good office job; and (4) follow all the standard operating procedures for going after something you want. That is, although you conduct the interview, you must *behave* as if you were being interviewed in the hope of, say, securing a job. After all, you are asking for something and normally not offering much in return. As interviewers we are generally guests in other people's offices or homes. So we sit when invited, and we terminate the interview and leave if asked. Smoking is a bad idea. We should not doodle during a boring discourse, or stare out windows, or wander around distractedly, even when accompanying someone else who may be asking the questions. All attention must be focused on the respondent and, in general, we should follow the lead of our respondent. Every move must be calculated as a reflection of respect for the other party. And even if we do not really feel any particular respect, we should recognize that we seek something, and, however painful it may be, we should humble ourselves accordingly. Rebellion and the conduct of research are not especially compatible, even though the questions we ask and the manner in which we deal with the results might be very rebellious indeed.

The Language of the Interview

With regard to the conduct of interviews, one point should be emphasized concerning foreign languages. We must appreciate that weakness can be turned to advantage. Whereas it is best for the respondent to speak clearly in his or her native language, that may not always be best for us. We are always inclined, of course, to attempt the language of the respondent. But if we are invited to proceed in our own language, we ought to recognize the advantages: (1) we will obviously understand more; (2) we will be able to ask our questions more precisely; and (3) we will control more thoroughly the course of the interview. A respondent can always explain or clarify in native tongue an obscure or difficult-to-express point. Furthermore, we will not need to translate the data later. Offers to speak in our native language may come from the Italians, for example; they are less likely to come from the French, and when they do they may also yield disdainful answers thereafter. In some instances, of course, delicate subjects will be discussed more openly with someone who seems a "member of the family" (speaks the native language). Germans do not like to explain antisemitism to outsiders (i.e., non–German speakers). In general, nevertheless, speaking in the language most comfortable for us is beneficial. We should recognize, too, that some languages may be neutral or preferable for the discussion of sensitive subjects, whereupon neither the interviewer nor the respondent will speak in native tongue. Finally, if we profess weakness in a language, we can be forgiven asking deceptively simple questions that are often valuable but resented when language comprehension is assumed or apparent. Thus, any weakness we have with a language should be exploited to invite repetition, clarification, and simplicity where otherwise points may have been deliberately obfuscating.

Getting and Exchanging Information

As I said earlier, we offer very little in exchange for the information and cooperation we ask. A respondent might imagine being recorded for posterity or might hope to gain some advantage over opponents. A respondent might find us more worthy than a journalist and hope we will retell a story to set straight a previously distorted record. For these reasons we should begin interviews by restating the purpose of our research and by reassuring the respondent of his or her singular importance and knowledge. When a respondent is self-deprecating (seriously or facetiously), we should indicate how pleased we are with the opportunity to interview him or her, perhaps offering specific examples of the respondent's appropriate expertise. On the other hand, a respondent may have no need or desire to inform despite flattery. Although granting an appointment, a respondent may not be prepared to say much. We have only one thing available to pry loose information, and that is information itself.

A respondent is always interested in knowing what other people have been saying and is always keen to pry loose information that might have come to us in confidence. Because the confidentiality of our work and its integrity are almost all we have, we must protect with extreme caution any assault on it. We should not quote and attribute information from one interview in another. If asked, "What did X say?" we must indicate that we are not at liberty to respond. Unfortunately that answer is precisely the answer we can then anticipate from our respondent to our questions.

To get around this problem, we should be prepared to reveal information, though always without attribution. We can say, "We have heard from some people . . ." without jeopardizing confidentiality. In general we should prefer not to trade information this way, but we must be prepared to do so. It should be done sparingly and only when necessary. It also must be done cautiously so that the respondent does not fear that we might do the same with his or her testimony. But information is all we have to trade and we must be prepared to trade it.

Comparative research has particular advantages in solving this problem. Information collected in another city or another country is far less sensitive than information collected in the same neighborhood or in the same parliament or within the same union or club. But we should recognize that such information piques curiosity no less. Thus, we should exploit, though again with a sparing tongue, the fact that we may be familiar with a similar case about which a respondent may be curious but know nothing at all. Furthermore, the less the respondent knows in advance, the less need be told to seem like making a trade.

The reverse of the last point should be emphasized. The less we know the less we can hope to learn. Later interviews will be more productive than earlier ones, which means that, in general, we should save the most knowledgeable people for last or arrange to see them at the beginning—when they may save us considerable time—and again at the end, when we have more to discuss. Respondents will detect the depth and breadth of our knowledge just as we will detect our respondents' familiarity with particular subjects when the inevitable trading of information develops. It is better to trade the information that is most remote to the respondent for that with which he or she is most familiar. Apparent openness on our part normally can bring such an exchange about. However, we must always remember that this rule is most useful to comparative research where our access to remote yet interesting information is greatest.

Let us consider for a moment the problem of "probing," especially in the context of closed interviews or when written questions have been submitted in advance. Let us imagine the following exchange. Written question: "Do you approve of General de Gaulle's nuclear policy?" Spoken answer: "I have always believed France must be strong and must use whatever means available to deter aggressors." We might interpret this answer affirmatively inasmuch as General de Gaulle's policy involves French strength, or we might interpret it negatively inasmuch as the program is deliberately limited in scale and scope. We do not repeat the question. Rather, we might go on to say, "General de Gaulle's nuclear policy involves cutting back the overall defense budget. Do you oppose defense cuts, and would you question the nuclear policy if it contributed directly to such cuts?" This question was not on our submitted list, but an answer will probably be offered. It is possible that the respondent will challenge our probe on the grounds that it is a different question; therefore, we should always be prepared to explain honestly and directly the meaning and purpose of our probe.

Even in a closed interview such probing may be necessary. For example, we ask, "How many people do you support in your household?" Answer: "Well, there is my wife, two daughters, my mother-in-law every evening, and my son's college roommate every weekend." We have to do some mental arithmetic, and we do not have an answer we can record. Does the mother-in-law live elsewhere and dine with our respondent every evening? Or perhaps he is being facetious and complaining about his wife's long-distance telephone calls. Is the son at home? Does the roommate visit every weekend all year? When the answer we are given is unclear or impossible to code, we must be prepared to ask further questions that are not necessarily on our form in order to secure the information we seek. We might ask the respondent in this instance, "You support five people including yourself, then?" The respondent will then sort out an answer.

We should always be cautious when probing. The manner in which a question is posed may influence the answer. For example, our French respondent might say "yes" if we ask, "General de Gaulle is really a great man, don't you think so?" A less leading question might have produced a more subtle answer. Or let us suppose that we are asking whether respondents perceive a "special relationship" between Canada and the United States. If we ask about the "special relationship" directly, they may discuss relations between the two countries as "special." If we never refer to the relations as "special," however, perhaps the respondents will not either. If they do not, it may indicate that relations are not perceived this way; the phrasing of our question may have precluded the possibility of discovering whether our very terms helped create answers.[6]

As researchers we must be self-conscious about avoiding advocacy. Often we will find ourselves with people who are making statements with which we strongly disagree. We may want to take issue with them. We must always remember the purpose of our business. We came to inquire and to find out, not to advocate. However painful it may seem at the time—or, for that matter, even in retrospect—we must reserve the advocacy for the presentation of our results when the data collection is complete. The sometimes fine distinction between prodding and advocating must be respected.

Keeping a Record of the Interview

An important decision concerns how we will keep a record of the interview. One possible way is to bring someone along who will take notes; another is to work as a team with someone else; a third way is to take notes ourselves; a fourth method involves using a tape recorder; and a fifth method is to write out everything from memory after the interview. Let us consider these possibilities in order.

The Silent Partner. It is generally not a good idea to bring along a notetaker. The silent, recording presence in the room, however self-consciously unobtrusive, is likely to constrain responses even more than the tape recorder, which we will discuss in a moment. The notetaker is like an audience, and however trusted the person may be, the respondent is unlikely to feel capable of speaking confidentially. There are exceptions, of course. But generally other methods for keeping records are preferable.

Interviewing as a Team. Team interviewing is quite different from having someone along as notetaker, as we will see in a moment. Team interviewing has the special advantage of allowing one person to take notes while the other concentrates on a line of questioning. But team interviewing can be difficult and usually requires more preparation than an interview conducted alone. More preparation is needed because we must coordinate carefully with our partner. On the one hand, we do not want to let a line of questioning fall unpursued, yet we must be wary not to interfere with the technique and style of our partner (who may inquire more or less directly, more or less quickly, than we would). On the other hand, we want to avoid the pregnant pauses when we anticipate incorrectly what our partners may do next. Lines of questioning must be agreed upon in advance, and the interview should have a leader. Moreover, the leader should arrange the interview, for the respondent will assume that the same party who made the arrangements will also conduct the interview (respondents always will consider a professor the leader when accompanied by an assistant, however).

Partners should be aware of each other's technique and style and should avoid interfering as much as possible. Many of these problems are subtle. Team interviewing can benefit from the presence of two minds and two pens, but it can also suffer from a lack of coordination. This method works especially well when there are linguistic problems requiring extra concentration but can be especially awkward when crossed signals lead to saying or asking the wrong things. Above all, we must not correct our partner or indicate any disagreement; nor should we offer an answer to our partner's question. There may be a reason of which we are unaware for asking a particular question in a particular way, and in any case we must be what the name implies—a team. Team interviewing, therefore, may seem a relief to the novice, but it is usually most effective when done by a skilled pair. The inexperienced researcher is most often better off alone.

Notetaking. Whether you take notes yourself or in coordination with a partner, you must come prepared. Before setting out for an interview you should always check for plenty of paper and pens with ink that will not run out. The paper should be attached in a notebook of manageable size that can rest comfortably on your lap during the course of the interview; you cannot expect to have a writing surface available, and you should never presume to set yourself up on someone's desk or table. In fact, notes should be taken as inconspicuously as possible, which means it is best to take them in a small notebook on your lap or in your hands, away from open view.

The page onto which you will record the notes should be prepared in advance. We are not acrobats, but social scientists; we cannot, therefore, plan to juggle papers while posing questions and taking notes. We must remember that there are two sets of notes at an interview: the notes we are taking and the notes that are guiding our questions. Since many interviews on the same subject will need to be completed before a researcher can rely on memory to conduct an interview, where shall we keep the notes we are using? If possible, they should be written on the same page as the notes we are taking. I like to carve out a corner where I list my questions in short form, leaving the rest of the page to record answers. In this way I have nothing to juggle.

Many researchers feel insecure without a list of fully written questions. Writing out questions can be helpful, and no interview can be prepared without serious reflection on what the questions will be about and what purpose must be accomplished. However, writing out questions in full normally precludes taking notes on the same page. The size of the sheet containing the questions should be approximately the same size as that on which the answers will be recorded. The questions should be kept within easy view, organized in front of us so that we can take notes without shuffling papers to find the questions or to find blank paper.

It is very important not to pursue an interview by burying our heads in our questions or notes. We must concentrate on what we are being told if we hope to ask coherent and logical questions. Therefore, when we take our notes, we must plan to take *only* notes—not long statements verbatim. Our priorities must lie with the relationship we can establish and maintain with our respondent. Furthermore, if our respondent indicates at some point that something about to be said is strictly confidential or off the record, it is important that we give some physical sign acknowledging this wish. If we are taking notes, the best way is to set down pens conspicuously, even fold hands, so that it is clear we are listening and not writing. After the confidential statement is complete, during some other discussion, we can then record quickly the main points not recorded earlier. Confidential remarks cannot be used with attribution, but in other ways or for other purposes they may well be remarks we want to remember.

We should recognize that taking notes and paying attention to what is being said while thinking of the next question involve mental acrobatics no less challenging than the shuffling of papers. And just as we can reduce the paper problem by preparing these materials thoughtfully before arriving at the interview, we can also make some preparations for the mental problems.

If we plan to refer to our notes only rarely in order to concentrate on the respondent, we must make a special effort to know the content of our notes, committing the better part of our questions to memory. Before setting out for certain kinds of elite interviews, we should also make a routine of checking *Who's Who*, or some appropriate equivalent, so that we are fully familiar with a respondent's background. Something is liable to come up during an interview that relates to a respondent's past, and it is much better to be fully acquainted with that past so we are not obliged to make superficial historical inquiry. We should also be familiar with public statements made by the subject and should be familiar with whatever the respondent has written. Government officials may publish under a pseudonym; we should try to locate and read any such writings. It is better to commit these things to memory than to rely on notes during an interview, and the more we can cite the individual's own background the better, for it flatters the respondent at the same time that it advances the discussion beyond public knowledge that otherwise would be repeated.

Using a Tape Recorder. The tape recorder is a technological device designed to meet many problems. In theory it should solve all problems of notetaking at interviews. Unfortunately, it is not the panacea it may seem, though in some instances it can be invaluable. Let us consider first when it might be used, and then what some of its advantages and disadvantages are.

Again, in theory, the tape recorder might be used at any interview. It is often helpful to ask over the telephone when completing the final arrangements for an interview whether it will be possible to bring a tape recorder. Such warning is sometimes preferable to merely arriving with tape recorder in hand, but the respondent who asks that a tape recorder not be used might have felt differently had we arrived ready to go. It is difficult to judge which strategy to adopt; my own experience suggests that there may be a small advantage in arriving with the tape recorder in hand. It is impossible to tape, of course, if the respondent—for whatever reason—prefers not to have the tape recorder present. In general, officials in England and in Italy will reject the use of a tape recorder on the grounds of confidentiality; in France there is in contrast a certain enthusiasm sometimes expressed, as if to suggest that the tape recorder is proof of a serious purpose and that remarks will be reported accurately and for posterity. In the United States there is relative indifference.

When the tape recorder is allowed (and even with it in hand we must ask whether we can use it before setting it up), we must take a number of mechanical precautions. First, we must be sure the batteries are fresh. We should also have enough clear tape, which usually requires overestimating the probable duration of the interview. The equipment must be prepared so that we need only plug in the microphone, press the record button, and begin. Whatever tape recorder we have, we should be sure that (1) it registers voice to be sure it is recording, and (2) it shows clearly that the tape is turning. During the course of the interview we should be sure to shut off the tape recorder when told something confidential, and we must remember that restarting usually requires holding down the record button again. Finally, in the category of mechanical concerns, we should know how long our tape will run and remember to turn it over or change it (for this reason, among others, we should be sure to wear a watch to an interview). These points may appear obvious or trivial, but on the first few tries, some or all of these errors are likely. The major portion of an interview can be lost by forgetting to bring enough tape or forgetting to turn over or change the tape. Finally, we need to mark the tape after it has been used so that we do not accidentally erase an interview.

The tape recorder is especially helpful when we are dealing in foreign languages. In fact, foreign language use is often an ideal excuse for securing consent ("Forgive me, but since my French is not that good . . ."). It is also helpful for recording material that can be quoted directly without paraphrase, since it helps us to concentrate more on the line of questions than on taking notes. Finally, a tape recorder may encourage people (as is often the case in France) to speak out.

There are many disadvantages as well. The tape recorder can inhibit a respondent (even when the respondent may claim otherwise), so for this reason the tape recorder we use should be small and unobtrusive. We should put the microphone midway between ourselves and the respondent (and leave it there, not keep emphasizing its presence by moving it about or making adjustments), and we should let the cord run so that the recorder itself is more or less out of the respondent's view. Locating the recorder this way cuts down on the motor's background noise feeding through the microphone as well.

We should also remember that tape recorders tend to lull us into a technological dependence with two major drawbacks: (1) if for some reason the recording fails or the quality of the tape is poor, we may have no notes or material from the interview, and (2) we cannot digest the many, many hours of tape recording that we will accumulate in the course of a project. For these reasons we cannot permit the tape recorder to substitute completely for notetaking. Not only do we need a few notes to jog our memories in case of mechanical failure, but also, when something of particular interest is said, we should record in our notes the number on the tape counter so that we can find the important segment of tape later on without having to listen to the whole tape.

It is impossible to know in any given case whether it would be better to tape or not to tape. We must make personal judgments concerning the respondents. We always risk inhibition, but we always stand to gain a documentary record. In addition to taking into account the general national and cultural tendencies suggested above, the researcher must judge each case independently.

Writing Notes After the Interview. The final method we have suggested for recording an interview is to write out everything after the interview is over. This method relies, of course, on superior memory. Even the best of us will probably need a few notes to remember everything. Summarizing our notes should be standard practice after all interviews, however, regardless of how we take notes during the interviews.

Concluding the Interview

Whatever method we have chosen for keeping a record of our interview, there are some standard procedures that might be followed as the interview comes to a conclusion. First we should always clarify whether we can quote our respondent. We should also ask whether it will be possible to return if the research seems to require a subsequent visit. (Each interview should be conducted, however, on the assumption that we will never see a given person again, unless we have already arranged a series of meetings.) If a series of meetings is planned, we may set aside areas of inquiry, but if there is no such prior agreement we cannot assume later access; for this reason our planning notes should identify priority items that must be pursued if the interview threatens to be briefer than we had anticipated. And for this reason we should request the possibility of returning.

We should also ask whether the respondent knows of other people we ought to see, and in sensitive subject areas (especially policy research) we should appreciate hints about who *not* to see, for the unsympathetic can make access to others difficult. If we are with a partner, the leader should ask the partner if he or she has any further questions. We should ask the respondent if there are any points that he or she would like to clarify or emphasize. Second-hand data (when we are told, for example, what a third party thinks) are as legitimate as direct testimony, for we cannot be sure that what we are told about someone is less true than what they tell us themselves. It is useful, therefore, to ask a researcher what someone else thinks. And I often ask, finally, "Given the subject we have been discussing, is there anything you think I should have asked or that I have neglected?" Responses to this question can be surprisingly useful. No matter how unsuccessful or disagreeable the interview may have been, gratitude for time and trouble should be expressed clearly, and every effort should be made to depart on congenial terms.

After the Interview

Immediately after an interview we must find a place (perhaps a nearby café, or in summer a nearby park bench) where we can spend approximately an hour with our notes. Even if a tape recorder was not used during the interview, it may now prove useful for pouring out our thoughts. All points should be clarified. Memory should be purged. All full statements that may be quoted later should be written out. Questions should be checked to see if everything was satisfactorily answered, and we should be sure all answers were recorded. As we become more experienced, this exercise becomes less time-consuming, but no matter how experienced we are, we must devote some time for this purpose.

* * *

There are a number of further concerns surrounding interviewing and pursuing research that we must now consider. For one thing, we have not yet discussed how to organize a work schedule; for another, we need to consider how to maintain our data. In Chapter 4 we will address these matters and a number of other peculiar field problems, such as gaining access to people in bureaucracies, and what we need to consider when the research is completed and we are ready to go home.

Notes

1. See my discussion of related problems in "An Antidote for Apology, Service and Witchcraft in Policy Analysis," in Phillip Gregg, *Problems of Theory in Policy Analysis* (Lexington, Mass: Lexington Books, 1976).
2. William F. Whyte, *Street Corner Society: The Social Structure of an Italian Slum* (Chicago: University of Chicago Press, 1955).
3. Elliot Liebow, *Tally's Corner: A Study of Negro Streetcorner Men* (Boston: Little, Brown and Co., 1967).
4. Edgar Morin, *The Red and the White: Report from a French Vil-*

lage, translated by A. M. Sheridan-Smith (New York: Pantheon Books, 1970).

5. Laurence Wylie, *Village in the Vaucluse* (Cambridge, Mass.: Harvard University Press, 1954); and Laurence Wylie, ed., *Chanzeaux: A Village in Anjou* (Cambridge, Mass.: Harvard University Press, 1966).

6. See the results of such inquiry in Elliot J. Feldman and Lily Gardner Feldman, "The Special Relationship Between Canada and the United States," *Jerusalem Journal of International Relations* 4, no. 4 (June 1980), pp. 56–85.

4

Organizing and Managing Field Research

Field research involves so many unexpected events that it is extremely difficult to organize a routine. Nevertheless, it is important to develop one so that data are well preserved and we do not slide into the idleness that can result from unstructured and undisciplined work.

Structuring Your Day

Let us consider how we might organize a "typical" day of field research. We have already discussed the actual conduct of research, but we have not placed those activities in the context of a work day. How do we get to an interview? How many interviews can we do in a day? What should we do with the time between interviews? And what happens when the last interview of the day is completed?

As I mentioned earlier, it is important not to be late for appointments. In cities such as London and Paris it is difficult to know how long it will take to reach a certain address. The Metro might break down; a bus might be caught in traffic. Our first rule, then, is to allow more time than we think conceivably necessary. We cannot overcome natural disaster, but we can anticipate natural conditions to some extent at least. If all goes smoothly and we arrive well in advance, we can sit in the car or find a café or bar in which to wait. We should not, because we are early, seek an early entry to the appointment. We should be on time. However, we might occasionally arrive for an interview in a residential neighborhood by bus or taxi in a driving rain one-half hour early. There is no café or bar or shop. There are only private residences, pavement, and rain. This situation is the exception—we will have to ring the doorbell. But conditions should be this extreme.

The distance between interviews will determine how many interviews can be managed in a given day. In rural America it may be possible, traveling by car, to cover seventy-five miles and conduct as many as six interviews between 8:30 A.M. and 10:00 P.M. But in London during the same time period, three interviews may be the most possible. Let us consider some of the constraints.

Unless interviews are in the same neighborhood, at least one-half hour must be allowed for travel. If the location of an interview is unfamiliar, another half hour must be allowed for getting lost. A minimum of one and one-half hours must be allowed for the interview itself, for the respondent may be delayed or late or sufficiently open that the interview extends beyond anticipated limits (a standard interview length is one hour). And one hour must be allowed for memory "purge." Thus, from the time we leave home to the time we arrive at the second interview in another neighborhood we have had to allow a minimum of three and one-half hours. Barring loss of way and excessive delays, if we leave home at 8:00 A.M. we can begin a second interview no earlier than 11:30 (experience will shorten the "purge" time, which may also eventually be consolidated with travel between appointments, but at most one full hour could be saved). If we are working in the same neighborhood, of course, much time is saved, and more work is possible.

As a rule, if we have an interview scheduled to follow one just conducted, we should travel to the site of the second interview before going through our notes. This way we remove the anxiety of having to get to the next place while trying to concentrate on the previous interview. But in any event, we should allow reasonable time between appointments.

There are few people in Europe, especially on the official level, whom we will be able to see earlier than 9:00 A.M. (in England, earlier than 10:00 A.M.). Furthermore, unless we have a luncheon appointment, we will not be able to see anyone between 11:30 A.M. and 2:30 or 3:00 P.M. Thus, we may only be able to manage one appointment in the morning, with possibly a second over lunch. Luncheon appointments, moreover, may take the entire lunch period, which means that when the hour's "purge" is counted in, an afternoon appointment could not begin before 4:00 or 4:30. Obviously, except possibly for dinner or evening, a 4:00 appointment will be the last of the day. Finally, due to the nature of a European dinner, no appointment can be planned for after dinner. The most complete possible day in a European city (and these points apply almost equally to the countryside) will consist of appointments in the morning, over lunch, in the afternoon, and over dinner. More probably and normally, however, interviews will be scheduled only in the morning and in the afternoon. If we see more than one person in the same building or in the same organization, we can accomplish more. Otherwise, these are the limits.

It is possible to do more in the United States or Canada for several reasons: Meals are less formal and time-consuming; offices open earlier in the morning and stay open through the lunch hours; adjustments in schedule can be made more easily over the telephone, with last-minute luncheon dates normal—in sharp contrast to what would normally be possible in Europe. In any event, we must be aware of the occurrences in a day that will take sizeable periods of time. And we must remember that interviewing can be both exhilarating and exhausting. Several interviews in one day ultimately prove counterproductive in terms of our own sharpness and receptiveness and may render us less than effective the next day.

Having our own car is indispensable in rural areas and advantageous even in cities. We can more readily carry a tape recorder, extra batteries, tapes, notes, etc., and we can more readily control our own travel time. In traffic-congested urban centers, public transportation may be faster, but our own car may be more reliable. And although impoverished researchers do not imagine themselves the users of taxis, we must be prepared to hail a taxi if we have no car and we must reach an appointment.

Our days can also be organized around the use of archives, or we can plan to spend the morning in a library and the afternoon conducting an interview. However we organize in this regard, we must remember to leave time to prepare interviews, not merely to conduct them. That is, we must track down public statements, personal histories, and so forth, and we must prepare questions both for full, methodical interviews and for interviews that may unexpectedly be cut short.

I mentioned earlier that we should arrange interviews by writing letters. Unfortunately, we usually have to write a number of letters at the same time for interviews to be conducted during the same period. Once the letters have been sent we wait in dread that nine people are all eager to see us for lunch on the same day. Rarely, in fact, do serious conflicts arise, but frequently we may be forced to set up more appointments in a given day than we might have wished while leaving other days free. One rule might be followed here: It is better to lose one interview entirely than to jeopardize the quality of two or three in an effort to squeeze too many into too little time.

After the Day's Work

If we are studying citizen groups or trade unions, we are likely to attend a fair number of evening meetings. Other objects generally do not require this particular demand on our time, however. We may decide to reserve the evenings for ourselves, but we must also remember that other important activities related to the day's work ought to be undertaken then.

Every interview requires a thank-you note. If we intend to see someone again, we might time the note to arrive a couple of weeks before we renew contact for another meeting. This method reminds the respondent who we are while extending a positive impression. The note might also be sent as we near the end of our field work, whereupon we might be able to write more personally about how the interview fit into our overall work. In general, however, it is probably best to write a note soon after the interview. If our notes reveal further brief questions or points yet needing clarification, we can request written answers at the same time that we express thanks for the interview. If materials are sent by the respondent after an interview, a note is also required. Evenings are a good time for this activity.

Project data should be maintained in at least three organized files, the development of which is a daily (or regular evening) task. First, we should maintain a file of contacts. We should list each person we see, their address, official position, where and when we saw them, and a few notes, perhaps, about our impressions of them. We should list how we came to see them (Did someone else make the contact for us? Did someone else recommend this person?) and whether it was agreed we could see them again. From our notes of the day, we should add to our contact file all names, addresses, and other pertinent information concerning other people recommended by the people we have interviewed that day.

After we have completed the contact file for the day, we should file and catalogue all documents and written materials we have collected. There almost always comes a point when we discover ourselves being offered materials we already have. If we have not catalogued, we are liable not to realize we already possess something. It is better to have more than less, but it is also better not to clutter our data with extra copies of the same documents. Also, if our field research relies more on collecting documents than on interviews, it is essential that we organize what we have collected. Not only should we catalogue generally, but we should examine the document to have an idea what it contains. There is a tendency in field research to collect documents and then examine them when we leave the field. If time allows, this tendency should be avoided. For one thing, documents may provide information that we might, if ignorant, try to uncover in interviews. For another thing, the documents may point us in important directions that would be impossible to pursue once we have left the field.

The third file we should maintain contains the interviews themselves. We should take our notes from the day and write them up in detail. For interviews we have taped, we should make an index of what the interview covers. These complete reports will likely be our principal data when the time to analyze and write up our results finally comes. Therefore, although again there is a tendency after a long and tiring day not to bother with these activities, it is crucial that we push ourselves. If we establish a routine of completing these files every day, the perception that they are an unnecessary bother will begin to fade.

In addition to these formal files, it is helpful to keep a notebook with us at all times in which we can record anything that occurs to us. As we get involved in the research, ideas will spark when we least expect them. We need a place to record these ideas, or we will later discover ourselves with countless little bits of paper, relatively useless. Some ideas may seem absurd or irrelevant at the time; we should record them anyway. When we write up results, we should refer to this notebook, for it may well lead us down the most profitable analytical paths. And before we leave the field we should consult this notebook; it may remind us of things needing to be completed. Finally, although the notebook need not become a diary, each evening we should consider—on a routine basis—whether something struck us during the day. If any thought or line of reasoning occurs to us, we should record it in this special notebook.

The special notebook may be of greatest use when we think we are stuck and have lost our way. Research is easily derailed by broken appointments, data that do not correspond at all to hypotheses, or simply lack of cooperation from many people. At such times we should look to this notebook and write ourselves memoranda: What are we trying to find out? What have we learned so far? What are the unanswered questions? Reflect on the objects in the hypotheses. Have we explored all of them? Writing out answers to such questions can get us back on track.

Every researcher will organize materials to suit personal preference. Some people like file cards, others notebooks, and so on. Although we should choose on the basis of our personal preferences, we should be guided by the facts that (1) materials need to be carried easily and perhaps frequently; and (2) our notes may be consulted by others.

Bureaucracies and Hard-to-Get Information

I wish to make a few brief remarks about getting to see the right person in a bureaucracy and getting information that seems inaccessible. There is one principle that governs both problems: We should try to go around instead of through the obstacles.

Buildings that house administrators have countless obstacles, usually human. In Italy there is likely to be a porter at the front door, at the end of every hallway, perhaps near every elevator entrance. In England there will be a guard at the front door; these guards are usually more efficient than the Italian porters and will not let a visitor past without authorization. For this reason it is hazardous just to show up saying, "I would like to see someone who can tell me about . . ." One solution to this problem, when in fact we do not know what branch of the particular bureaucracy will have an answer for us, is to begin with the telephone. We can let the switchboard operator route us through the organization until, as we keep saying, "Yes, that's right," we are given the name of the department we want and perhaps even the name of the responsible person there. Then we can show up at the door and announce that we are going to this or that department or to see this or that person. It is best if we can tell the guard we have an appointment, but we should be careful not to lie; the guard will probably telephone upstairs to check. And through our conversations on the telephone we should be sure to get names. We should never end a conversation with a bureaucrat without knowing to whom we have spoken.

Although more manpower will be distributed to block our path in the Italian system, the greater number of people generally proves a far less formidable obstacle than the English guards. The important rule is not to talk with anyone stationed outside an office and never to hesitate or seem uncertain of where we are going when we are in public view. There should be no hesitation at the front door. We must enter directly, perhaps extending a warm and familiar "good morning" or "good afternoon"—in the native language—to the guard. We should make our way directly to stairs or elevators without hesitating. A second rule is that, unless we are studying office personnel, low-level bureaucrats, or staff, there is no one on the lower floors of a multistoried building whom we want to see. Decision makers and authorities, like the aristocrats of old, ascend to the high places and tend to occupy offices on the upper floors. We want to get to the upper floors, therefore, before someone detains us.

Almost every building will have a general directory on the first floor. However, every floor should have a directory as well, or at least names on doors. Therefore, we should tend to consult directories on the upper floors instead of below. And we should remember that, whereas it is the job of the guards to block us, secretaries have no similar task. Here is someone we can usually ask. A courteous inquiry will often produce a courteous and helpful reply. Once in the office area, a secretary may guide us to our desired destination. Moreover, it is better to ask secretaries than officials as they pass in the corridors. The latter will direct us to the guards or, worse, question our presence. The secretaries probably will not.

People who work in bureaucracies are often hard to locate. Bureaucracies also contain information that the staff may be reluctant to share. Public records, we may be told, are not public because they are too disorganized. In England, each ministry of state has its own library, and we can often find material there. But in Italy, for example, we may not find libraries and we may find a pattern of secrecy that seems to make everything pertinent unavailable. One solution to this problem is the corollary of our description of entering buildings: Go to the top. Another rule is never to waste time negotiating with someone at a level where the materials are kept but where release of them to the "wrong" people could bring severe internal retribution. We should seek permission from above for nonsensitive materials.

Sensitive materials, of course, are another matter: For these we must try the lower echelons first and hope to find either a disgruntled worker or someone who will make a mistake. If we were to begin above, we might generate a proclamation that would seal off all materials definitively. We must always remember that relationships within bureaucracies are hierarchical and continue after the episode of our visit passes. Those in the upper echelons have a stake in being regarded as superior by those below. That means that those above are always prepared to contravene what has already occurred below. If below we are denied something, those above may order it opened. Unfortunately, the reverse is also true, though probably less frequent.

When the way is blocked above and below, we can only seek the help of others inside or outside the bureaucracy. One idea is to look for someone no longer working there who might have friends or who might have kept materials. Secretaries also can prove remarkably helpful sometimes. In each instance where the way seems blocked, we must try another way before bulldozing straight ahead. That said, we should sometimes be prepared, as a last resort, to bulldoze. We need only say we are about to publish and that their side of the story, given the paucity of information available, is not very favorable. Such a veiled threat, after repeated efforts to secure help, can sometimes produce wonders.

Bureaucracies are not alone in making materials difficult to obtain. One other pertinent case that is an especially frequent impediment to young historians involves access already granted to some senior scholar. The senior scholar may, in turn, assert exclusive access. If we want the materials for the same purpose as the person who has exclusive access, there is not much we can do. If, however, our research merely intersects over these materials and we want them for different purposes, we need to appeal both to those who have granted the rights and to those who hold the rights, emphasizing the special need we have. We can employ the journalistic tactics I have already noted with regard to getting interviews. Finally, we can threaten to publish the fact that another scholar is blocking access to important research materials for apparently selfish purposes. Usually materials can be pried loose from their most selfish guardians if access has already been granted to someone.

Hanging around a bureaucracy or an organization or meeting people casually in a cafeteria or at evening meetings (of, say, a citizens' group) can make a face familiar and, eventually, more welcome. There is a high risk in overexposure, but when direct efforts fail, the subtler but equally eager approaches can be fruitful.

Team Research

Most of our discussion has assumed that we are working alone. Although thesis research will be independent, other research often involves teams. When teams work in the field, there are a number of rules to follow.

First, the team must have some place where all members pass every day. Ideally the team will share an apartment or a house. If it is not possible to arrange accommodations this way, then a common office is desirable. At the very least, all members of the team must be in daily contact with one another.

There are many reasons for following this rule. Although each member of a team may have a separate assignment, data that will serve more than one person often can be found in the same place. It is always preferable for one person to collect the pertinent data that can serve two. Thus, if more than one researcher seeks information in a provincial office, it is best if everyone provides a single researcher with all requests for the provincial office.

As another example, the same person might be the potential respondent to two different interviews. Where two members of a team want to interview the same person, they should either organize and conduct the interview together, or one person should conduct the interview in behalf of the team. Only under extreme circumstances should more than one interview of the same person be conducted by different members of the same team on closely related topics.

To avoid the embarrassment of unwittingly harrassing the same person through separate contacts for separate appointments, a research team ideally should meet every evening—perhaps over dinner—to discuss contacts and the next day's research plans. When letters are to be sent requesting interviews, all team members should be informed so that each has an opportunity to indicate whether a given person appears on two lists. Only one letter should go to that person. A research team needs to avoid the pitfall of becoming its own bureaucracy.

For the best coordination of a research team there must be a leader. The leader assumes responsibility for guaranteeing regular contact among the members and for avoiding multiple interview contacts. The leader should also coordinate data collection so that each trip to a place by a member of the team is profitable to everyone concerned. Thus, in the review of the next day's plans, each member of the team should report on what they will do, whom they will see, and what exactly they will seek. Each member must then be sure to ask every other member if a given trip can be of mutual service.

Research teams also need to avoid the tendency to fall into mutual dependencies. If there are four team members working approximately forty hours per week, there will then be one hundred sixty working hours. If the team tends to interview in pairs, however, then the time that could have been spent in independent data collection begins to lose value. Ideally the team will be composed of individuals with independent assignments closely related. Sometimes these assignments will require team interviewing; more often they should involve independent work serving more than one of the team's interests.

Combining Personal Life with Field Research

Field research can become all-consuming, but (as with all activities) complete devotion to it is not necessarily healthy. If field research is being conducted in a strange environment, however, there may be many constraints on leading a normal social life.

The greatest intellectual problem involves the degree of contact possible with people being studied. Anthropologists seek such contact, and the "participant-observer" school of sociology encourages it. For examining the internal dynamics of single groups or populations there is probably nothing better than participant-observation—sharing responsibility while watching closely all the actors. However, if we are studying conflict between or among groups, institutions, or individuals, contact may compromise our independence. If we frequently socialize with one group, we may begin, unconsciously, to lean to its side. Even if we resist this tendency, a competitive group may perceive that we are leaning this way and refuse to deal with us or prove less than cooperative. We are especially inclined to the side of one party when that party treats us very well and the other party treats us badly. We are then inclined to ask ourselves, "Why not return their invitation?" The answer must lie in the purpose of our research.

If we hope to know all we can about a group of people—be it

a trade union or a board of trustees—the best possible way to accomplish our objective is through frequent and varied contact. Thus, we should seek contact whenever there is an opportunity. If, on the other hand, we are studying relations between the trade union and the board of trustees, inviting the chairman of the board home to dinner is not likely to help much with the trade union. And if we think all will be satisfactory as long as we have the union leader in the next evening, we need to consider what they will surely consider: Who was invited first? In short, if we choose to integrate our social lives with the social lives of our respondents, we must appreciate that there is a strong and inescapable political content in our choice.

Our greatest problem in this regard is to avoid becoming identified with one side of a conflict or with one group of people. We do not want to be drawn into the conflict itself, nor do we want to incur anyone's hostility. In general, therefore, we must be reticent about extending invitations ourselves and cautious about accepting those of others. Even when studying the union, we risk becoming ensnared in an internal conflict by being identified with a faction or with certain individuals.

There are three main reasons why these constraints are particularly painful to confront. For one thing, we derive a much greater sense of satisfaction out of meeting the people we are studying informally as well as formally; we sense that we understand and know them better when we deal with them on a more personal level. For another thing, we find ourselves in strange settings where our only human contact may be with the people we are studying. Not only is it alienating to convert people into objects of observation, but it is isolating if we see only people with whom we must maintain formal relations. Finally, as we cut off our own social lives, we tend to cut off the social lives of family members who may accompany us. The social and personal alienation faced by a researcher may therefore be more serious for a spouse or for children. They may have no professional activity available, and they also find themselves in a strange setting. They are probably less equipped to adapt to the new environment because of language deficiency (not having been trained for this work or place), and they may be asked to limit their social contacts because we worry about being compromised.

All these problems are greatest in small communities where we feel greater pressure to socialize with the same people we are studying because the apparent alternative is loneliness. In urban settings we can perhaps find other company. We cannot set down absolute rules concerning social contact. But, again recognizing that the lack of social contact is fundamentally alienating, we must try to consider our professional and personal needs separately. We must recognize that social contact must be weighed in terms of the purpose of our study. It is perhaps cynical to pursue social contact merely to help collect data, but field research is a special, not a normal, condition of our lives. And it is at least realistic to recognize that although our motive may be innocent, it can still bring on damaging consequences.

Once these risks and constraints are understood, we must then, as always, make our own choices. Extended, isolated field research has risks not only for the research, but also for our own mental stability. If we are reduced to a choice between the two, then we must risk some feature of our research in behalf of our mental health. But perhaps being aware of the dangers in advance can reduce the risk of such a choice being forced upon us.

One way or another we will have to make our way in the community where we are conducting our study. Thus, it is perhaps wisest to seek social contact deliberately with people unrelated to our research as early as possible. Such contact can serve to reduce the problems that may develop later on. We must not forget our own personal needs, for they will not forget us. In the end, the success or failure of a project may depend on whether we have been able to make ourselves comfortable enough to pursue our research effectively.

Finishing and Going Home

We never really finish field research. There are always more people to see, more questions to ask, more material to collect. However, we cannot go on forever. Knowing when we have enough data is largely intuitive. For example, we may collect a whole new version of a given event each time we speak to someone, but at some point we must say simply, "I have enough versions to get the idea." Often we will have to approximate a story and assume we have enough information.

We stop collecting data when (1) we run out of money; (2) we have to meet a publication or contract deadline; (3) we run out of time; or (4) we run out of patience. At any of these points, the research is not really finished; rather, the research ends. Perhaps we sense diminishing returns, perhaps we don't, but at some point we must stop and depend upon what we have already collected. The study will be a snapshot of events and opinions and perspectives and documents of a moment in time. We cannot expect more from the data, and we cannot do more ourselves. At that point we collect our things to go home. And if we are home already, we halt the field work and begin the systematic analysis of the data collected.

Finally, let me mention a couple of important considerations about moving after the completion of field research away from home. If we plan to travel by car, bus, train, or boat, there is perhaps no problem in carrying the fruits of our labors with us. But if we fly, or if we need to carry suitcases of clothing and other possessions on some other form of public transportation, then we must separate ourselves from our data. There are three partial solutions to this potential problem.

The most irreplaceable materials, such as contact lists, interview reports, and secret documents, should be separated from the other materials. If at all possible, these materials should be kept with us at all times. Thus, if we are flying, we should plan to carry these materials on board. We should recognize, however, that they will probably be heavy and that someone at the airline may oppose our refusal to check the bag in. To mitigate some of the potential calamity in such a confrontation, the airline representative should be told that we have research materials—the products of months or years of work—from which we do not intend to be parted. Whatever arrangement need be made, we shall declare, we must carry this baggage on. We should plan, at the same time, to be relatively unburdened of other carry-on things so as to reduce any clamor over this particular bag.

Replaceable materials can be mailed, shipped, or flown, either as extra luggage or air freight. If we choose the mails, we should send two separate packages with everything duplicated.

This way we double the expense but significantly multiply the probability that we will see our materials again. We also need to pack well; scrambled computer cards in a mail sack are as good as lost. And if at all possible, we should avoid putting materials on boats. Final shipping costs, when we finish with forwarding agents, packers, etc., will not be significantly less than air freight costs would have been, and since there is much less handling by air freight, there is much less risk of pilferage or loss. Furthermore, we can send papers as air freight or as extra baggage on the same plane that we are traveling on and greet the data at the other end. The carrying capacity of jumbo aircraft has reduced significantly the cost of such shipping. The material we have collected is simply too valuable to take any unnecessary risk. We should pack accordingly.

Getting our data safely home is the last field aspect of a field research project, and perhaps the most important single task we face. When successful, we can proceed to produce the results of our work; when unsuccessful, there is nothing to be said—and perhaps nothing to be done.

A Final Word

We have now considered most of the more important aspects of field research in the social sciences. This little guide has advised on formulating research tasks, selecting appropriate methods for pursuing them, organizing strategies for overcoming research obstacles, and structuring time and effort in the conduct of field research. It has warned of pitfalls while, it is hoped, encouraging adventure. It may be both useful in the field as a reminder and useful for preparing your study before going into the field. With the companionship of these tips and the experience that has led to them, students will perhaps make fewer mistakes and suffer less anxiety. Most of what I have warned about, after all, I know because I was not warned myself and had to learn through often painful experience. I have stood in the rain waiting for appointments without an umbrella, arrived at incorrect addresses, forgotten to press the record button of a tape recorder, carried too few pens with ink, and lost irreplaceable data in the international mails. I have seen others depend for years on access to resources that will never be opened, receive mail sacks of scrambled computer cards, forget crucial personal details of someone they are interviewing, and miss appointments because of failed public transportation. Research ought not to be painful. This guide is intended to help relieve some of the pain—or at least some of the anxiety—and thereby increase the many pleasures.

Appendix:
An Illustrative Interview

Good interviewing technique comes with practice, with experience, and with reflection on why interviews succeed or fail. The annotated and edited transcript that follows should provide insight into the actual conduct of an interview and into how and why valuable answers—revealing sometimes new and startling information long after events have passed—can be elicited.

The respondent in this interview, Max Lejeune, was chosen because of his particular experience, expertise, and position of responsibility. The interview was organized around questions of fact as well as opinion and aimed, above all, at bringing out attitudes and perceptions on central questions of policy:

- How did a Socialist government minister responsible for the policies governing the armed forces of France in Algeria reconcile his socialism with the colonial objectives of the war?
- How did he perceive the enemy? Was their terror different from the later terror of the OAS?
- How did he distinguish the Algerian experience from the recently terminated war in Indochina? How was the 1956 Suez invasion related to French military efforts in Algeria?
- What did he understand to be the role of the French nation, and what were the relationships between the nation and the army and the army and the Algerians?
- What lessons from the war in Algeria were learned about

the army and the nation? What is the utility of an army now, and what is the utility of conscripts?

The main objective of the interview was to explore the perceptions of the responsible government minister and to establish whether the consequences of sending French conscripts (the *contingent*) were understood in advance. A second objective was to establish the strategic perceptions of the government and, hence, the role of the army in Indochina, Algeria, and Suez. As a third objective, I sought to clarify the French definition of the national obligation for military service through the specific experience of Algeria. Similar questions, with similar purposes, were put to a number of other prominent participants in this period of French decision making, including Robert Lacoste, Jacques Soustelle, Christian Pineau, Maurice Bourgès-Maunoury, and General André Zeller.

Max Lejeune was secretary of state for the armed forces in France from 1948 to 1950 and in 1956-57. He was also president of the National Defense Commission of the National Assembly during 1954-55 and vice president of the National Assembly in 1947-48, 1967-68, and 1970-71. During 1956-57 he bore direct responsibility for the decision to send the *contingent* to fight in Algeria.

This interview with Max Lejeune was conducted at the Assemblée Nationale in Paris on April 28, 1971. He warned at the outset that the interview could last no more than thirty to forty-five minutes. The transcript here was prepared from a tape recording in French by Leonie Gordon and edited from our sixty-minute discussion.

ML: I can give you a half-hour or three-
quarters--no more.

EJF: I will try to be direct and to the
point. I would like to begin with this
question: when it was decided to send the
contingent in March 1956, the decision was
taken, if I understand correctly, because
it was thought necessary to establish a
French military presence throughout Algeria?

ML: Yes, the decision was taken because in
France, at that time, we considered Algeria
three departments of France. We sent the
soldiers of the contingent there because it
was France. In contrast, we did not send the
contingent to Indochina because Indochina
was a protectorate, not a state of the French
Republic.

No conscripts to Indochina
an important difference
between France and the U.S.
He raised the point here;
pursue it right away, even
though it comes later on
my list.

EJF: But, at the time of Dienbienphu, did not
one say, "Perhaps we must send one Frenchman
to come to the aid of another?" Even at that
time was it not possible to send the contingent?

ML: No, it was impossible. They thought, at
the time, of sending volunteers from the contingent, but it was absolutely impractical for
the military administration.

"Absolutely" means move on;
he also said, in the first
question, that Algeria was
a French domestic problem.
How domestic?

EJF: Do you believe, in that case, that
one can use the army domestically? For
example, there was much talk during May
1968; might it have been possible, at
that time, to use the army, say, to stop
the strike?

ML: Well, in 1948-49 there were general
strikes, and as the Minister of the period
said, they could have become insurrectional;

the army was used to confront the danger
and to maintain order in the northern
departments and in Pas de Calais.

EJF: So you think Algeria was to be treated
in the same way, just as if it were metropolitan France?

ML: Algeria? Yes, yes. Because, according
to military regulations one mission of the
army is not only to defend the integrity of
the national territory, but also to assure
the maintenance of public order.

EJF: You introduced a system of rotation
for the contingent in Algeria, in a sense
seeking to assure equal service for everyone
by requiring everyone to do a tour of service
there.

ML: Yes.

EJF: Did you mean truly to involve <u>all</u>
the nation in Algeria through this involvement of the contingent?

ML: Yes. We did not want only the presence of a professional army, which would
have given the impression of a colonial
war. Algeria was part of France, because
the definition of a nation is not racial.

He is convinced Algeria was a domestic problem; no use debating the point more.

EJF: After some time in Algeria the
generals complained about the contingent,
the conscripts....*

ML: Not at all.

They most certainly did; how far will he go with this disclaimer?

EJF: You don't think so?

ML: Not at all.

EJF: That is to say that...

ML: When I was Secretary of State for
Military Affairs in Algeria I spent over
eighteen months, during which 10-12 days of
every month were devoted to visiting every

soldier. At no time did general officers
complain about the attitude of their men.
Just the contrary.

EJF: OK.

ML: There was nothing comparable, even at
the worst moments, to what seems to be
taking place now in Vietnam with American
conscripts.

* NOTE: Ellipses indicate
editing in the tape.

Press a specific instance.

EJF: In April 1961, nonetheless, the
contingent went on strike....

ML: But in April 1961 it was because the
French Government changed its policy.
General de Gaulle declared that Algeria
was to be Algerian, so young soldiers said,
"So, what do we do now? Why should we risk
our lives if the leader of France says
'Algeria for the Algerians'?" To the contrary,
for these young guys they said, "It is
finished."

There was a strong insur-
rectionist movement within
the contingent seeking to
end the war; will he admit
it?

EJF: But you believe, then, that they simply
followed General de Gaulle, and it was not
something else affecting their decision to
strike?

ML: No. They were scared, especially of
following the military chiefs who wanted to
maintain the former policy of a French
Algeria. Naturally, they followed the
government, but they did so as boys of 20
and 21 years old. I would like very much
to be able to say that they thought, "It is
the law we must follow," of course. But for
most the truth is they realized their own
lives were at risk.

His view is clear; what,
then, was the military
strategy? Quote him.

EJF: In 1956 you said, for example,
"Hundreds of thousands of men will not
suffer," and you insisted that the army's
problem in peacekeeping in Algeria required

a change of habits.

ML: A change of methods.

EJF: But do you believe, then, that this task was accomplished?

ML: We were involved, always, in a rebellion of people who were prisoners in Indochina, in the Vietnamese camps of political propaganda with the Vietminh; they returned to Algeria after the Geneva accords had ended the Vietnam War. I said to President René Coty that it was absolutely indispensable to end the affair very quickly, to do so by exceptional means, not of a massive military force but by severe and swift police tactics.

EJF: M. Lacoste, at the same time, wanted the infusion of some 100,000 men....

ML: When I arrived on the scene in 1956 I did not want an immediate increase in the number of men. I asked only that the methods be changed. M. Lacoste, however, demanded a French presence in Algeria through the use of the contingent; I was not in favor, but I went along out of party solidarity. When there are military forces in a country, despite everything the local population very quickly feels the weight of this presence, which can degrade the climate, the atmosphere. For this reason I understood very well when you said, "In sending the soldiers of the contingent to spread out through Algeria you implied that France intended to stay," but at the same time it is important to create illusions. One accentuates the weight of the military presence on people who have their own civilian problems. Naturally, the army provided many services, building roads,

Show you know the facts and the personalities so that he cannot simply change the subject.

He has indeed understood me; and he has begun to explain more.

teaching children, managing civilian administration which did not exist before, but it
was no less true that it was necessary to
separate the promoters of rebellion from the
life of the state as quickly as possible.

Fighting a rebellion through road construction? That wasn't his policy.

EJF: Do you think this civilian role for the
army is proper? Does it always exist for
an army?

ML: No, it does not always exist....The

For a period Challe con-ducted a conventional war.

directives given General Challe, to apply
firm military force, were dictated by me in
1956. I was attacked, of course, by certain
communist newspapers, but I had a mission to
accomplish, and I defined it at the time
as the mission undertaken by General Challe--
which led to the pacification when, to the
army's great surprise, General de Gaulle
decided to deal with the leaders of the
rebellion when they pleaded for peace.

So much for his military preferences; what of military politics? Begin with speci-fic case.

EJF: Could you tell me something about the
resignation of General Guillaume in 1956?
ML: General Guillaume was a problem that
involved M. Bourgès-Maunoury, who was Minister
for National Defense, more than me.

(...I know you were both involved.)

EJF: Yes, but...
ML: Because General Guillaume at the time,
if I recall correctly, was in Morocco. It
was another problem, not precisely military....
EJF: A political problem?
ML: Yes.
EJF: Could you...

He really does not want to answer. Return to his perception of the war.

ML: You know, my memories are quite fluid.
If I had the time to look at my notes from
the period I would say, but I fear going back
too far beyond what I remember and I do not
want to give you a wholly personal and superficial impression.

EJF: I understand. You described the
enemy at the outset of problems in Algeria
in very specific terms--that they were
assassins, fanatics....

ML: I said it and I take none of it back.
I still think it.

Does he object to terror
or to the rejection of his
plan for a French Algeria?

EJF: How would you like to describe, then,
the terror of the OAS that followed, for
they seem quite similar to me?

ML: Don't you see? I am a socialist who,
as early as 1936, supported French citizen-
ship for the moslems in Algeria....It is
important to understand that I was, in 1958,
alongside General de Gaulle when he said,
"Long live French Algeria." He descended
from the podium and said to me, "So, Lejeune."

("I felt personally
betrayed and still do....")

"Oh, my general, you have called for a French
Algeria. That means integration. Hurry to do
it. It is possible, but you must hurry." I
myself continued to believe in my own formula
of Algeria within the Republic. This cry of
"Long live Algeria," the famous "I have understood you," all that--the French recorded that,
the Europeans of French Algeria, with eight
years of formal conflict and you must then
understand that for them there was immense
disillusionment when General de Gaulle abandoned
this policy. And for the army, there was
anger, for they were asked suddenly to play
a different part. To protect France, this
army thought, it would now be necessary to
control and manage themselves, for they had
been betrayed. One should never involve
an army in political activity; yet, from the
moment they were involved, above all by someone like General de Gaulle--with the prestige
he enjoyed in the army--they sensed the
betrayal.

Obviously he thinks they're different, but make him draw a clear distinction.

EJF: Do you believe, then, that these activities were similar, the acts of terror driven by the same political rationale for the OAS as for the FLN?

He sees the point; he also sees the political awkwardness of his opposition to ultimate French policy.

ML: There was at the time, in France and in Algeria, provocation. It is very delicate for me to deal with this question with you.... The terror of the OAS was a reaction against those who appeared to abandon the French cause. I do not justify it, but there is this sentiment, that the army was repressed. It is necessary to speak of the terror of the FLN.

He still leaves open my question; try one last time.

What is dramatic for armies is the violence--violence engenders hate, and hate engenders more hate.

EJF: That is exactly what I am asking. I would like to know whether you wish to differentiate between the reasons on each side for apparently similar acts. That is precisely the question.

ML: I hold responsible for all that those who failed to keep their involvement with an eye for the interests of the country. Voilà.

Let him continue; he is now telling his cosmic view of the war's relationship to the destiny of France.

EJF: OK.

ML: For me, the guy responsible is General de Gaulle. I wrote him, fifteen days before he died when he sent me a copy of his book, dedicated to me. I thanked him for the book, but I told him the reading of it gave me enormous pain because when he came to power those who helped him get there--the French people--expected a guarantee of domestic peace. I insisted that the policies he followed returned France to a hexagon, no longer the great power for which he had hoped himself, having lost access to Saharan oil--which meant the

loss of France's energy independence. General
de Gaulle perhaps counted greatly on the more
rapid development of nuclear reactors. He left
France much smaller and much weaker, despite
all appearances.

Was the war not already
lost?

EJF: Do you believe Algeria could have
been retained, even in 1958?

ML: Yes. It is not a matter of keeping
Algeria in the form of French departments.
One could have given it its own evolutive
statute to keep for the long future a common
destiny with France.

EJF: Before May 1958, was your government
on the way to...

ML: Indeed. The special outlined bill
[loi-cadre], it was already before the

I've already interviewed
Soustelle; no utility in
pursuing this line; he
is baiting.

Parliament. And who fought it? M. Soustelle.
I am sure M. Soustelle stayed faithful to his
ideas, but I am obliged to insist that he
fought the bill, and in 1958 General de Gaulle
did not want to take it up again....A minority
of fanatics could not lead me to condemn more
than a million brave Europeans who considered
the place their home.

EJF: This evolution you are talking about--
in what direction were things to evolve?

The concept was never taken
seriously; it is amazing he
still clings to it, but
there is no point in seeking
an explanation here.

ML: I don't see why it was not possible, for
example, for the status of a French union under
the sign of the French Republic--alongside the
metropole and the departments, other territories,
Gabon and the Ivory Coast, for example, which
entered the community.

He still has not clarified
the role of the contingent;
try it again by asking him
to attack his critics (since
he seems to like that).

EJF: There are many critics who think
non-military tasks for the army, and
especially for the contingent, were very
difficult--I'm speaking of psychological
warfare, for example. Do you think the
critics are right?

ML: No, because I would like to say simply
that I like professors when they do psychology and I like military men less when they
try psychology too much. To each his own
mission. There is a tendency to forget the
essential and rudimentary mission of the army.

Don't accept his metaphor-
ical answer; I want some-
thing more specific.

EJF: What do you think, then, really was
possible for the contingent in Algeria?
What could the conscripts accomplish? Were
they to go into battle, to secure areas, or
what exactly?

ML: You know there were conscripts who fell
in Algeria. Of course, there were some. But
it is important too to tell the truth. It was
the special forces, especially paratroopers,
foreign legionnaires, and professional soldiers
who, every time, were in the major operations
in the front lines. That conscripts were
caught in ambushes occasionally, yes. But in
this war, which did witness conscript losses
at unacceptably high levels, we know equally

He never accepted Lacoste's
position and he thinks the
contingent simply got caught
in the line of fire. He sees
no role for them in Algeria
beyond avoiding the appearances of colonial war.

well that an enormous number of these high
losses were attributable to accidents.

EJF: You have said that during the period
in question one preferred well educated and
trained soldiers and that one no longer had
soldiers who simply would follow unexplained
orders. Do you think it is possible to have
an army in which the soldiers are very well
educated and with whom it is possible to have
something of a dialogue before they follow
orders, an army that does not march solely
on discipline?

He seems to like the pro-
fessional army; go directly
to the key dilemma.

ML: Oh, you know, an army without discipline
is not an army. Voilà.

EJF: Can you establish true discipline with

well-educated men?

ML: I don't understand.

EJF: Well, certainly in the traditional army the generals preferred men who would follow orders without question. But when the army is populated by men who question, is it possible for the army to work?

ML: Well, my dear young man, the China of Mao Tse-tung has many admirers, not only intellectuals. If Mao's régime were installed here you would see discipline in work, under arms. It is the weakness of democracy not to accept the necessity of discipline, not only in work, but equally for defense.

"You can **discipline** anyone"; the **contingent** can be **disciplined.** **Move** on.

EJF: Might I ask a question which might seem tangential to the subject of Algeria? I'd like to know what role Suez played, coming in the midst of the conflict in Algeria. Many people wondered at the time whether entry into the Suez crisis in 1956 would detract from the effort in Algeria, whether there would be enough men to fight, and so forth. Was there a technical or strategic problem in pursuing the Suez invasion at the same time?

ML: During the War in Algeria, you know very well, the rebellion would not have been possible without support from the Arab League and more particularly from Egypt. You know that arms were smuggled across the desert. If hostilities at Suez had not ceased for another ten hours, it would have been the end of Nasser. Paratrooper columns would have entered Cairo and it would have been over. The entire situation in the Middle East would have changed.

EJF: Are you saying that the Suez operation was conceived as part of the Algerian War?

Yes; OK, was there a
strategic problem?

ML: It is obvious that everything took
place at the same time.

EJF: To pursue the two operations simultaneously, did you require many more troops?

ML: No, no, no. What we had was sufficient.

By all subsequent accounts,
not so; press him with facts.

EJF: But there were only two divisions....

ML: No, no. It would have been all over
when Nasser...when Cairo was reached, it
would have been finished. The Eden-Guy
Mollet conversations during the critical days
were central to the future of the Middle East.

He said "ten"; the point is he
thinks he was betrayed again.
Will he admit the manpower
shortage if I show him where
the troops came from?
Yes, he admits the problem,
but he minimizes it because
of the objective.

What I regret, simply, and I repeat, was that
we did not have another 24-36 hours.

EJF: Do you think NATO was weakened at all
during the invasion when divisions had to be
withdrawn from Germany?

ML: We did not have to withdraw so many men.
With the forces deployed in Egypt--French
units--with the air force and the presence
of massive naval forces in the eastern
Mediterranean--had the affair lasted another
24-36 hours it would have meant the fall of
Nasser, the end of hostilities and for a
moment, at least, the possibility for a total
change of political conditions in the eastern
Mediterranean with a very substantial influence
on events in Algeria.

There ensues a discussion of military involvement in Chad
and the American military effort in Vietnam. Then...

Time is running out; get to
the contemporary questions;
start with an easy confirmation of his credentials.

EJF: You are still a member of the National
Defense Commission....

ML: Yes.

EJF: What do you think of the proposed legal
changes in the law governing national service?

ML: We are generally in agreement for one
year of military service because, unless we

want to collapse--that is, no more military
service....Well, all republicans are still
frightened by the thought of entrusting the
defense of their country to a professional
army. I realize I do not have the right,
given my formal responsibilities, to ignore
technical requirements which today involve
long instruction for handling the new weapons--
and that implies a professional, not a conscript
army--yet the conscript army can be used today
for surface defense of the territory. The real
problem remains, as I have said, that demo-
cracies today are very weak; they do not provide what is necessary, nor the discipline,
for defense.

He is addressing the modern   EJF: Then you do not accept that a period of
dilemma; pursue it.   one year for military service is sufficient
                                  for training an army?

                                  ML: Yes I do, but on condition that the
                                  training is well done. During the last
                                  world war we trained soldiers in six months
                                  and sent them all over. They blended in
                                  with the forces in place. But to extrapolate
                                  from that experience to peacetime--with the
                                  psychological impact of a liberal climate,
                                  individual freedom, leisure time, etc., well.
                                  In wartime, training went from dawn to dusk.
                                  They knew more about military service than
                                  going to the toilet. But we must remember
                                  the difference between service in peacetime
                                  and service in war. For peacetime forces
                                  there must be a popular public respect for a
                                  national defense as necessary and indispensable.

He has said something differ-   EJF: You think, then, that for defense a
ent, but see how far he might   professional army might be better?
finally go--probe.   ML: I did not say it would be better. It is
                                  obvious, however, that those with the respon-

sibility to govern will be so inclined, for
they will have more confidence in the professional army's technical ability. The army
today is founded on the use of tactical nuclear
weapons; we should be under no illusion that
such use must lead to using the atomic bomb;
then we see that in the last twenty-one years
the character of national defense has changed
brutally.

He won't concede on training,   EJF: Then one has reduced effectively the
but perhaps he will on   importance of the army, given the dependence
strategy--it led the British   on a nuclear strategy.
to abandon conscription.
                                 ML: Yes, well, the French government thinks
                                 it has built its defense policy on dissuasion,
                                 with France having an independent capacity.
                                 In any case military service, as presently
                                 conceived, with one year's service and some
                                 peacetime tasks to keep fit, ought to maintain
                                 the accord of democrats and republicans. It
                                 does not exactly provide for the national
                                 defense, but it does not turn over the national
                                 defense simply to a professional army. Never-
                                 theless, I should say that the army has emerged
                                 from the last twelve years profoundly troubled.
                                 Its efforts have been forgotten. It is in
                                 grave condition, a bit like France.

He made the key concession:
compulsory military service is a
political choice whose military
vitality under modern arms and
with present strategy is marginal.
But he is too wedded personally to
the traditional army to pursue this
proposition successfully any further.
He also looks tired and we have gone
much longer than he had offered. Stop here.

EJF: That is a sufficiently pessimistic
note; perhaps we should stop. I have no
further questions, but perhaps there is
something on this subject I have neglected
to ask. Is there something else you might
want to say, or some ground I have failed
to cover?

ML: No, I have spoken freely but I have not
had a chance to think of anything I have
forgotten to say.

EJF: Are there others you think I should
see on some of these subjects?

Good. I have seen them both,   ML: Yes, of course, you should probably
which means I am on the right   talk to M. Soustelle, for example, and M.
track.   Pineau for Suez.

EJF: Thank you very much for your generous
help. Perhaps I could speak with you again
if it seems appropriate?

ML: As you wish.

Much has been learned by inference which must be confirmed by
interviewing others and corroborating this testimony with his public
statements.

Selected Bibliography

The recommendations here are drawn from several social science disciplines. Anthropologists have been the leading observers of research abroad and of the field experience; sociologists have given the most attention to participant-observation; psychologists have worried most about aspects of interviewing, political scientists about comparisons and evaluation, and so forth.

Many of the works in this bibliography are useful in areas other than the categories in which they have been placed here. The general readers, especially, can be helpful for a variety of purposes, and each has a special utility. Miller's volume, for example, provides guidance in grantsmanship particularly appropriate for sociologists; Murphy offers a useful discussion of elite interviewing, not only for policy evaluators; Barzun and Graff provide very practical guidance for all social science and humanities researchers, not only for historians. On the other hand, one should beware of misleading titles. Shively and Holt and Turner, for example, tend to equate political research with quantitative methods; Wax's account is very personal and lessons often are implicit. Students and scholars should not fear crossing disciplinary lines for practical guidance in using the readings suggested here, however. All address the same means of collecting research data: hearing, reading, and speaking.

General Readers from Disciplinary Perspectives

Barzun, Jacques, and Graff, Henry F. *The Modern Researcher.* New York: Harcourt, Brace and World, 1957. HISTORY

Bickman, Leonard, and Henchy, Thomas. *Beyond the Laboratory: Field Research in Social Psychology.* New York: McGraw-Hill Book Co., 1972. SOCIAL PSYCHOLOGY

Cicourel, Aaron V. *Method and Measurement in Sociology.* Glencoe, Ill.: Free Press, 1964. SOCIOLOGY

Cole, Stephen. *The Sociological Method.* Chicago: Markham, 1972. SOCIOLOGY

Epstein, A. L., ed. *The Craft of Social Anthropology.* London: Tavistock, 1967. ANTHROPOLOGY

Festinger, Leon, and Katz, Daniel, eds. *Research Methods in the Behavioral Sciences.* New York: Holt, Rinehart and Winston, 1966. PSYCHOLOGY and SOCIOLOGY

Forcese, Dennis P., and Richer, Stephen, eds. *Stages of Social Research: Contemporary Perspectives.* Englewood Cliffs, N.J.: Prentice-Hall, 1970. SOCIOLOGY

Glaser, Barney G., and Strauss, Anselm L. *The Discovery of Grounded Theory: Strategies for Qualitative Research.* Chicago: Aldine Press, 1967. SOCIOLOGY

Hammond, Phillip, ed. *Sociologists at Work: Essays on the Craft of Social Research.* New York: Doubleday & Co., 1967. SOCIOLOGY

Jongmans, D. G., and Gutkind, P.C.W., eds. *Anthropologists in the Field.* Assen, Netherlands: Van Gorcum, 1967. ANTHROPOLOGY

Miller, Delbert C. *Handbook of Research Design and Social Measurement.* New York: David McKay Co., 1977. SOCIOLOGY

Powdermaker, Hortense. *Stranger and Friend: The Way of an Anthropologist.* New York: W. W. Norton & Co., 1967. ANTHROPOLOGY

Shiveley, W. Phillips. *The Craft of Political Research.* Englewood Cliffs, N.J.: Prentice-Hall, 1974. POLITICAL SCIENCE

Thomas, D. H. *Figuring Anthropology.* New York: Holt, Rinehart and Winston, 1976. ANTHROPOLOGY

Williams, Thomas R. *Field Methods in the Study of Culture.* New York: Holt, Rinehart and Winston, 1967. ANTHROPOLOGY

Defining Problems

Dubin, Robert. *Theory Building, A Practical Guide to the Construction and Testing of Theoretical Models.* New York: Free Press, 1969.

Kaplan, Abraham. *The Conduct of Inquiry: Methodology for Behavioral Science.* San Francisco: Chandler Publishing, 1964.

Kuhn, Thomas. *Structure of Scientific Revolutions.* Chicago: University of Chicago Press, 1970.

Weber, Max. *The Methodology of the Social Sciences.* Glencoe, Ill.: Free Press, 1949.

The Field Experience

Fichter, Joseph H. *One-Man Research, Reminiscences of a Catholic Sociologist.* New York: Wiley-Interscience, 1973.

Junker, Buford H. *Field Work: An Introduction to the Social Sciences.* Introduction by Everett C. Hughes. Chicago: University of Chicago Press, 1960.

Wax, Rosalie H. *Doing Fieldwork: Warnings and Advice.* Chicago: University of Chicago Press, 1971.

Classic Field Experience Examples

Liebow, Elliot. *Tally's Corner: A Study of Negro Streetcorner Men.* Boston: Little, Brown and Co., 1967.

Morin, Edgar. *The Red and the White: Report from a French Village,* translated by A.M. Sheridan-Smith. New York: Pantheon Books, 1970.

Whyte, William F. *Street Corner Society.* Chicago: University of Chicago Press, 1943.

Wylie, Laurence. *Village in the Vaucluse.* Cambridge, Mass.: Harvard University Press, 1954.

Wylie, Laurence, ed. *Chanzeaux: A Village in Anjou.* Cambridge, Mass.: Harvard University Press, 1966.

General Advice on Collecting Data

Bardach, Eugene. "Gathering Data for Policy Research." *Journal of Urban Analysis* 2 (1974):117–144.

Bernstein, Carl, and Woodward, Robert. *All the President's Men.* New York: Simon & Schuster, 1974.

Charnley, Mitchell V. *Reporting.* New York: Holt, Rinehart and Winston, 1966.

Douglas, Jack D. *Investigative Social Research.* Beverly Hills, Calif.: Sage Publications, 1976.

Johnson, John M. *Doing Field Research.* New York: Free Press, 1975.

Murphy, Jerome T. *Getting the Facts: A Fieldwork Guide for Evaluators and Policy Analysts.* Santa Monica, Calif.: Goodyear, 1980.

Phillips, Bernard S. *Social Research: Strategy and Tactics.* New York: Macmillan, 1971.

Sanders, William B. *The Sociologist as Detective: An Introduction to Research Methods.* New York: Praeger Publications, 1974.

Schatzman, Leonard, and Strauss, Anselm L. *Field Research.* Englewood Cliffs, N.J.: Prentice-Hall, 1974.

Sigal, Leon V. *Reporters and Officials: The Organization and Politics of Newsmaking.* Lexington, Mass.: D. C. Heath & Co., 1973.

Surveys and Sampling

Glock, Charles Y. *Survey Research in the Social Sciences.* New York: Russell Sage Foundation, 1967.

Hyman, Herbert. *Survey Design and Analysis: Principles, Cases, and Procedures.* Glencoe, Ill.: Free Press, 1955.

Leuthold, David A., and Scheele, Raymond J. "Patterns of Bias in Samples Based on Telephone Directories." *Public Opinion Quarterly* 35 (1971):24–57.

Sudman, Seymour. *Applied Sampling.* New York: Academic Press, 1976.

Interviewing

Cannell, Charles F., and Kahn, Robert L. "Interviewing." In *The Handbook of Social Psychology,* edited by Gordon Lindzey and E. Aronson, vol. 2, pp. 526–595. Reading, Mass.: Addison-Wesley, 1968.

Dexter, Lewis A. *Elite and Specialized Interviewing.* Evanston, Ill.: Northwestern University Press, 1970.

Gorden, Raymond L. *Interviewing Strategy: Techniques and Tactics.* Homewood, Ill.: Dorsey Press, 1969.

Hyman, Herbert H. et al. *Interviewing in Social Research.* Chicago: University of Chicago Press, 1975.

Merton, Robert K. et al. *The Focused Interview: A Manual of Problems and Procedures.* Glencoe, Ill.: Free Press, 1956.

Participant-Observation and Passive Observation

Bogdan, Robert, and Taylor, Stephen J. *Introduction to Qualitative Research Methods.* New York: John Wiley & Sons, 1975.

Bruyn, Severyn T. *The Human Perspective in Sociology: The Methodology of Participant Observation.* Englewood Cliffs, N.J.: Prentice-Hall, 1966.

Collier, John, Jr. *Visual Anthropology: Photography as a Research Method.* New York: Holt, Rinehart and Winston, 1967.

Friedrichs, J., and Ludtke, H. *Participant Observation, Theory and Practice.* Lexington, Mass.: D. C. Heath & Co., 1975.

Jacobs, Glenn, ed. *The Participant Observer.* New York: George Braziller, 1970.

McCall, George J., and Simmons, J. L., eds. *Issues in Participant Observation.* Reading, Mass.: Addison-Wesley, 1969.

Schwartz, Morris S., and Green, Charlotte. "Problems in Participant Observation." *American Journal of Sociology* 60, 4 (1955).

Vidich, Arthur J. "Participant Observation and the Collection and Interpretation of Data." *American Journal of Sociology* 60, 4 (1955).

Webb, Eugene J.; Campbell, Donald T.; Schwartz, Richard D.; and Sechrist, Lee. *Unobtrusive Measures: Nonreactive Research in the Social Sciences.* Chicago: Rand McNally & Co., 1966.

Statistics and Quantitative Methods

Alker, Hayward. *Mathematics and Politics.* New York: Macmillan, 1965.

Blalock, Hubert M. *Social Statistics.* 2d rev. ed. New York: McGraw-Hill Book Co., 1979.

Coleman, James S. *Introduction to Mathematical Sociology.* New York: Free Press, 1964.

Doran, J. E., and Hudson, F. R. *Mathematics and Computers in Archaeology.* Cambridge, Mass.: Harvard University Press, 1975.

Edwards, Allen L. *Statistical Methods.* New York: Holt, Rinehart and Winston, 1967.

Hays, W. L. *Statistics for the Social Sciences.* 2d ed. New York: Holt, Rinehart and Winston, 1973.

Kemeny, John G., and Snell, Laurie. *Mathematical Models in the Social Sciences.* Cambridge, Mass.: MIT Press, 1962.

Ostle, Bernard, and Mensing, R. *Statistics in Research.* 3d ed. Ames: Iowa State University Press, 1977.

Comparative Research

Armer, Michael, and Grimshaw, Allen, eds. *Comparative Social Re-*

search: Methodological Problems and Strategies. New York: John
Wiley & Sons, 1973.

Holt, Robert T., and Turner, John E., eds. *The Methodology of Comparative Political Research.* Glencoe, Ill.: Free Press, 1970.

Vallier, Ivan, ed. *Comparative Methods in Sociology: Essays on Trends and Applications.* Berkeley: University of California Press, 1973.

Index